Advanced Poetry

BLOOMSBURY WRITER'S GUIDES AND ANTHOLOGIES

Bloomsbury Writer's Guides and Anthologies offer established and aspiring creative writers an introduction to the art and craft of writing in a variety of forms, from poetry to environmental and nature writing. Each book is part craft guide with writing prompts and exercises, and part anthology, with relevant works by major authors.

Series Editors:

Sean Prentiss, Vermont College of Fine Arts, USA
Joe Wilkins, Linfield College, USA

Titles in the Series:

Environmental and Nature Writing, Sean Prentiss and Joe Wilkins

Poetry, Amorak Huey and W. Todd Kaneko

Short-Form Creative Writing, H. K. Hummel and Stephanie Lennox

Creating Comics, Chris Gavaler and Leigh Ann Beavers

Advanced Creative Nonfiction, Sean Prentiss and Jessica Hendry Nelson

The Art and Craft of Asian Stories, Xu Xi and Robin Hemley

Advanced Fiction, Amy E. Weldon

Forthcoming Titles:

Experimental Writing, William Cordeiro and Lawrence Lenhart

Poetry 2nd ed, Amorak Huey and W. Todd Kaneko

Environmental and Nature Writing 2nd ed, Sean Prentiss and Joe Wilkins

Fantasy Fiction, Jennifer Pullen

Advanced Poetry

A Writer's Guide and Anthology

Kathryn Nuernberger and Maya Jewell Zeller

BLOOMSBURY ACADEMIC
LONDON • NEW YORK • OXFORD • NEW DELHI • SYDNEY

BLOOMSBURY ACADEMIC
Bloomsbury Publishing Plc
50 Bedford Square, London, WC1B 3DP, UK
1385 Broadway, New York, NY 10018, USA
29 Earlsfort Terrace, Dublin 2, Ireland

BLOOMSBURY, BLOOMSBURY ACADEMIC and the Diana logo are trademarks of Bloomsbury Publishing Plc

First published in Great Britain 2024

Cover design: Rebecca Heselton
Cover image: Porcelain figures by Sophie Woodrow | sophiewoodrow.co.uk

A catalogue record for this book is available from the British Library.

Library of Congress Cataloging-in-Publication Data

Names: Nuernberger, Kathryn, author. | Zeller, Maya Jewell, author.
Title: Advanced poetry : a writer's guide and anthology / Kathryn Nuernberger and Maya Jewell Zeller.
Description: New York : Bloomsbury Academic, 2024. | Series: Bloomsbury writer's guides and anthologies | Includes bibliographical references and index.
Identifiers: LCCN 2023025529 (print) | LCCN 2023025530 (ebook) |
ISBN 9781350224582 (paperback) | ISBN 9781350224575 (hardback) |
ISBN 9781350224599 (epub) | ISBN 9781350224605 (pdf)
Subjects: LCSH: Poetics. | Poetry–Authorship.
Classification: LCC PN1042 .N84 2024 (print) | LCC PN1042 (ebook) |
DDC 808.1—dc23/eng/20230605
LC record available at https://lccn.loc.gov/2023025529
LC ebook record available at https://lccn.loc.gov/2023025530

ISBN: HB: 978-1-3502-2457-5
PB: 978-1-3502-2458-2
ePDF: 978-1-3502-2460-5
eBook: 978-1-3502-2459-9

Series: Bloomsbury Writer's Guides and Anthologies

Typeset by RefineCatch Limited, Bungay, Suffolk
Printed and bound in Great Britain

To find out more about our authors and books visit www.bloomsbury.com and sign up for our newsletters.

CONTENTS

Foreword: The End & the Beginning xi
An Invitation to Compose an Ars Poetica Before Reading *xi*
Introduction and Notes to Readers, Writers, and Teachers *xi*
Some Notes on Teaching This Book *xiv*

Pathways into Poetic Lineages

1 Sound, Shape, & Space: Received and Invented Forms 1
A Few Poems to Start Us Off . . . 2
Rebecca Tamás, "Interrogation (1)" 3
Mai Der Vang, "Dear Exile," 6
Jawdat Fakhreddine, translated by Hudo Fakhreddine and Jayson Iwen, "Bird" 7
Rosebud Ben-Oni, "Poet Wrestling with Atonement" 8
Mita Mahato, Excerpts from "Extinction Limericks" 9
Douglas Kearney, "Afrofuturism (Blanche says, "Meh")" 10
Discussion 11
The Oral Tradition and Technologies of Sound 14
Forms for Slowing Down, Doubling Back, Reading Again 16
From Page to Stage, Stage to Page 18
Further Experiments in Form and the Open Field 19
Invitations to Reflect 20
Writing Exercises 21

2 Telling Secrets: Confessions, Epistolaries, & the Lyric "I" 23
A Few Poems to Start Us Off . . . 24
Toi Derricotte, "Speculations about 'I'" 25
Jorge Luis Borges, translated by James. E. Irby, "Borges and I" 28
M.L. Smoker, "Letter to Richard Hugo (1)" 29

Margaret Atwood, "Siren Song" 30
Christopher Soto (Loma), "Those Sundays" 31
Discussion 32
The Poem's Rhetorical Situation 32
Poetic Subjectivity and The Origins of the Lyric "I" 36
Confessional Poets vs. Confession 38
Confessions and the Epistolary Mode 40
Invitations to Reflect 43
Writing Exercises 44

3 The Poem in Telephone Lines & Other Thoughts on Tone, Talk, and Voice in Poetry 47
A Few Poems to Start Us Off . . . 48
Barbara Guest, "Eating Chocolate Ice Cream: Reading Mayakovsky" 49
Craig Morgan Teicher, "Why Poetry: A Partial Autobiography ["How tense it makes me, reading . . ."]" 51
Daniel Borzutzky, "Lake Michigan, Scene 18" 53
Debora Kuan, "Minority Assignment #2" 55
Louise B. Halfe—Sky Dancer, "*ê-kwêskît*—Turn-Around Woman" 56
Discussion 58
The New York School 59
Experimental Voices 62
More Experiments with the First Person Speaker and the Power of Connection 65
Invitations to Reflect 67
Writing Exercises 68

4 Writing Out of Surrealism 69
A Few Poems to Start Us Off . . . 70
Gérard de Nerval, translated by Louis Simpson, "Lines in Gold" 71
Marosa di Giorgio, translated by Peter Boyle, two untitled poems from *La falena* (The moth) 72
Eduardo Corral, "Self Portrait with Tumbling and Lasso" 73
Zbigniew Herbert, translated by Alyssa Vales, "Hermes, Dog, and Star" 75
Jose Hernandez Diaz, "The West" 76

Discussion 77
Non-sense and the Ecosystem of Surrealism 78
Fur Cups & Saucers 79
Global and Intersecting Implications 80
Further Arcs and Mysteries of Ancestry 82
Invitations to Reflect 86
Writing Exercises 87

5 Duende, Deep Image, & The Poetics of Spells 89
A Few Poems to Start Us Off . . . 90
Josefina de la Torre, three untitled excerpts from *Poemas de la Isla,* translated by Carlos Reyes 91
James Wright, "Milkweed" 93
Diane Seuss, "[I dreamed I had to find my way from the city where I live now]" 94
Brigit Pegeen Kelly, "Song" 95
Jennifer Givhan, "After Emily" 97
Rachelle Cruz, "Self Portrait as Blood" 98
Discussion 99
A Little on Lorca and Ingredient-gathering Friendships 100
A Brief History of the Duende 101
Living Metaphor: A Form and a Radius of Action 102
Duende, James Wright, and Deep Image 103
The Poetics of Deep Image and the Shadow Self 105
Contemporary Feminist Renditions of Image as the Poetics of Spells 107
Invitations to Reflect 110
Writing Exercises 111

6 The Poetics of Liberation 113
A Few Poems to Start Us Off . . . 114
Monica Hand, "Black is Beautiful" 115
Laura Hershey, "In the Way" 116
Roy G. Guzmán, "Queeradactyl" 118
Naomi Shihab Nye, "A Palestinian Might Say" 119
Kenji C. Liu, "Warding Spell Against Trump v. Hawaii :: 585 US ___ (2018)" 120
Discussion 122

The Liberatory Poetics of Surrealism 123
The Black Arts Movement 125
Accessibility and Liberation 127
Poetic Liberation through a Community-Building Practice 129
Invitations to Reflect 131
Writing Exercises 132

7 Writing the Body 134
A Few Poems to Start Us Off . . . 135
Debjani Chatterjee, "What I Did Today" 136
Bruce Snider, "Frutti de Mare" 137
Ama Codjoe, "On Seeing and Being Seen" 138
Meg Day, "10 AM Is When You Come to Me" 139
CA Conrad, "(Soma)tic 5: Storm SOAKED Bread" 140
"One Day I Will Step from the Beauty Parlor and Enlist in the Frequency of Starlings" 141
Cameron Awkward-Rich, "[BLACK FEELING]" 143
Discussion 145
Pleasure, Pain, and the Source of Feeling 146
What a Metaphor Is to a Body 148
Genre / Gender Blur 151
Invitations to Reflect 152
Writing Exercises 153

8 The Racial Imaginary 154
A Few Poems to Start Us Off . . . 155
Roger Reeves, "In a Brief, Animated World: The Marriage of Anne of Denmark to James of Scotland, 1589" 156
Aracelis Girmay, "& When We Woke" 157
Jaswinder Bolina, "Partisan Poem" 159
Leanne Betasamosake Simpson, "this accident of being lost" 161
Tess Taylor, "Downhill White Supremacists March on Sacramento" 162
Discussion 163
Telling and Re-Telling the History of Racism 164
Race and the Relationships between Author, Speaker, and Reader 166
That Art of Looking Inward 170

Invitations to Reflect 173
Writing Exercises 174

9 Writing in the Field 176
A Few Poems to Start Us Off . . . 177
Vievee Francis, "Another Antipastoral" 178
Jos Charles, from *FEELD* 179
Gerard Manley Hopkins, "The Windhover" 180
Kim Hyesoon, translated by Don Mee Choi, "All the Garbage of the World, Unite!" 181
Inger Christensen, translated by Susanna Nied, from *alphabet* 182
Discussion 183
Attention, Wonder, and Some Global Origins 184
Devotionals, Moments of Time, and other Celebratory Poetics 185
The Three E's: Ecopoetics, Ethnopoetics, and Ethical Positionality 187
The Antipastoral, Necropastoral, and Field of the Page 189
Invitations to Reflect 193
Writing Exercises 194

10 Docupoetics & Other Forms of Lyric Research 197
A Few Poems to Start Us Off . . . 198
Layli Long Soldier, "38" 199
Paisley Rekdal, "Assemblage of Ruined Plane Parts, Vietnam Military Museum, Hanoi" 204
Craig Santos Perez, from "Understory" 206
Philip Metres, *"Black Site (Exhibit 1)"* 209
Marwa Helal, "Census" 210
Kiki Petrosino, "Instructions for Time Travel" 212
Discussion 213
Written in the Grass 214
A Brief History of Docupoetics from Virgil's *Georgics* to the Present 215
Putting the Documents in Docupoetics 218
Questions of Voice & Witness 220
Invitations to Reflect 224
Writing Exercises 225

Afterword: The Beginning & the End 227
An Invitation to Revisit Your Ars Poetica 227

Mentor Poets and the Making of Personal Canons 227
Making More Space in the Field 232

Appendices: Mapping Your Writing Life 233
Creating an Inspiring and Supportive Workshop Community 234
Strategies for Revision 240
Some Notes on Assembling a Collection 244
Submitting Poems for Publication 247
Writing an Artist Statement 251

Acknowledgments 255
Index 262

FOREWORD

THE END & THE BEGINNING

An Invitation to Compose an Ars Poetica Before Reading

We often tell students that we know the ending of a poem is working when it makes you want to go back to the beginning. And we know a title is working when it rewards that return.

So, before you dive into the contents of this book, we invite you to reflect on your own poetics knowledge and beliefs, aesthetics and influences, styles, and ways of making language magic. We suggest that before you even start reading this textbook you begin by writing an ars poetica, a poem or poem-like prose piece on the art of poetry, specifically focusing on your own beliefs about and approaches to writing craft and inspiration, draft and revision, the effable and ineffable. Put your most-you voice into this work, documenting yourself as a writer now. (As a practicing poet, you may already have a sense of what an ars poetica entails, but if not, you can find lots of examples in the online companion to this textbook.) And, when you finish the chapters, come back and write another one from zero draft. Compare the two. How has your voice transformed? What new beliefs and approaches do you have? How have your thoughts on the art of poetry changed? What parts of your voice and style have remained steadfast?

Introduction and Notes to Readers, Writers, and Teachers

Who is this book for?

Most introductory and intermediate poetry-writing courses and self-directed studies lead you quite engagingly into inspiration and craft decisions regarding image, voice, music, poem shape, and other forms of language play that will help you create compelling verses. We intend for *Part 1:*

Pathways into Poetic Lineages to be useful to those writers who have been working in the genre a while and now hope to deepen their relationship to poetics, to experiment and take risks with forms and styles, and to push their writing and reading into new understandings and innovations, across varied and inclusive global aesthetics.

How is this book organized?

We have organized this book into two parts, "Pathways Into Poetic Lineages," a set of 10 chapters that each introduce a potential lineage in which a poet might be writing; and then "Mapping Your Writing Life," a set of appendices that cover practical matters, as outlined below. We hope that these reflective and practical approaches to poetic identity empower writers to both recognize received traditions and to imagine their ways into new ones.

Pathways into Poetic Lineages

The first part of this book, which is the majority of its content, contains 10 chapters that each discuss a lineage or tradition in poetics. Within each chapter, we:

- open with a very brief overview of that chapter's focus;
- include five to six poems representative of this lineage;
- offer context for the lineage by defining terms, discussing literary histories, and referring back to the chapter's opening poems as examples;
- invite the reader to reflect on that particular lineage and its relationship to their work; and
- provide a range of craft exercises to help writers practice techniques that might contribute to styles / poems that could be in conversation with this lineage.

Appendices: Mapping Your Writing Life

The second part of the book offers several appendices, designed to help you navigate practical parts of writing, from revising and submitting work for publication to developing sustainable writing communities for a lifetime of writing.

Why begin each chapter with poems, instead of saving them for an appendix, or anthology?

As we state in our preface to the first chapter, we like to begin all conversations about poetry with poems. We ourselves are poets and believe that most of us came to this genre not because we loved reading and studying what *others* thought of a poem, but because we delighted in language as an art, first. Once an aspiring poet experiences this delight, they might wonder about how it came to be—in terms of craft, influence, ancestry. The poems come first in order to ground the whole study in that which can teach us the most.

Do I need to read the chapters in order?

Not at all. You'll notice that there's lots of overlapping and entangling of traditions in this book. For example, we discuss epistolary poems in both Chapters 1 and 2, or the field of the page in 1 and 9, and Surrealism in 4 and 8. This is because lineages aren't really linear. Like poets, whose influences and traditions often overlap into webs and rhizomatic tangles, our ancestries and their forms and styles are integrated into one another. One might easily write these chapters using different titles or controlling ideas, as one might also create sub-chapters within some of them: "Writing in the Field," for example, could also have been called "Writing Place," or have been split into a chapter on the pastoral, one on the necropastoral, and one on devotionals. At one point in one of our author's lives, someone called her a "nature" poet, and she balked—the term was too married to a specific version of poet in her mind. Likewise, you do not need to define yourself by how we name these lineages, but you might say your work is influenced by documentary poetics, field poetics, and epistolary traditions. You might also say you are interested in duende, writing the body, and the confessional mode. None of the categories we describe are mutually exclusive.

What pedagogical principles guide this textbook?

We wanted this book, like our classrooms, to be rooted in a social constructivist pedagogy based in community building, shared knowledge and expectations, and student choice underscoring each assignment. So, while we have tried to represent a wide and deep range of voices, aesthetics, and identities, we are wary of authoritative canons, and hope students will continue to challenge and build upon any suggested reading list. We also invite poets to imagine new ways of framing lineages and to write new chapters as exercises in their own authority.

Some Notes on Teaching This Book

We imagine several approaches to using this book. If a poet would like to consider a broad, aerial perspective before getting into specific lineages, they might first read through all the small paragraphs that open and overview each chapter, to get a sense of the depth and breadth of those particular poetics. Or, you might choose to open your study with the poetic lineage map assignment we describe in the afterword, which one might develop throughout the term. Or, you might choose to use a mix of these approaches, and study one chapter per week, adding a stand-alone contemporary collection of poetry to augment each chapter or set of two or three chapters. (As we mention above, many of the lineages we discuss overlap and many contemporary poetry collections exist at the confluence of multiple influences.) Another approach would be for an instructor to pick just those chapters most relevant to their pedagogical interests and invite students to use the other chapters for independent study.

Still another possibility would be to start with Part II of the text, Mapping Your Writing Life (our appendices), and ask poets to identify their individual goals, and then allow them to chart their own course through the chapters in Part I as a journey in search of a personal poetics, perhaps sharing summaries and responses to their individualized reading with their cohorts along the way.

Because each chapter can also operate entirely on its own, this text could also be adapted to a four-to-six-week community class or writing group, with leaders and / or members choosing those parts most relevant to their writing goals.

Finally, while we wrote this book with a *writing* course in mind, we also recognize its potential for use in advanced or graduate-level poetics form-and-theory courses. In these courses, teachers could augment their students' prior knowledge of poetic terminology with overviews of influential lineages, using each chapter as a jumping off place for study of that tradition. In this case, the writing exercises at the end of each chapter might serve to experiment with that style of poetics. Students could then write accompanying analytical pieces in which they discuss how an element within this tradition helped them more fully understand their own poetic practice.

One might easily build an entire course of study around just this textbook plus the online companion—which contains links to additional texts available online: poems, craft works, scholarly essays, and other works that augment or expand the chapters' discussions.

We recognize that anyone teaching this book is likely a poet, too, with your own take on the last several thousand years of writing. Obviously, please feel free to adapt any of our writing exercises, reflections, and assignments to your own style.

Kathryn Nuernberger & Maya Jewell Zeller
July 2023

1

Sound, Shape, & Space: Received and Invented Forms

A FEW POEMS TO START US OFF . . .

We like to begin all conversations about poetry with poems. In this chapter we'll introduce you to a few received forms poets can adopt, reinvent, even explode. Here are five examples we'll discuss in this chapter.

Rebecca Tamás

Interrogation (1)

Are you a witch?

Are you

Have you had relations with the devil?

Have you

Have you had relations with the devil and what took place?

I kissed him under the tail, it was a bit like soil, a bit like road tar
when it heats up, he was flickering in pleasure, the field would
be just the same when I tongue that, the bird's feathers parting.

What knowledge did the devil give you?

I built a house next to the sea, the roof is red / orange, the sky
is a shaking plate of light peeling you back, there is grass
out the front, some metal bins, you can see a lighthouse. I began
to sleep with the windows open, I began to creep along the bed
to my own globe face in the mirror. Sitting rubbed up in myself
is this fierce fire, it does not come from me, even the stones in
the drive are crackling with it.

What did the devil make you do under his control?

His mother had just died. We ate mint ice
cream by the coffin, he was missing her,
my sock was loose, we kept laughing.

What is magic?

Picture an egg yolk, that huge yellow throw up sun.
Dementedly shining, falling out of itself, birthed and
reverent.

What is magic?

Little cracks coming in, small flaws in the glass,
and the air slapping itself, you stand on a hill,
things are mainly green and breakable,
you think ok I'm not alone, but mainly,
ok I was never alone, on a far off hill the
earth is breaking up against the gas pressure
of the sun, if there was ever anything to miss
this is what you miss, how it's beginning.

What crimes have you enacted?

Love makes me forget myself sometimes.
I am horribly angry, I am sick with it,
my vomit turns black, but this love.
I can't explain it, beyond that it is exactly.

What other witches / sorcerers have you conjured with?

S couldn't eat. The food was poor and cheap but not that.
She had these violet eyes.

Have you taken black mass?

I've wondered why things turn. Rustling and fluttering cells,
the nib of the chest where what you might call soul slides out
and enters a hyena fucking happily amongst the fruit rinds.

What did the devil make you do under his control?

What you should do is go out and get really drunk.

What did the devil make you do under his control?

What you should do is get a sleeper train.

What did the devil make you do under his control?

I can pack everything and I can carry the suitcases up
staircases and along roads. I can go, even though
I am not importantly myself. Some of the things
that are me can go.

Have you profaned holy scripture?

The biggest fear is that reality itself starts to curdle,
stiffens into waxy stops.

Were you born to witches?

Were you

Who have you used spells against in this parish?

I can't say that I've met god directly, but I
can tell you how I think of it. God holding my heart
in a palm as it flexes from blue to green to white.
God being really tired, haar of sea fog.
I've had to decide what it looks like, what it is.
Shiver of the long world, cold feet,
a small, bright, filthy song.

Mai Der Vang

Dear Exile,

Never step back   Never a last
Scent of plumeria

When my parents left
You knew it was for good

    It's a herd of horses never
        To reclaim their   steppes

You became a moth hanging
Down from the sun

Old river   Calling to my mother
Kept spilling out of her lungs

Ridgeline vista closed
Into the locket of their gaze

                It's the Siberian crane
        Forbidden   to fly back after winter

You marbled my father's face
Floated him as stone over the sea

Further   Every minute
Emptying his child years to the land

You crawled back in your bomb

        It's when the banyan must leave
    Relearn to cathedral its roots

Jawdat Fakhreddine, translated by Hudo Fakhreddine and Jayson Iwen

Bird

1.
The heart lies,
and drops in the pit of the body
heavy beats.
The heart lies,
and sends to the far limbs lightning
and night-long shivers.

2.
The heart plays, it does not lie.
It plays, drumming among lowly organs.

3.
It is the heart then,
the bird of this body.
In its pit it plays.
In its pit it strives.
It forever flies wingless within its thoracic cage.
Wrestling with echoes,
choking sometimes,
shy as shy words,
noble as noble words.

4.
It is the heart.
It will fall asleep tomorrow.
Then, would the bird break free from the pit of this body,
a bird promised beyond these arid skies,
slaking the skies?

(April 1995)

Rosebud Ben-Oni

Poet Wrestling with Atonement

So I turn you into a horse but you are jealous of that horse.
& so you've chosen to die.
Or rather: the horse will not
not be skinned. There. {There.} Feel better. Next year
I'll teach you to swim & you'll carry us north
for wintertime.
So I turn you into
a horse, a water horse, with sealskin & steely
fins that never tire, but still you are jealous
of some distant & parched mire
wanting to bury me
in a rusted flask.
Wanting all my bare skin
skunned in wineflesh.
As proof
of first horse-&-human debt,
unborn seed
far away from smokeless winter
chimney & singed
evergreen
kicked[straight]
to the curb.
& even if we'd return
{minutes} before the world's end, still
I'd turn you into a horse who would die
dying for the music.
Underneath ivory
tabernacle, under holy child.
& still you lament the tusk
warped into wings,
the horns hammered for organ keys.
& now you're a songless thing tearing through
the middle of this horse, who(m) if I don't finish,
will be left swimming
in loose folds of ocean
for eternity
—so I turn you into a horse
& you say the ice is not a place for sacrifice.
So I turn you into {a horse} & you say: *turn me*
into a drop of rain & I swear by the *skun*
of our sins you[& I]
will never see land again.

Mita Mahato

Excerpts from "Extinction Limericks"

Douglas Kearney

Afrofuturism (Blanche says, "Meh")

won't you let me take you on a ~~*sea*~~ *cruise?*

ROCKETS

so far ahead
it's behind us.
Moses tote her
raygun saying
moonwalk or git
disinigrated!

TAKE ME TO
TAKE ME TO
TAKE ME TO
TAKE ME TO
TAKE ME TO
TAKE ME TO
TAKE ME TO
TAKE ME TO
TAKE ME TO
TAKE ME TO
TAKE ME TO

pharaohs go far away-o, no rid-
ing place
down dere!

thrones
thrown up
like they
just don't care!

[eject]

MOONSHOTS

what our antenna said we was bugged,
so us eyed the light up to light out.
whole of "... the place" blacked up so blacks out
this terra. o great gettin up launchin!
spacesuited Q.U.E.E.N.S. in foil to fly.
flightsuited kings sky around shinin.
zip zip zip off the planetation,
beyond the stairs to nigga heaven.

ROCKETS

TAKE ME TO
TAKE ME TO
TAKE ME TO
TAKE ME TO
TAKE ME TO
TAKE ME TO
TAKE ME TO
TAKE ME TO
TAKE ME TO

IT'S AN ESCAPE CRAFT
FROM NOW&THEN
BY WAY OF THEN&SOON.

"yeahyeahyeahyeah"
"yeahyeahyeahyeah"

MOONSHOTS

"who you callin BUCK Rogers?!"

it's the Where,
the When we go
when the Call
gets no Response.
[do you read?
over.]

ASTROSHEEN®
REMY MARTIAN®
~~CADILLITE®~~
~~CADILACTIC®~~
SPACEY ADAMS®

TAKE ME TO
TAKE ME TO
TAKE ME TO
TAKE ME TO
TAKE ME TO

ROCKETS

are we *there* yet?
are we *we* yet?
are we *we* there?
are there *we* there yet?
are we here *yet* there?
there, there.

ooo–weeee!

"NASA been good to us!
Dogonnit, I'm serious!"

MOONSHOTS

"who you callin StarBUCK?!"

"pilot...
"pilot...
"pilot...
"pilot...
"pilot...

DISCUSSION

Some of the most resonant poems are those invented by children, or by adults trying to delight children. Magpie rhymes, for instance, beg to be reinvented as you walk along with a grumpy preschooler or two in tow—*One for sorrow, two for mirth, three for a wedding, four for a birth*. Or how about this one? *One for giggling, two for gloom, three for rocket ship, four to the moon.* Now you try. *One for sunshine, two for rain, three for adventure, four and we're home again.*

Or maybe you are more familiar with "Down by the Bay," that rhyming game of a song with the refrain, "Down by the bay, where the watermelon grows, back to my home, I dare not go. For if I do, my mother will say—" and now comes the moment in the verses where the only rule is to rhyme as absurdly as you can within the steady rhythm:

> Did you ever see a goose dancing with a moose, down by the bay?
> Did you ever see a llama spinning her mama, down by the bay?
> Did you ever see a lady penning some poetry, down by the bay?

Poetry is the art form most closely knitted to oral traditions. Poetic elements like rhyme and rhythm have long served the crucial function of helping griots, troubadours, and other storytellers remember the important and sacred knowledge of their communities. (Sometimes that help comes in the form of a missed beat or rhyme tripping the performer up because they've begun to go astray.) But even when print media is readily available, the oral tradition remains alive in poetry. Four Guns, an Oglala Lakota tribal judge in the nineteenth century, critiqued Eurocentric notions of literacy as an advancement over this oral tradition, saying,

> Our host has filled many notebooks with the sayings of our fathers as they came down to us. This is the way of his people; they put great store upon writing; always there is a paper. But we have learned that there are many papers in Washington upon which are written promises to pay us for our lands; no white man seems to remember them. The Indian needs no writings; words that are true sink deep into his heart where they remain in silence; he never forgets them.

It's an ambitious, but worthy, goal for a poet to consider deeply how they might use language with the degree of care and integrity described by Four Guns.

The Song Poet is a recent memoir by Kao Kalia Yang, which celebrates the ways a rich oral tradition can be a source of strength and solace. As part of a larger story about her Hmong-American childhood and her family's journey through refugee camps after genocide was declared against the

Hmong people who had assisted US soldiers during the Vietnam War, Yang writes about the first time she heard her father perform *kwv txhiaj*, traditional Hmong song poetry:

> In his song I was no longer young. I was one with a people who had lived for a long time, traveled across many lands, a people clinging to each other for a reminder, a promise, of home, that place deep inside and far beyond where the Hmong people had hidden our hearts so that we could heal.

While only some of us have the chance to spend significant portions of our lives immersed in oral traditions that remain vibrant through careful and steadfast preservation, any time we write, especially using traditional forms, we connect ourselves to that long tradition of passing knowledge across time and place, farther than we could imagine a single person or their lone voice ever reaching. Here are just some of the ways that commonly used forms connect us to a chorus of voices and ancestors:

The elegy was originally created by the Greeks, with strict metrical forms to be used in response to a death. More recently, in the English language, it has evolved away from metrical constraints and is defined as any poem whose subject is a lament for the dead.

The ode is another Greek invention. Designed to be sung, they were works of praise and celebration, composed of three verses: the strophe, antistrophe, and epode. In contemporary poetry the three stanzas are no longer considered an essential element, though odes do commonly follow an *ababcdecde* rhyme scheme. But it is primarily the theme of celebration or praise, not the rhyme scheme, that makes an ode an ode.

The haibun is a form originating in Japan that features a combination of a prose poem and haiku. The prose poem usually describes a scene or moment in an objective manner, avoiding the use of the first person. The haiku then follows, communicating either subtly or quite directly with the material in the prose portion.

The ghazal is an Arabic form that was embraced by medieval Persian poets, who often used the form in writing about erotic longing, religious belief, or mysticism. Ghazals are composed of a series of stand-alone couplets that each end on the same word or phrase (the *radif*), which is preceded by the couplet's rhyming word (the *qafia,* which appears twice in the first couplet). The last couplet includes a proper name, often the poet's.

The sonnet is a fourteen-line poem written in iambic pentameter, containing a volta, or turn, and using one of several regular rhyme schemes; *ababcdcdefefgg* was the one Shakespeare used (with the volta occurring between lines 12 and 13), while a Petrarchan sonnet uses *abbaabbacdecde*. Often the first eight lines (octave) describe a problem, while the last six lines (sestet) offer its solution (with the volta occurring between the octave and the sestet). Choosing a form of sonnet involves, therefore, deciding when the turn should occur—does the sonnet require more suspense before concluding, or less? One also may relate this decision to the rich tradition of using the sonnet form when composing a love poem, its most common subject, though a sonnet can really have any theme.

The litany was initially used as a prayer or supplication in religious processions. More recently it has been adapted as a poetic form that catalogs a series. The form often features repetitious phrases or movements, such as anaphora, epistrophe, and other forms of syntactical parallelism.

The tanka, which translates as "short song," is one of the oldest Japanese forms. It was developed in the Japanese imperial court, where nobles engaged in tanka writing contests, and tankas were also exchanged between lovers as part of courtship and seduction. After spending an evening together, one might send their beloved a tanka as a kind of note of thanks. There are some challenges to translating this form from Japanese into English, but one Western way to think of the form is as a five-line poem with a 5/7/5/7/7 syllable count.

The pantoum is a traditional Malay form that was appropriated by French poets after Europeans colonized Malaysia in the sixteenth century. A pantoum is composed of a series of quatrains wherein the second and fourth lines of each stanza are repeated as the first and third lines of the next stanza. The pattern continues for any number of stanzas but in the final stanza, the first and third lines of the last stanza are the second and fourth of the penultimate. The first line of the poem becomes the last line of the final stanza. The meaning of lines should shift as they are repeated; a feat of word play achieved via shifting punctuation, punning, or recontextualizing. In Malaysian literary traditions, the pantoum is often treated as a whimsical or mischievous form of poetry.

A traditional Hmong song poem is not typically described as a poetic form with particular rules. Instead, Kao Kalia Yang explains the form by describing the way her father has carried the tradition forward. "In perfect pentatonic pitch my father sings his songs, grows them into long, stretching stanzas of four or five, structures them in couplets, repeats patterns of words, and changes the last word of each verse so that it rhymes with the end of the next. He is a master at parallelism, the language is protracted, and the notes are drawn deep and long. The only way I know how to describe it as a form in English is to say: my father raps, jazzes, and sings the blues when he dwells in the landscape of traditional Hmong song poetry."

Anglo-Saxon charms are a form of spell and a form of poetry that can be traced back at least to the twelfth century, when a few were recorded in medical texts written in Old English. They were very likely abundant in the oral tradition for a long time before that. A charm, which uses regular metrical forms, gives a set of instructions. They might be a recipe for a remedy or describe a series of ritual actions, or a combination of both. Their purpose is to heal or protect. Among the handful of traditional charms that remain with us today are charms to protect one on a journey, to aid in the delivery during a difficult childbirth, to protect against a swarm of bees, to ward off sickness, and to heal soil that has become barren from poor land management.

As you can see, embracing poetic forms means so much more than just committing to following a set of tricky rules around rhyme or rhythm. Rather, it is a complicated and inspiring task that requires willingness to tap into the spirit of the oldest songs of human experience and emotion. These rhymes and rhythms aren't arbitrary—they are the ways our ancestors and forebears found to express love and grief, longing, and wisdom. When we write in these forms, we are embracing the possibility that we might hear some echo of them in ourselves.

The Oral Tradition and Technologies of Sound

Rebecca Tamás's "Interrogation (1)" is an example of a poem deeply rooted in the oral tradition even as it takes full advantage of the technologies of ink, paper, and alphabets. In this poem there are two very distinct formal influences at play. One is the tradition of magic, which involves the use of poetic forms like charms and incantations. While we mention charms above, we will talk more about the tradition of spells in "Duende, Deep Image, and the Poetics of Spells." A common definition for a spell is: Words that make something happen. With this definition in mind, we hope you will never doubt that your work as a poet is pure magic.

In Tamás's poem we see this influence unfold in lines that itemize ritual actions like, "Picture an egg yolk, that huge yellow throw up sun." There is also the recitation of transcendent visions of a kind of divine presence, which echoes the spiritual function of literary expressions in magical traditions. "Ok I was never alone, on a far off hill the / earth is breaking up against the gas pressure / of the sun." These incantatory lines of communion with the natural world and shameless sensuality are juxtaposed against the poem's other influence, the court records and transcripts of witch trials.

Unlike the ancient agrarian shamanic traditions sometimes referred to as Paganism, which largely rely on oral traditions, the witch trials adopted the language of logic and reason, while the inquisitors generated extensive paper trails to justify their torture and executions, as well as to intimidate others. The question-and-answer format of an inquisition, especially the cruel and detached tone when articulating absurd fantasies about sex with demons, is also closely aligned with the form and content of witch trial records. The trial records were kept by court reporters, so it's difficult to say now what was added or omitted, and though they claim to be perfect records of human voices, we have no doubt they are classic examples of the kinds of rhetorical manipulation and subterfuge the written word can allow, and against which Four Guns cautioned.

However, Tamás applies this rhetoric in her poem to critique the patriarchal and theocratic oppression of this tradition. The speaker's answers adopt a tone that is at times defiant or visionary, always unapologetic, and often conveying transcendent descriptions of what is beautiful and life-affirming about the spiritual (and literary) traditions that pre-date Christianity. Through this ingenious fusion of two very different forms, Tamás is able to create a form that can imagine "God holding my heart / in a palm as it flexes from blue to green to white" while also asserting the pleasure of singing such "a small, bright, filthy song."

Jawdat Fakhreddine's "Bird" is another example of a poem in conversation with an ancient tradition of poetry passed down through the generations. As you read the poem, you will notice how the translators have attempted to carry rich sound effects from the poem's original Arabic form into English. There is the litany wherein "the heart drops" and "the heart lies" and "the heart plays." There are also repetitions like "In its pit, it plays. / In its pit, it strives." You could amuse yourself for quite a while noting the instances of alliteration, assonance, and internal rhyming that weave this poem together in a symphonic fashion that echoes the musical effects of experiencing the poem in Arabic, while also accommodating for the different possibilities and limitations for musicality in English. We also want to highlight this work because of the poet's strategy of alluding to Classical Arabic poems in each of his own poems. While this may not be readily apparent to English-language readers who aren't well-versed in Arabic literary traditions, the translators explain in their introduction to the collection where "Bird" first appears that "nearly every poem in the book begins with an allusion to a Classical Arabic poem, sometimes a poem that has become almost commonplace in daily Arabic parlance. Fakhreddine then personalizes and adapts the spirit of that poem to the conditions of his own life."

Throughout this textbook we will be introducing you to trends, lineages, and schools of thought in twentieth and twenty-first-century poetics. In many cases just one or two poets will serve as emblematic examples of a style or tradition we see influencing many contemporary poets. Our hope and intention is that any time you encounter a poem in this book that resonates with you deeply, you will refer to our online companion to find your way to many other poets working in those traditions. Our goal is that you make your way to the poems and poets that speak so deeply to your life that, like Jawdat Fakhreddine, every poem you write will feel rooted to those old songs, whether heard in childhood or a dream more ancient than that, that animate your poetic spirit.

Forms for Slowing Down, Doubling Back, Reading Again

Certainly, a poem destined for the page is not quite the same as one that will only live on the tongue. A poet who composes for the stage must consider how silence or volume or cadence might amplify the effect of each word, while the poet with their eye on print must consider how a rhyme lands differently when the eye perceives it before the ear. A poet performing must consider how an audience will process lines they must catch as they drift from the body of the poet through the audience into their own minds, which may be distracted or uncertain. With pen in hand, the poet writing for the page must consider what will surprise a reader who can always slow down, double back, and read it over again. In her meditation on the tension between the oral and the written in poetry, Mai Der Vang writes in "Poetry as Homeland: Reflection on Hmong American Exile and a Literary Future," that "I see my work attempting to retain what it means to be descended from a people whose way of life relied on the spoken word, while braiding that notion together with the need to pen one's voice onto paper in order to survive this era and the next." Traditional forms offer poets so many ways to evoke, to play, to sculpt, and to push an idea further. They also offer ways to hear the voices of the ancestors and to answer back.

"Dear Exile," by Mai Der Vang, is another poem rooted in the relationship between song and memory. This poem, an elegy for the land and those lost in the genocide against the Hmong people, uses couplets and repeated words to tell the story of almost unbearable loss. The poem also uses an epistolary form. Epistolary poetry, which we will discuss further in Telling Secrets, is a tradition of writing poems as letters; they always use a direct address; that is, they speak directly to a "you," a real person, while the reader imagines themselves having stumbled upon this artifact of an authentic communication. The epistolary form here is particularly haunting because readers must consider that, for a speaker in exile, there is no longer a home address such a letter can reach. Thus, the paradox of sending an epistle to the nature of exile itself.

This poem is notable for its use of sound effects—there is the repetition of the word "never" for example, and the alliteration in lines like "My father's face / Floated him as stone over the sea." In keeping with oral traditions, though, it also uses couplets as a way to hold a litany of images and memories, as well as metaphors for how this grief feels. Each couplet features a different enigmatic image. Some clearly connect to the experiences of the speaker and her family in exile—"Old river calling to my mother / Kept spilling out of her lungs." But other stanzas intentionally avoid a clear first-person subject, making it possible to hear the poem as if it were being spoken by voices in a chorus, allowing the reader to appreciate how wide-ranging and collective this grief is. "It's a herd of horses never / To reclaim their steppes."

You might also notice the use of irregular pauses indicated by extra spaces in Vang's lines, which suggest something like the drawing of a ragged breath or a mind that falls silent for a moment in unspeakable reveries. Such thinking about form as a way of controlling the breath and pace of the poem to match its meaning owes much to the mid-twentieth-century innovations with form that Denise Levertov helpfully described as "organic form" in her essay "Some Notes on Organic Form" (which you can read in its entirety, alongside some other notable essays on poetics and form, in the online companion to this chapter). According to Levertov, "During the writing of the poem the various elements of the poet's being are in communion with each other, and heightened. Ear and eye, intellect and passion, interrelate more subtly than at other times." The poet then, in crafting such a vision for the page, must try to intuit "an order, a form beyond forms." In organic forms, Levertov writes, "content and form are in a state of dynamic interaction; the understanding of whether an experience is a linear sequence or a constellation raying out from and into the central focus or axis, for instance, is discoverable only in the work, not before it."

Mai Der Vang's "Dear Exile" is an excellent example of how organic form might be employed. Another interesting use of form following function—or maybe we should say form following emotion—can be seen in Rosebud Ben-Oni's "Poet Wrestling with Atonement," where the page is treated as an open field wherein the mind can wander, then stall, reverse course, find a groove of understanding that is then interrupted or compounded. Ben-Oni's is not a form that aids memorization or invites audience repetition through call-and-response or the use of refrains. Rather, hers is a form that thwarts easy repetition, that relies on the technology of print to allow the poem to operate as a song. Though it is often beautiful to read out loud, this poem exists primarily as an object made of words you can hold before your eyes. The page becomes an aid in contemplation of what it means and how it feels to try to stop a romantic relationship from disintegrating.

From Page to Stage, Stage to Page

No discussion of poetic forms or the oral tradition would be complete without talking about how spoken word poetry has transformed the landscapes of contemporary poetry. Spoken word poetry is a twentieth and twenty-first century continuation of ancient oral traditions. It encompasses all kinds of poetry recited aloud, including work performed at poetry readings and slams, jazz poetry, and hip-hop music. The emphasis in spoken word is on the aesthetic effects of sound and the quality of the performance. Contemporary spoken word poetry is deeply influenced by the poetry of the Harlem Renaissance, though its lineage can be traced back to precolonial African literatures, including the great griot epic from Mali, *The Epic of Sundiata*. More recently, Button Poetry and the Nuyorican Poets Café have been crucial hubs and incubators for spoken word poetry.

While there is no shortage of poets writing out of slam or spoken word poetry scenes who we love to recommend (and in fact that list can be found in our online companion to this chapter), we want to focus on Douglas Kearney's work as an example from a poet who is deeply attentive to questions of sound and musicality and who has also made the open field of the page a fascinating playground for exploration and experimentation with poetic forms. Kearney's early work made extensive use of sound effects and repetition to explore themes of trauma, racist violence, and the ways Black people's pain is made into spectacle by a dominating, racist culture. While people sometimes describe poets who publish books after launching their careers as performers as making a transition "from stage to page," Kearney, who describes his work as closely related to the lineage of performance art, which is in kinship with but not the same as Slam poetry, uses the open field of the page to evoke the sonic textures of his performances. The page becomes a technology that can both translate and archive a work of performance art that might otherwise have been held only by a passing moment in time and space.

We strongly encourage you to listen to his recording of "Afrofuturism (Blanche says, 'Meh')" to better and more fully appreciate how the typography conveys sonic effects from Kearney's performance of the poem. Through auditory and typographic collage, Kearney reflects, with some notes of skepticism, on optimism about future technologies and innovations. The poem, with its allusions to Moses leading people out of slavery with her ray gun, or people in space suits working in plantations beyond the stars, suggests cynical frustration with fantasies that don't seriously contend with how a truly remarkable future would prioritize justice and equity over moonshots and rockets. The collage of voices is reminiscent of the chaotic chatter of advertisements, political speeches, and other forms of empty promises. Meanwhile, Kearney asks, "Are we there yet," over and over again, inviting readers to contemplate what "there" they really want to reach, or if "an escape craft from now and then" is really the way.

Further Experiments in Form and the Open Field

The question of form in contemporary poetry certainly flourishes as much in the open field of the page as it does in the space before an open mic. Poet and collage artist Mita Mahato creates poetry comics that merge the visual arts with language to create a poetic experience. Her sequence of poems, "The Extinction Limericks," calls back to a familiar poetic form to create space for grief over the many and mounting losses from climate change.

The limerick is a poetic form that combines a sing-song rhythm and rigid rhyme scheme to tell bawdy jokes. The form is often associated with bars and drunken revelry. A particularly iconic example is:

There was an Old Man with a beard,
Who said, "It is just as I feared!
Two Owls and a Hen,
Four Larks and a Wren,
Have all built their nests in my beard!"

In "The Extinction Limericks," Mahato sets us up for this kind of jolly rhyming. "There once was a tiger from Java," she writes, and we readers await eagerly the tiger's antics. In that silence we linger over the word "was" and slowly begin to understand what the past tense, in this poetic moment, really means. There are no more stories, jokes, or tales of wonder for an extinct creature. The poem creates a feeling of anticipation for a rhyme that cannot complete itself. This realization transforms the good humor we associate with limericks into a lamentation. Moreover, in that silence is the image—Mahato's striking fragmentation, by torn paper—of the creature that "once was." In this way, the erasure of the rest of the limerick creates a moment of meditative reverie, or poetic elegy, on how the lives lost had value, meaning, beauty, and wonder. The lives we could still see vanish do too.

As you can see, while poetry is rooted in ancient techniques and traditional forms, these are invitations to play, explore, and experiment with how sounds, shape, and meaning can call forth new forms of expression. Finding your voice as a poet involves finding forms that fit with your ways of thinking, speaking, relating to others, and the particular magic of an empty page conjuring your voice into being, first in your own mind, and then in the minds of your readers and listeners.

INVITATIONS TO REFLECT

Discuss Together

What kinds of oral traditions have shaped your relationship with your language or languages? What experiences have you had with telling or being told stories, jokes, little games? Reach back to your memories of abuelas and aunties and grandfathers and barbers and kindergarten teachers and ladies from the neighborhood at the salon. But don't hesitate to acknowledge that in this digital age Ms. Frizzle or Mr. Rogers or Elmo or LeVar Burton or K-pop bands like BTS might also be major influences on the way you understand the lyrical possibilities of language. In what ways is your understanding of the oral tradition you have inherited similar to or different from the ones described in this chapter?

For Further Study

Many poetry collections, like those whose works are listed in this chapter, draw from various received traditions, both poetic and cultural. Rebecca Tamás's *Witch,* as stated in our chapter, draws from the forms of inquisition and trial, and might be considered in poetic lineages with lyric "I" / confessionalism, ecopoetics / writing the field, Surrealism, spells and the occult, as well as other ancestries. Find a copy of her book and trace as many such influences as you can find. Do this again with Diane Seuss's *Frank Sonnets,* Mita Mahato's *In Between,* or other books you've read that engage quite directly with conversations about form. Now, look at your own manuscript in process or latest set of poems. What ancestral conversations, traditions, and forms do you tend to engage? With what others might you like to study and pursue? Which ones do you wish to push against?

Writing Exercises

1 The Listening Poem

Collect an oral history. Find a story that is unique to a community of which you are part and transcribe (that means copy word for word) the story you are told. You could call up a grandparent and ask about their youthful adventures. You could call up a friend from high school and ask them to remind you of some legend from your high school days. (How many high schools are allegedly haunted by a cheerleader from the '50s?) Maybe you belong to a church where people share testimonies about spiritual experiences—that's also a form of storytelling, although a more serious and earnest kind than teenage ghost stories would be. Please note that transcribing a story means that your work as the writer is not to tell the story yourself, it is to get someone else to tell you the story, while you record it word for word. Once you have recorded and transcribed the oral history, cut all of your questions and comments, and also cut any preambles or slow starts to the interview, as well as any winding down dialogue at the end to create a found poem. You might also choose to add commentary or insert questions where the original conversation had none. The key here is to first create a transcription and then discover the poetic possibilities that exist within such deep and careful listening.

2 Nursery Rhymes Remix

Revisit the little poems of your childhood—nursery rhymes or riddles or commercial jingles, cartoon theme songs, lullabies, fables, fairy tales. Pick one style or category and collect as many examples as you can remember or find—ideally at least five, though as few as three will work, into a mini-anthology. Then write a poem that imitates the tone and form of these little poems, even quotes or samples lines from them. But the subject of the poem should be about the experiences of adulthood—sex, drugs, rock and roll, paying the rent, scheduling a colonoscopy, finding a babysitter, going to a funeral etc.

3 The Poem Will Teach You Its Form

Take a journal entry or a failed poem and read it carefully to understand the patterns of thought in that writing. Draw an illustration or diagram to more fully internalize your understanding of the way you are thinking in the piece. Then choose one of the traditional forms described in this chapter that most closely matches your rhetorical impulses. (You also have the option to do a little googling and find one of the hundreds of other poetic forms to guide you.) Rewrite the piece, hewing as closely as you can to the rhyme schemes, meters, and other rules associated with that form. But also bear in mind that poems often teach us how to write them, so the poem may insist you break some of the form's rules or impose new formal limits. Try to learn from the elegance of the form, while giving yourself permission to let your poem stretch its wings.

4 **Into, Beneath, Beyond the Page**

Gather up 5 days of junk mail and create a poem by erasing words and images from one of the pieces. You can erase using black ink, white out, other colored paints or inks, or by pasting / collaging words or images from other mail over this piece.

5 **Response and Mimesis** (mimesis: from the Greek, "to imitate")

One of the oldest traditions in studying craft and form is writing an imitation poem, or poem that typically takes as its shape the exact syntactical, lineation, and grammatical rules of an existing poem (for examples of imitations, and more conversation about them, see our online companion). When we write using received forms, we are engaging in a form of mimesis. Same as when we add to "Down by the Bay." Yet another way to engage in mimetic traditions is through response poems, those that call back to, but don't exactly replicate, the inspiring poem. Choose a form or a poem you admire and write "back" to it, hewing as closely to your source as possible, but then, when your poem starts to leap in its own direction, allow yourself and your writing the freedom to become something entirely your own. When the poem is complete, you will have to decide whether it has verged away from the source poem enough to be its own poem and not a work of plagiarism. If the poem is very close to the original, let it remain an exercise in your notebook that you learned from, not a work you try to publish. If you feel it has become a piece that can rightly be called your own, you may still want to add a note at the beginning or end that says "after" and names the poet and poem that originally inspired you. You will see such notes on many contemporary poems, and it is a lovely way to acknowledge the writing ancestors who have helped shape your work. When done artfully, citation can be thought of as another poetic form.

2

Telling Secrets: Confessions, Epistolaries, & the Lyric "I"

A FEW POEMS TO START US OFF . . .

Poets writing in a voice that speaks specifically from an "I" to a "you" are often said to be writing in direct address, or apostrophe, and when composed as a letter, this is called epistolary (poetry or prose). Likely you picked up on this when discussed in the last chapter, but we'll talk more about it here. Related to epistolary is the confessional mode, an oft-referenced but frankly little-understood way of truth-telling in a poem—often mistaken for autobiographical, but also making use of persona, or a created character, to voice sometimes surprising realities. Both poetic styles have their history in the Lyric "I," one of the oldest and most intimate points of view and literary moves—the first person, in high lyric mode. Poems and discussion of these poems in this chapter will help you make sense of these techniques and their history and think about how they might be of use to you (I?).

Toi Derricotte

Speculations About "I"

A certain doubleness, by which I can stand as remote from myself as from another.

—Henry David Thoreau

i

I didn't choose the word—
it came pouring out of my throat
like the water inside a drowned man.
I didn't even push on my stomach.
I just lay there, dead (like he told me)

& "I" came out.
(I'm sorry, Father.
"I" wasn't my fault.)

ii

(How did "I" feel?)

Felt almost alive
when I'd get in, like the Trojan horse.

I'd sit on the bench
(I didn't look out of the eyeholes
so I wouldn't see the carnage).

iii

(Is "I" speaking another language?)

I said, "I" is dangerous.
But at the time I couldn't tell
which one of us was speaking.

iv

(Why "I"?)

"I" was the closest I could get to the
one I loved (who I believe was
smothered in her playpen).

Perhaps she gave birth
to "I" before she died.

v

I deny "I,"
& the closer
I get, the more
"I" keeps receding.

vi

I found "I"
in the bulrushes
raised by a dirtiness
beyond imagination.

I loved "I" like a stinky bed.

While I hid in a sentence
with a bunch of other words.

vii

(What is "I"?)

A transmission through space?
A dismemberment of the spirit?

More like opening the chest &
throwing the heart out with the gizzards.

viii

(Translation)

Years later "I" came back
wanting to be known.

Like the unspeakable
name of God, I tried

my 2 letters, leaving
the "O" for breath,

like in the Bible,
missing.

ix

I am not the "I"
in my poems. "I"
is the net I try to pull me in with.

x

I try to talk
with "I," but "I" doesn't trust
me. "I" says I am
slippery by nature.

xi

I made "I" do
what I wasn't supposed to do,
what I didn't want to do—
defend me,
stand as an example,
stand in for what I was hiding.

I treated "I" as if
"I" wasn't human.

xii

They say that what I write
belongs to me, that it is my true
experience. They think it validates
my endurance.
But why pretend?
"I" is a kind of terminal survival.

xiii

I didn't promise
"I" anything & in that way
"I" is the one I was most
true to.

Jorge Luis Borges, translated by James. E. Irby

Borges and I

The other one, the one called Borges, is the one things happen to. I walk through the streets of Buenos Aires and stop for a moment, perhaps mechanically now, to look at the arch of an entrance hall and the grillwork on the gate; I know of Borges from the mail and see his name on a list of professors or in a biographical dictionary. I like hourglasses, maps, eighteenth-century typography, the taste of coffee and the prose of Stevenson; he shares these preferences, but in a vain way that turns them into the attributes of an actor. It would be an exaggeration to say that ours is a hostile relationship; I live, let myself go on living, so that Borges may contrive his literature, and this literature justifies me. It is no effort for me to confess that he has achieved some valid pages, but those pages cannot save me, perhaps because what is good belongs to no one, not even to him, but rather to the language and to tradition. Besides, I am destined to perish, definitively, and only some instant of myself can survive in him. Little by little, I am giving over everything to him, though I am quite aware of his perverse custom of falsifying and magnifying things.

Spinoza knew that all things long to persist in their being; the stone eternally wants to be a stone and the tiger a tiger. I shall remain in Borges, not in myself (if it is true that I am someone), but I recognize myself less in his books than in many others or in the laborious strumming of a guitar. Years ago I tried to free myself from him and went from the mythologies of the suburbs to the games with time and infinity, but those games belong to Borges now and I shall have to imagine other things. Thus my life is a flight and I lose everything and everything belongs to oblivion, or to him.

I do not know which of us has written this page.

M.L. Smoker

Letter to Richard Hugo (1)

Dick: The reservoir on my end of the state is great for fishing. Some of the banks are tall and jagged, others are more patient, taking their time as they slope into rocky beaches. If you were the kind of fisherman I imagine, then you might have considered it a great place to cast from. My family has gone up there ever since the water on the Mni Shoshe was damned off. My grandparents put on their moccasins and beadwork and danced for FDR when he rode the train out to see the finishing touches of this great industrial project. I haven't yet decided if this is something I wish to be proud of. Maybe this summer I'll spend more time up there, on the edge of a lake that was never meant to be a lake, and form an actual opinion. Maybe too I'll write you again. But you have probably already figured as much. I almost thought of not returning to finish the writing program you began with your own severe desire for language. But I did. And now I'm at the end. Already though, I'll admit to you, I'm thinking of home. I have been this whole time.

Margaret Atwood

Siren Song

This is the one song everyone
would like to learn: the song
that is irresistible:

the song that forces men
to leap overboard in squadrons
even though they see the beached skulls

the song nobody knows
because anyone who has heard it
is dead, and the others can't remember.

Shall I tell you the secret
and if I do, will you get me
out of this bird suit?

I don't enjoy it here
squatting on this island
looking picturesque and mythical

with these two feathery maniacs,
I don't enjoy singing
this trio, fatal and valuable.

I will tell the secret to you,
to you, only to you.
Come closer. This song

is a cry for help: Help me!
Only you, only you can,
you are unique

at last. Alas
it is a boring song
but it works every time.

Christopher Soto (Loma)

Those Sundays

My father worked too many hours. He'd come home with his
cracked hands and bad attitude. & I'd rather talk about Rory now.
[His blond locks] How the sun would comb crowns into his hair.
Rory was my first love, before he killed himself.

> My father hated faggots. The way my cock looked beneath a
> dress. The mismatch of his chafed knuckles and my cut cuticles.
> A scrambling of hands. I was always running. Mascara. Massacre.
> My momma would wash the red paint off my nails and face.
> She'd hold me like the frame of a house. No, the bars of a
> prison cell.

"Mijo, your father is coming home soon. Hide your heels." I'm
the donkey clanking down the hall. Click, Clack, Click, Clack.
Over Momma's body [he'd grab me] & throw me against the
wall. My bruises dark as holes, he punched into the wall. His
hand was the hammer. I was the nail. & I want to talk about Rory
now.

> That night, after my father smashed the television glass with his
> baseball bat, I met Rory at the park. We made a pipe out of a
> plastic bottle and aluminum foil. [He watched me undress & run
> through ticking sprinklers]. I fell beside him then; beneath the
> maple tree. & he saw my goose bumps from the cold. & he felt
> my bruises, as they became a part of him.

Rory, I want to say that death is what you've always wanted. But
that can't be the Truth. [This time] we can blame it on me. I'll be
the packing mule, carry all the burden. & you, you can be a child
again; fold your church hands like dirty laundry [crease them tight].
Nobody has to know about us, not my father nor yours-
                    No, not even God.

DISCUSSION

If you have memorized a poem, or scrap of poem, or excerpt of lyrics from a song, recited it for years in wind and rain or joyful weather, until its music feels part of your cellular makeup, essential to your existence, mapped into your synapses and tissue so that one day you mistake the voice of the poem for your own voice, if you find yourself saying certain lines to a significant other to explain or express your deepest sentiments, as if those lines have their own coded meaning, as if they are, in fact, a kind of language, you might just know what we mean when we claim the speaker of a poem can feel permeable enough to be the bear suit or bird suit any of us wear as we stumble across the tundra or sing on our little islands or pen letters to our ancestors, that in fact the more intimate or personal the poem's *rhetorical situation*, the more universal the poem's *rhetorical exchange*.

Rhetorical exchange sounds complicated and formal, but if you know about gossip, then you know about rhetoric. Mary Ruefle, in *Madness, Rack, & Honey,* writes: "Everybody loves secrets—that's why you are here . . . I know with absolute certainty that each of you, as you entered this room, passed through the doors, found your seats, carried a secret inside you." Indeed, it is a truth universally acknowledged that poets . . . love to dish.

How does the deep mystery and gravity of the inner life move from the author-self through the poem and into the reader and then live—bloom more!—in that confidant? As poets, how do we begin to approach the Lyric "I" or other point of view? And how might that be related to the intimacies of poetic exchange?

The Poem's Rhetorical Situation

As an exercise in thinking about a poem's point of view and its relationship to authorial intrusion, self-reflexivity, and other matters of address and exchange, we often begin a poetics class by asking students to apply what they know of rhetoric to discussing poetry. This may sound counter, but a poet's inherent—learned or born-knowing—understanding of the lyric "I" or the lyric "you" or the lyric "they / them, she / her, he / him, ze / zou" is useful for crafting / establishing a relationship based on trust, which is one way of knowing what a poem can do: share an intimate secret between two parties.

Many creative writing professors talk about the author-speaker relationship, and also the speaker-listener relationship. We refer to the lines between these entities as *membranes*, borrowing the scientific term, because we find it useful to track permeability. Begin with the author, drawing a circle—or elliptical shape—around the word "author" on the board. That elliptical shape might be made up of a series of dashed lines, to indicate permeability, such as when the author writes autobiographical, first person poetry, in what is commonly referred to as the Confessional mode (though not all first person poetry is Confessional, and not all Confessional poetry is first person—we'll talk more about that in a minute); or the shape might be made up of a more solid line, to indicate that the author has constructed a border between themselves and their speaker, and is using a *persona*, which you are familiar with as poetry's term for character (as *speaker* is a poet's term for narrator). However, because some personas are really past or adjacent versions of the author themselves (with whom the late essayist Joan Didion famously suggests "We must keep on nodding terms"), the membrane may remain permeable. Also, because writing in the voice of another often—paradoxically—allows the self to be more honest, the line between them may remain "dashed" (in our visual representation) and permeable even for a persona. In fact, whether the poet writes in first, second, or third person, this line could be more or less porous.

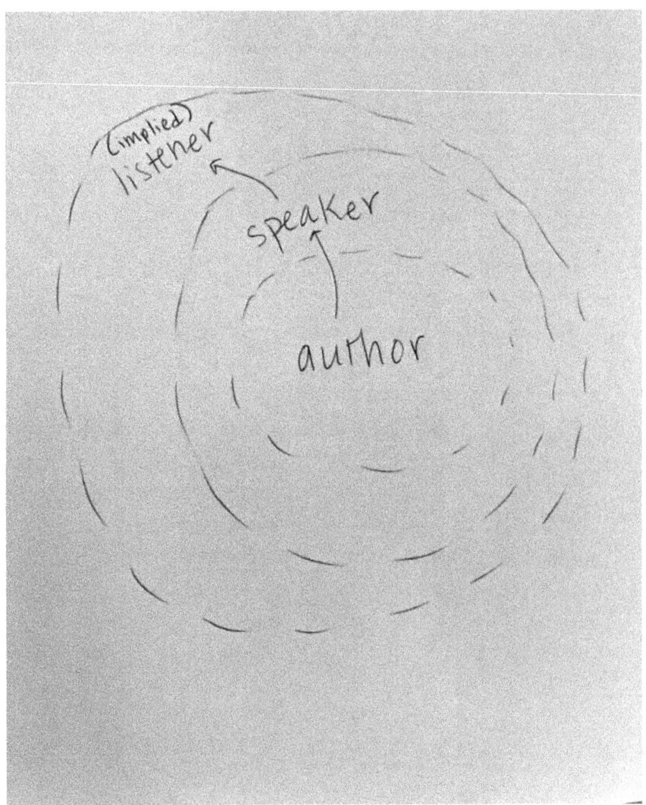

Beyond the listener is the *intended* audience—that is, who the author intended to have read the poem, and / or to whom their publishers marketed it (at the time and place of publication / re-publication), and beyond that, the reader—who is actually experiencing it now.

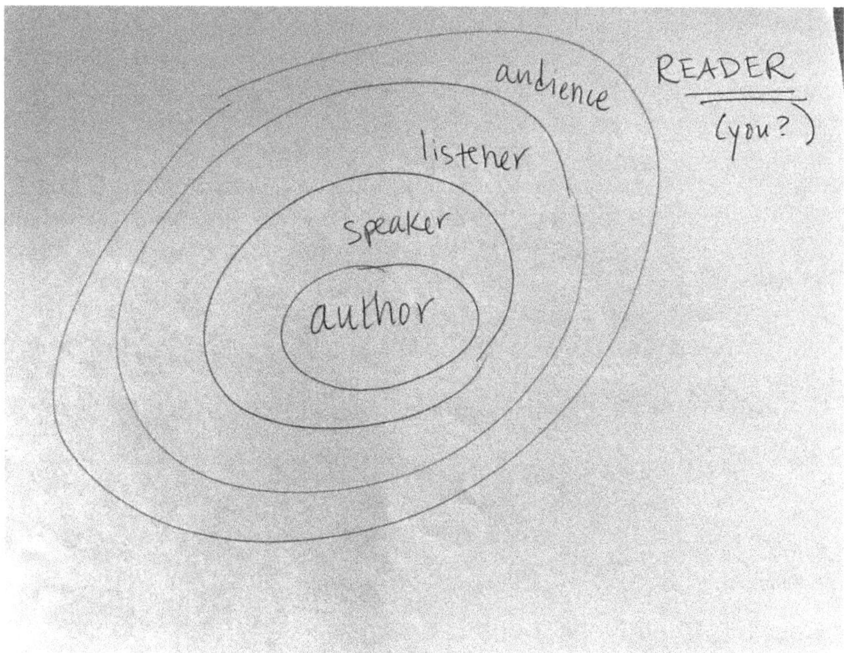

Of course, you can add extra layers to indicate things such as *setting*—and put it between the speaker and listener, like a sea one must cross to reach the other, or you could put it after the listener, and before the audience, to indicate that the audience, and the reader, are *witnesses* to an exchange that takes place in a shared setting. You could do this with many literary devices and affects, and pretty soon the diagram is a hot mess (like a "hot goss" phone call with a friend, or like a poem, or any other rhetorical situation). Additionally, the lines you draw between the author / speaker / listener / audience / reader can have more or less permeability depending on the reader's perspective, which is informed by cultural contexts, and also publishing concerns—and which might make the content, and voice of the poem, feel more or less intimate, depending on how "relatable" the subject and speaker are to them.

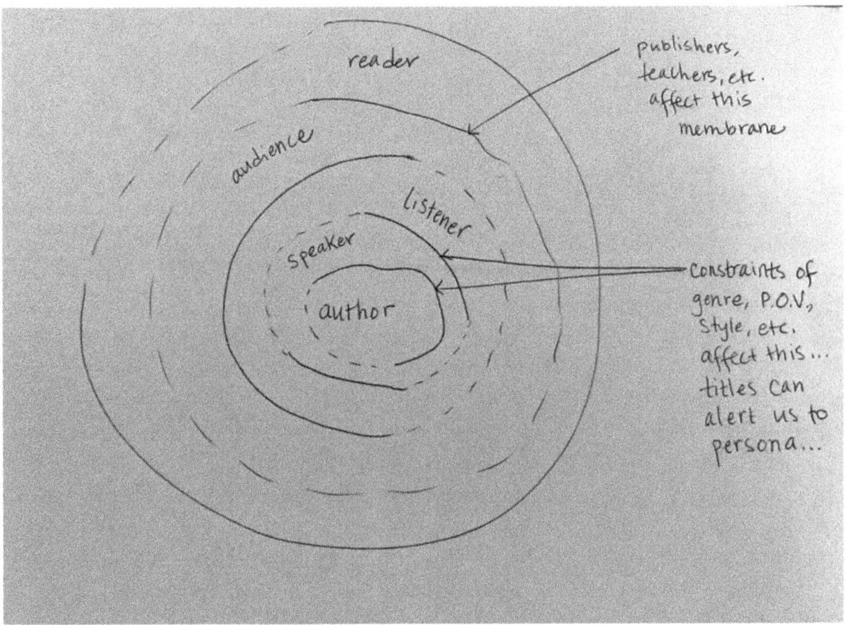

Let's look at a few lines from Margaret Atwood's "Siren Song," which you remember from the opening poems of this chapter, to get us started on one example of these membranes. We'll begin at the fourth tercet:

> Shall I tell you the secret
> and if I do, will you get me
> out of this bird suit?

In Atwood's poem, it is one of the traditional sirens—those that lured sailors to their deaths, those to whom Odysseus avoided falling prey by having his men tie him to a mast—that serves as the speaker. In the lyric tercet shared above, the siren woos a listener, asking them, "Shall I tell you the secret," and confessing "I don't enjoy it here / squatting on this island / looking picturesque and mythical // with these two feathery maniacs," that intimate confession of misery building trust with the listener. We might feel the humor and the seduction, too, Atwood pulling us in, a suspense that spans stanzas: "I will tell the secret to you, / to you, only to you. / Come closer," she writes, the speaker pulling in her listener—a sailor—but readers might mistake it for themselves, and "come closer" to the poem in terms of reading / feeling. The siren continues, jumping the stanza break as the sentence enjambs, rhythm matching the rhetoric, "This song // is a cry for help: Help me!," suggesting, almost, as we imagine that we are the sailor, that we breach the membranes of the poem, as the sailor might leave their ship; each sentence stretches and breaks like a wave crest in the succeeding tercet: "Only you, only you can, / you are unique // at last," croons the siren.

And here—at this "at last," *there is a shift in implied listener*. What follows moves the listener from *sailor* to true confidant: "Alas / it is a boring song / but it works every time." The sailor, devoured by the siren, can no longer hear her song; she speaks at the end to either herself, and her fellow sirens, or to us, the *implied listener,* expected to have been eavesdropping on the whole exchange. The audience all along is us (the reader), the lyric "I" functioning as performative as it often is in a Confessional poem; and the resulting intimacy is inferred to have been artifice—so that the poem becomes a missive about what the lyric can do (an ars poetica, perhaps!), and the self-reflexivity (traditionally thought of as referring to writing the poem as part of the poem, or, the speaker acknowledging the authorial intrusion into that imagined world) becomes part of the siren's rhetorical space. Speaker= siren; listener= sailor / *then shifts to* listener= us, readers of poems, those who wish to learn how to make such seductive songs. "It works every time," the siren-speaker tells us, meaning it works to draw in your audience, and devour them with your art. Then there's Atwood, both *under* the membrane of the speaker and hovering *above* the whole poem's rhetorical context, laughing *with us*, so that the author-audience relationship, too, is built upon the reflexivity of the siren-as-speaker, and our shared knowledge of how easily a song can seduce a sailor and bring him to his death.

Poetic Subjectivity and The Origins of the Lyric "I"

Now that we understand author-speaker-listener membranes, let's look back at the early history of the lyric mode, often said to be in conversation with narrative, meditative, and dramatic modes, with which you may also be familiar from Aristotle's *Poetics.* (If you aren't familiar with this, don't worry—you can look it up any time, when you are ready—it's available fairly widely.) The lyric mode, especially via direct address from a speaker to a listener, stretches back to the earliest poet on record, when in 2300 BC the Sumerian high priestess Enheduanna (𒂗𒃶𒌌𒀭𒈾) composed on stone tablets 42 hymns, collectively referred to as "The Sumerian Temple Hymns." Each of these hymns were written to a city's temple, as if it held the consciousness of its deity, the patron of its city. For example, in Temple Hymn 15, *The Gishbanda Temple of Ningishzida,* the Betty De Shong Meador translation, Enheduanna addresses the temple as "dark shrine frightening and red place / safely placed in a field," suggesting a kind of holy contradiction and possibly reproductive protection, but also giving that temple's god a kind of agency. And in Temple Hymn 22, *The Sirara Temple of Nanshe,* Enheduanna writes:

> O house you wild cow
> there to conjure signs from divination

you arise splendid to behold
bedecked for your princess

Again, the apostrophe to the house (listener / you) as a "wild cow . . . bedecked for your princess," suggests a power in feral and decorated female form—not unlike the speaker's own "wild" self. In some translations, the poet / speaker is named as "I" in these, but in most, the authorship is implied through ode-like collapse of that speaker-listener membrane—the "you" deity taking so much focus in the poem's address that the "I" feels almost unnecessary to declare, name, or detail in terms of identity. So, while there isn't a Lyric "I" in these, Enheduanna does name herself at the end of the last tablet in the collection, Temple Hymn 42, *The Eresh Temple of Nisaba Ezagin,* declaring "the person who bound this tablet together / is Enheduanna," imploring then: "my king something never before created / did not this one give birth to it," asking the deity to recognize her authorship! And—we might note—doing so by using a metaphor of female reproduction. In one of her other lasting works, a devotional ode to Inanna, queen of heaven—the Sumerian equivalent of Aphrodite—Enheduanna does employ the subjective I, with quite a permeable membrane since she also names herself in the poems, as in "I, Enheduanna will offer supplications to Her, / My tears, like sweet drinks." The poet / subjective self is here embodied in the "I," in the first recorded written poetry.

Some 1700 years later, the Greek poet Sappho, with whom you are perhaps more likely familiar, wrote similar poems of direct address and supplication, often from a speaker to an intimate lover, seeking to thin that membrane between them. While these poems only come to us in fragment form, we can see the tradition today clearly sustains the kind of musical intention imbued from Sappho's own poetry—which she wrote to be sung accompanied by a lyre. Given its origins in music and direct address, Lyric poetry is often celebratory, ode-like, about something or someone (an object of affection), and sometimes both, with the object functioning as a kind of vehicle (the physical embodied image) to the metaphor's tenor (concept or subject to be embodied), and usually spoken, within the context of a poem, by a person. The lyric "I" refers to the first-person speaker of such a poem. It suggests a space in which the reader can imagine that identity, filling in gaps where concrete information is given in fragments, distilling an experience. A poem using the lyric "I" often assumes that we can participate as members of a larger shared culture.

Modernist women such as H.D. or Mina Loy used the lyric "I" in the 1910s, as did T. S. Eliot in his "Love Song of J. Alfred Prufrock" (which also, of course, takes epistolary form in its apostrophe, or direct address, to the "you" listener, who the speaker invites to go with him into the streets: "Let us go then, you and I . . ."). In 1960, Argentinian poet Jorge Luis Borges joked about the author-speaker and the lyric "I" in his poem, "Borges and I" (in the Spanish, "Borges y Yo"—the alliteration underscores the humor!), writing "The other one, the one called Borges, is the one things happen to," and "I know of Borges from the mail and see his name on a list of professors or in a biographical dictionary." Critics explain that this is Borges denouncing his fame and therefore public identity as a writer; while this is likely true, we would argue he is also just making a poet joke—he simply wants the reader to consider the ways the self is already split; the poem / page creates an attendant diagram. Years later, in her poetics-turned praxis, the poem "Speculations About 'I'," Toi Derricotte would write "I am not the 'I' / In my poems. 'I' / Is the net I try to pull me in with," with a reflexivity that belies and complicates the ways we think of the constructed self—not as autobiographical, but as artifice. But then also, not artifice so much as intentional expression, or in Derricotte's speaker's case, *un*intentional expression. Deriving from the German "das lyrische Ich," the term gives agency to that siren of Atwood's, asking if she can take off a layer of the lyric self—that "bird suit," that which also allows her the construct of power. The reflexivity of the speaker / persona here is embodied in an unlayering of secrets, which both empower and risk the self-as-speaker.

Confessional Poets vs. Confession

Confessional Poets, that famous group from the 1960s—Robert Lowell, Sylvia Plath, Anne Sexton, W.D. Snodgrass, infamously John Berryman, and more—made use of the lyric "I" to tell intimate stories of their speakers, to make confessions about feelings, emotional turmoil, and lives of suffering, often focusing on patriarchy and / or the complications of oppressive gender roles. They wrote in contrast to high Modernism, rejecting what they felt was the impersonal distance of that movement, and instead imbuing their poems with the consciousness of everyday—but very closely inhabited—people. They spoke out in opposition of New Criticism, which insisted on a firm boundary between author and speaker; the Confessional Poets claimed the boundary wasn't that starkly defined, that the poet, too, had a voice, and sometimes put themselves directly into their poems, in soliloquies and monologues of dramatic confession (Think of the famous example of Robert Hayden's "Those Winter Sundays"). However, while these confessional poems were sometimes autobiographical in emotional truth, they were not absolutely—and their descendants are not—always about *only* the factual truth(s) of the authors' lives. They are not memoirs. The confessional poets still utilized personas that traipsed into myth, Freudian theory, history, and other ways of knowing to create compelling first-person accounts, sometimes *combining those myths or fictions with their own lives*, offering voicy, intimate portraits, and therefore often getting closer to emotional truth(s). These poems were really something in between autobiography and myth; the confessional poets' poems had very permeable membranes, but membranes nonetheless.

The term "confessional poetry" was first used by the critic M.L. Rosenthol in his review of Robert Lowell's collection *Life Studies* (1959), and then applied to that generation, seen as precursor to many movements in following decades (including Adrienne Rich, who rejected the term, deeming it reductive, or Audre Lorde, who might have called the term a "convenient blanket"). Today's poets—those writing in the 2020s—are often using similar techniques as the confessional poets, recalling "the personal is political" as an aesthetic and practical stance, insisting upon the importance of identity politics as central to their verse as social activism, though it is important to note that today's poets using the lyric "I" are often more deeply rooted in the autobiographical than the mythical, less about borrowing and even more about relying upon the individually lived experience as subject matter and also as technique. In our chart, the membrane between author and speaker for today's poets seems even thinner than that of the particularly labeled Confessional generation, where the poem's secret relied more on the poem's construct than the poet's life. The lineage, though, is apparent—when looking at, say, contemporary poet Christopher Soto's "Those Sundays," which references Robert Hayden's famous "Those Winter Sundays" in its title and subject. Both poems wrestle with the realities of distant, even disapproving fathers, and Soto's also holds a direct echo of Anne Sexton's poem "Divorce," ending, too, in "Not even god" (Soto), which mirrors Sexton's "there is no one to cover me—/ not even God." Merging and questioning the confessionalism of Sexton's middle-class, white feminism and Hayden's racially aware, poverty-informed directness, Soto stakes a space that is neither and both, operating more in confession as practice than confessionalism as mode, Soto recalling the religious undertones of what it means to confess, but speaking to the dead lover as both supplicant and savior:

> Rory, I want to say that death is what you've always wanted. But
> that can't be the Truth. [This time] we can blame it on me. I'll be
> the packing mule, carry all the burden. & you, you can be a child
> again; fold your church hands like dirty laundry [crease them tight].
> Nobody has to know about us, not my father nor yours-
> No, not even God.

The speaker [membrane: thin; speaker is nearly Soto, as revealed in interviews with the poet] tells Rory—who is beyond the grave—that he, the speaker, will be "the packing mule, carry all the burden." The "dirty laundry" that the poem has revealed—the speaker's father's homophobia, his violence, his disapproval of his son's being and choices—can be folded (reversing the simile) like "church hands." The lovers themselves take the confession and hold it for themselves, removing "God" and "fathers" from the equation, so that the absolution *is* the confession itself. This confession is what a poem might achieve—the lyric mode might achieve—the intimacy of address from one voice to its listener, and too, to its eavesdropping reader (if he / she / they are not the already-intended listener). The world of the poem collapses these membranes so that we feel we are right in it, both speaking and receiving speech.

Confessions and the Epistolary Mode

Let's continue our discussion of Hayden to transition to speaking about the *epistolary, or letter-based, form*. What do confessionalism and the lyric "I" have to do with the epistolary? Confessional and epistolary are both modes in which a poem might establish intimacy. The lyric "I" in each does this by taking a specific kind of leap, assuming safety and knowledge in the recipient, the "you." In a letter, the "I" writes to the "you," a specific recipient, making use of direct address—a risk-reward system of intimacy—to convey information / updates, secrets, and confessions. Remember our talk of membranes, earlier? Here, that membrane between the speaker and listener is fairly thin and we, the readers, are rhetorically eavesdropping—the container of the poem is even more established as a holistic literary construct.

The epistle as literary construct works so well because the speaker is in full-on intimate address, leaving out only the boring details that a shared conspirator would already know, including those of place and sense and—here it is: gossip! (Why we are here, yes, and get your secrets ready.) The mode works well for those speakers and subjects in joy and in pain, in ode and in elegy (and perhaps, also, in curse—though the accursed might need to be a third party). For those of you coming to poetry from prose or hybrid forms, you might remember that Maggie Nelson famously does this in her hybrid prose poem-lets in *Bluets,* in which she declares that she does not "know how to compose otherwise, which makes writing in a prism of solitude, as [she is] here, a somewhat painful experiment" (number 108).

A somewhat painful experiment! A prism of solitude! Composing as a letter! These are the same aching qualities you might know from love songs, or from various epistolary traditions around the world. One such famous lineage traces to the Pacific Northwest, where Richard (Dick) Hugo penned his 1977 collection *31 Letters and 13 Dreams,* intermixing epistles with dream narrative, with first-person "I" address to the second person "you" in letters, and second-person "you" given agency / character in the dreams. We love this collection because it suggests what all good letters or dreams can do—blur the subconscious and the conscious mind, through states of sleeping and waking, each intimate expressions of one's combined consciousness (we'll talk more about this in Writing Beyond Surrealism, when we discuss Surrealism's connection to dreams).

If you've ever stood on a Northwest beach on a gray day, looking out across the waves toward the horizon, you might not be able to tell the difference between the sea and the sky, where they meet in a fine seam. This is what these poems are like—the sea is the dreams; the sky the letters. And from various iconic Northwest places, Hugo writes to different Northwest writers—among them "Letter to [David] Wagoner from Port Townsend," "Letter to [Carolyn] Kizer from Seattle," and "Letter to [James] Welch from Browning." Hugo signs each letter, "Love, Dick." Hugo also addresses a general "you" in the dream poems, which seem, at first glance, to be the first-person "you," but upon closer inspection, feel like choose-your-own-adventure dreams or those Old Spice commercials from the early 2000s, where suddenly "you're on a boat," or anywhere else the subconscious is said to transport you, as it might in a poem. And the combination of letters and dreams, of second person specific and second person ambiguous, plays with the membrane, as well as the idea of a poem. Is it a letter? Is it a dream? While they are clearly labeled as "Letter to" and "In your [adjective] Dream," their proximity asks us if what's under the surface of our consciousness could rise up and spill forth through either form.

Fast forward three decades from the late-1970s culture of *31 Letters* to the early 2000s, when Assiniboine / Sioux poet M.L. Smoker studied at the University of Montana with Richard Hugo's protégé James Welch—Blackfeet and A'aninin—a novelist and poet himself. Hugo learned from Roethke; Welch learned from Hugo; Smoker from Welch. You can see clearly how one thread of poetic lineage constructs itself here—and this is one such line many Pacific Northwest poets recognize and might trace on their own poet-maps (Maya, one of our co-authors, included). It isn't simple, though; such mixed positionalities of power involving race, class, and gender must be treated with nuance. Smoker makes it more possible for us to consider and discuss these nuances: in her thesis-turned-first-poetry collection, *Another Attempt at Rescue,* she frames her book in two prose letters, writing "back" to Dick Hugo—a complicated and beautiful move that is at once a nod to her poetic mentor(s) and a decolonizing of language and aesthetic. In these poems, Smoker collapses boundaries between the colonized and the colonial oppressor, the speaker capable of holding and addressing contradictions, which we see in the opening's epistle to Hugo:

> Dick: The reservoir on my end of the state is great for fishing. Some of the banks are tall and jagged, others are more patient, taking their time as they slope into rocky beaches. If you were the kind of fisherman I imagine, then you might have considered it a great place to cast from. My family has gone up there ever since the water on the Mni Shoshe was damned off. My grandparents put on their moccasins and beadwork and danced for FDR when he rode the train out to see the finishing touches of this great industrial project. I haven't yet decided if this is something I wish to be proud of.

Smoker uses the epistle to address a literary predecessor, but also to address her cultural ancestry, and the complications of how her family was made to participate in ongoing colonialism. She makes leaps of imagination and of conditional reflection, shown in "if" and "I haven't yet decided," allowing the reader to take part, by our own reflection, in how ensnared these connections must be, how difficult to untangle the lines of descent. Later, in the second "Letter to Richard Hugo," which closes the collection, Smoker goes deeper into landscape and relationship, noting what an "influence Jim

[Welch] has been," thanking Hugo—while also, in some ways, implicating him—for telling Welch to "write what he knew," saying "that allowed me to write what I knew, twenty-five years later, from another rez a little further down the road," and also notes that "the salmon are plentiful, even if they begin their lives in a hatchery down below the dam." Her language is plain-spoken and direct, and it implies its metaphors, or states them simply as concrete images that we can then make into metaphors, or leave alone, as she put them. The listener knows exactly what the speaker means, when she closes with "There's just something about the remissible wave of a cast which feels like the biggest commitment of all."

Remissable: able to be pardoned (as in, a sin) + wave of a cast: as in, casting out one's filaments (Whitman's spider), casting a line (fishing, poetry, poetic lineage), casting a confession (for absolution, or to establish intimate exchange) = "biggest commitment of all;" as in, the commitment of the poet / fisherperson / soul seeking something like connection. Poetry, as the impulse to risk connection. Poetry itself as the absolution, if you want to get religious about it.

Isn't that it? The calling out and expectation of—but not waiting for—response, as poetic impulse? This is how the epistolary feels like a kind of confession to the reader, and how the confessional poem feels like a letter to the reader. Both collapse imagined boundaries and show us how permeable those boundaries are, how ultimately we long for connection and sharing of secrets.

INVITATIONS TO REFLECT

Discuss Together

How thick or thin do the membranes between you and your reader tend to be in your poems? Choose the poem in this chapter that comes the closest to the kind of poet-reader relationship you strive for and explain the similarities and differences between that poet's approach and your own.

For Further Study

Choose a book or body of work by a poet in the confessional, epistolary, and / or lyric "I" tradition(s) and study that model for how it engages with intimacy and risk-taking in form and subject. What moves does the author make in their pursuit of intimacy or confessional writing? What do they borrow from and add to the sweep of epistolary and lyric "I" poetics? In addition to those poets, poems, and collections referenced in this chapter, feel free to reach across time and continent / read other translations, such as tenth-century Japanese writer Sei Shonagon's *Pillow Book*, Sappho's works collected in *If Not, Winter* (translated by Anne Carson); you might also look to collected works of H.D.; Remedios Varo in *Letters, Dreams, & Other Writing;* contemporary poets Melissa Kwasny in *Thistle*, Yanyi in *Year of Blue Water,* and Victoria Chang's novel-in-verse, *Love, Love,* as well as her hybrid collection, *Dear Memory.* How does this lineage / tradition continue, branch, and divide? How do you see it intersecting with others? Do you see yourself working in any of these other lineages, and how? What specific techniques and moves are you excited to further research and / or try?

Writing Exercises

1 The Poem as Letter (Epistolary poem)

A. Letter to an Ancestor / Predecessor

Write an epistolary poem to a literary predecessor, as Smoker does, or to someone you might intimately consider a literary ancestor, situating yourself in a physical place you both know. Remember to include specific details you'd both understand that don't need to be explained. Alternatively, write an epistolary to a literary contemporary (see Richard Hugo's examples), or to an actual friend, outside of poetry, but on a subject you both understand and for which the reader will be eavesdropping. Another variation: address a childhood friend with whom you are no longer in touch, but with which you have sharply defined memories. Think of the membrane between author and speaker as quite thin, between speaker and listener as very thin, and imagine the reader outside of that as nonexistent. For more examples, see Carolyn Forche's "Letter to Victoria," or the epistolary-turned-poetry exchange between Natalie Diaz and Ada Limon, published as "Envelopes of Air" in the *New Yorker.*

B. Letter to a Stranger

In the Surrealist painter and writer Remedios Varo's *Letters, Dreams, & Other Writings* (trans. Margaret Carson), we find she wrote intimate letters to strangers. To reveal herself a bit, she would conceive of the living room as a solar system and the objects of the home as orbiting some central object that she would designate as the sun. And, of course, she also constructed a unicycle-spine-person out of bones (homo rodans), and she talks about that. Finding a recipient randomly in the phone book, Varo invites him to a New Year's Eve party with her and her Surrealist pals (including Leonora Carrington, who we will talk about as part of her lineage in another chapter). Here is the start of one of Varo's letters:

> Dear Stranger,
> I haven't a clue if you're a single man or the head of a household, if you're a shy introvert or a happy extrovert, but whatever the case, perhaps you're bored and want to dive fearlessly into a group of strangers in hopes of hearing something that will interest or amuse you. . . . (p. 16)

Using Varo as inspiration, write a letter to an absolute stranger. In yours, choose a random person you don't know (but could perhaps find out a little about, perhaps on social media); maybe resist that impulse and instead rely on your imagination), and invite them to an upcoming event you plan to attend with friends and / or family. You do not need to actually send this invitation; just writing it will do. In fact, please be careful with letters to strangers.

C. Direct Address as Epistolary Elegy

In his poem "Separation," W.S. Merwin wrote of the strange relatedness of losing someone and how it changes the way his speaker sees the world around him:

> Your absence has gone through me
> Like thread through a needle.
> Everything I do is stitched with its color.

We can feel this poem on a blood level, how the absence of the "you" becomes the thread of the speaker, who becomes a needle. The "separation" is made manifest, more than metaphor, in the off-the-page actions of the speaker. "Everything I do," the speaker says, "is stitched with its color." The speaker is never the subject taking action in the poem; he / she / they remain passive—as the vehicle for absence, which is the subject of the first clause; as part of the noun clause "Everything I do" which then passively "is stitched." This is how one carries on in grief: as an agent without agency. "Your absence" has a "color" we imagine—in my mind, it is red as blood, or wine, or the neon of a flame. That color that means *gone*. Try to write something stitched with the color of someone's absence, or maybe with the color of his presence. It parallels something. Include that something.

(Soto's "Those Sundays" is also this form of elegy, weaving in references to a literary ancestor and a familial one to help the speaker mourn and address Rory, his deceased lover, who is also the listener.)

2 **Direct Address as Apology / Litany of Apologies**

Use the techniques suggested above but make it an apology. For further examples, look up and read Martin Espada's obsessive and humorous "I Apologize for Giving You Poison Ivy by Smacking You In the Eye with the Crayfish at the End of My Fishing Line" and Kaveh Akbar's lyric ode "Apology."

3 **Persona as Intimate / Familiar**

In "Siren Song," Atwood assumes the voice of a siren. Take on a persona from mythology and write in that voice, intimately, to a listener who would exist within the rhetorical context of the poem (e.g., in "Siren Song," the listener is a sailor, being seduced). You might note how you feel empowered by this voice to say things you wouldn't otherwise, but which feel somehow extremely close to you, emotionally.

4 **You Yourself and You**

Using Borges' "Borges and I" as a model, write an imitative poem that situates you and your lyric *self* against one another, as tandem (or, a term you may know: doppelgangers). Think of how Borges writes, "I like hourglasses, maps, eighteenth-century typography, the taste of coffee and the prose of Stevenson; he shares these preferences, but in a vain way that turns them into the attributes of an actor," and make a similar thread in your poem. Toward the end, begin a line like his: "Years ago I tried to free myself from him and went from the mythologies of the suburbs to the games with time and infinity," explaining how you tried to get away but ultimately fail.

5 **The Reclaiming Power of Collective Confession**

One powerful effect of confession or truth-telling is that it engenders more truth-telling from others who might have otherwise felt hesitant to go forward with their stories. Think of contemporary and historical movements in which collective voice, a shared consciousness, or even just joining a "we" for a moment has empowered individuals and therefore social stratums. One such example is the #MeToo movement of the late 2010s, in which many people came forward publicly with their stories of surviving assault. Literature written in the empowered "we" voice—from those of such survivor groups—has had enormous effect on justice movements. Think of a group to which you personally belong or identify and practice writing in "we" voice from that group's shared consciousness or experiences. Gwendolyn Brooks' "Kitchenette Building" and Robin Coste Lewis's "The Mothers," which responds to Brooks, are two such examples of poetry that uses such "we" voices to offer insight into justice movements—in this case, race / gender and sexuality / race / gender. (You can find these poems in our online companion.) This is also what Atwood might be doing with "Siren Song"—reclaiming or offering agency to a group otherwise seen as antagonists (sirens), who become the protagonists and recast their own story.

6 Memorize a poem by someone you consider to be a literary ancestor, for good or bad, and then once you have it solidly memorized, write "back" to that ancestor / poem. Try to repeat some of the moves of the original poem, either through direct syntactical / grammatical mimicry, or through general response. You may note moments of departure that surprise you, and you may note yourself speaking, as Soto does, to more than one ancestor or predecessor at once, redefining lines of descent and recasting your family ties.

3

The Poem in Telephone Lines & Other Thoughts on Tone, Talk, and Voice in Poetry

A FEW POEMS TO START US OFF . . .

One of the key questions to consider when reading and writing poems is who the speaker of the poem is and how that speaker's voice is meant to affect the reader. We started talking about those questions in the previous chapter, but we want to take the conversation further by talking about talk and tone among writers who are as attentive to the artistry in everyday uses of language as they are to the experimental possibilities that emerge from such attention to language. All the poems we'll discuss in this chapter experiment with how speakers, voice, and elements of personal nonfiction transform the way readers experience a poem. Here are five poems to help you think about voice, perspective, and intimacy in poetry.

Barbara Guest

Eating Chocolate Ice Cream: Reading Mayakovsky

Since I've decided to revolutionize my life
since
"
decided
"
revolutionize
"
life
"

How early it is! It is eight o'clock in the morning.
Well, the pigeons were up earlier
Did you eat all your egg?
Now we shall go for a long walk.
Now? There is too much winter.
I am going to admire the snow on your coat.
Time for hot soup, already?
You have worked for three solid hours.
I have written forty-eight, no forty-nine,
no fifty-one poems.
How many states are there?
I cannot remember what is uniting America.
It is then time for your nap.
What a lovely, pleasant dream I just had.
But I like waking up better.
I do admire reality like snow on my coat.
Would you take cream or lemon in your tea?
No sugar?
And no cigarettes.
Daytime is good, but evening is better.
I do like our evening discussions.
Yesterday we talked about Kant.
Today let's think about Hegel.
In another week we shall have reached Marx.
Goody.
Life is a joy if one has industrious hands.
Supper? Stew and well-cooked. Delicious.
Well, perhaps just one more glass of milk.
Nine o'clock! Bath time!
Soap and a clean rough towel.

Bedtime!
The Red Army is marching tonight.
They shall march through my dreams
in their new shiny leather boots,
their freshly laundered shirts.
All those ugly stains of caviar and champagne
and kisses
have been rubbed away.
They are going to the barracks.
They are answering hundreds of pink
and yellow and blue and white telephones.
How happy and contented and well-fed they look
lounging on their fur divans,
chanting, "Russia how kind you are to us.
How kind you are to everybody.
We want to live forever."
Before I wake up they will throw away
their pistols, and magically
factories will spring up where once
there was rifle fire, a roulette factory,
where once a body fell from an open window.
Hurry dear dream
I am waiting for you
under the eiderdown.
And tomorrow will be more real, perhaps,
than yesterday.

Craig Morgan Teicher

Why Poetry: A Partial Autobiography [*"How tense it makes me, reading . . ."*]

How tense it makes me, reading
poetry, knowing how much I miss, misunderstand,
how only some of the words
resolve under my eyes
                                        into sentences
while others slip by unnoticed,
like a note inscribed on a greeting card
by an aunt who never knew me well.
What I mean is the job is never
done, I'm never through. And I'm not made
for tasks that linger; some
of me is always considering
all the money I owe
to banks and credit card companies
and the kid
                    who kindly bought
me most of my high school lunches
because my dad forgot to send me to school
with a couple of bucks.
                                        Which is of course to say
reading poetry is a metaphor.
Nothing ever
finishes.

~

So why did I choose poetry?
Maybe because it acknowledges right away
what scares me most,
how the line breaks before
the thought is done, how the line,
a partial thing,
is the measure
and it's never enough. My
                                        college love
never did come running back
after I sent her
that photocopied pamphlet

of heartbroke verses,
and my lamentation
did not un-injure my son or
get me back my job.

~

I woke up panting and confused
from the same nightmare over and over
through childhood—I can't remember when
it stopped: my task was to build
with colored blocks atop
a floating green
island a kind of little city;
this was urgent—there would be no
forgiveness if it was not complete.
The dream ended
with me standing before
this hovering shard of land
as it hovered away,
my job still undone, and I was
dropped back into my bed to
beg my mother
for something she could
understand but not give,

It's hard now not to see it as
a premonition, maybe a preparation
for her dying only a few years
later, her life, my life
like all lives, unfinished.

~

And so I came to poetry.

Daniel Borzutzky

Lake Michigan, Scene 18

The beaches are filled with cages

And the cages are filled with bodies

And the bodies are filled with burdens

And the burdens consume the bodies

And the bodies do not know to whom they owe their life

I drop my body on the sand and someone tells me to pick it up

I drop to the sand to pick up my body and someone tells me to steal more hair to steal more flesh to steal more bones to steal more fingers

I tell them I cannot risk contaminating the data

I tell them that if I steal more hair then the data will not be clean

I tell them I cannot touch my own body out of fear of contaminating the data

I have a virus I say

I am contagious I say

No salt in my body I say no heat in my blood

The sand is dying slowly

It turns into a wall and in the wall there is a nook and in the nook there is light and in light there is god and in god there is nothing and in nothing there is hope and in hope there is abandonment and in abandonment there is wound and in wound there is nation and in nation there are bones and in bones there is time and in time there is light and in light there are numbers and in numbers there are codes and in codes there are mountains and in mountains there are bodies searching for bones and in the mountains there are tunnels and in the tunnels there is so much festering garbage

The men in uniform take the garbage away but they have a hard time distinguishing the garbage from the people so they scoop it all up and carry us into the next morning

And in the next morning there is a confession

I have put my burdens in the wrong body

I have framed my burdens in the wrong language

I have staked my burdens to the wrong nation

I need medicine to sleep

I need medicine to stop the shrieking in my ears

I need medicine to make the Chicago corpses turn into hydrangeas

I need medicine to make the immigrants turn into butterflies

I need an injection to make the bureaucrats turn into terrorists

It is raining again on Lake Michigan

Some say it is raining bodies   but really it is raining trash

The trash they bomb us with explodes when it lands near our bodies

And our bodies are tornadoes

And the joke turns into a mystery novel about how god keeps his hands from shaking when he is about to destroy the universe

I need my burdens   sing the bodies on the beach

I fight for my burdens   scream the bodies on the beach

I know the blankness of my burdens is a battle for love and country

I know the blankness of my burdens is a coda to the death of the city

I don't know why I can't see the moon anymore

I can't see the stars for the sky anymore

I don't even bother to look up

Debora Kuan

Minority Assignment #2

We sultry the lampshade & suture the lambchop.
We but windows wasp & swap.

We hookline&sinker gin our drink.
We water our bent-up Bible with ink.

We con & thereof canvass.
We nuclearize & notice.

We scrub our you skin, confess our cardboard sins.
We blunder the pure & blame the breast milk.

We but cowl necks, we but fur.
We noose-slip beneath the radar.

We anaesthetize our tribal bones.
We but nuns undo the union.

We capture the culpable bells.
We but soldiers wet ourselves.

We peep & spy & sleeper.
We exoticize our features.

We pry apart our private parts.
We don the nods & pocket the wads.

We hook our masks around our ears.
We prepare our rightful heirs.

Louise B. Halfe—Sky Dancer

ê-kwêskît—Turn-Around Woman

When I was growing up in the bush, on the hillside,
I watched the sun arrive from the dark, watch her slip
into the dark. I travelled. I didn't know the world back then.
I just travelled. I was afraid
I would never return. I tumbled that hillside
back into myself.

You can tell me
after you hear this story
if my name suits me.
I've yet to figure it out.

In Rib Woman
stories are born.
The Old Man called it psychology. Me,
I just dream it.

> *These gifted mysterious people of long ago,*
> Kiyâs e-matâhtâwisiwak iyiniwak,

my mother, Gone-For-Good, would say.

> *They never died. They are scattered here, there,*
> *everywhere, somewhere. They know the language,*
> *the sleep, the dream, the laws, these singers, these healers,*
> atayohkanak, *these ancient story keepers.*

I, Turn-Around, am not one of them.

I was taught by Old people.
An Indian Man, a White Man.
An Indian Woman, a White Woman.
They worked in lairs, in the full veins of
Rib Woman.
I sat in their thicket, wailing.
The old ones navigated through my dreams.
Sometimes they dragged, scolded, cajoled,
cheered and celebrated.
I wanted to be with them. Like them.

I am not a saint. I am a crooked good.
My cousins said I was easy, therefore
I've never been a maiden.
I am seventy, but still
I carry my sins. Brothers-in-law
I meet for the first time wipe their hands
as if I am still among the maggots. I didn't
know their women wept when their men
slept in my bed. I am not a saint.

I married Abel, a wide green-eyed man. Fifty years now.
Inside Rib Woman I shook hands with promise.
Promise never forgot, trailed me year after year.
His Big Heavens a morning lake
drowns me in my lair.
I learned how to build Rib Woman
one willow at a time, one skin at a time.
I am only half done. This is part of the story.

I, *ê-kwêskî*, am a dreamer.
I dream awake. Asleep. On paper.
The Old Man said the universe,
the day, was the story. So,
every day I am born.
The Old White Man taught me
to unfold night visits.

The Old Woman taught me
all of it was real.
The Old White Woman helped me
to cry with the Thunder.

DISCUSSION

One of our key takeaways from the our previous chapter discussion about the various membranes between a living writer and any one of their future readers is that the poet and the speaker of the poems cannot be assumed to be one and the same. We often point to classic persona poems like Robert Browning's "My Last Duchess," wherein the speaker of the poem is a serial killer, and then remind our students: "Say 'The Speaker,' because you wouldn't want to call the poet a murderer."

We like this extreme example, with its super-thick membrane between the ominously threatening speaker and presumably non-criminal author, as well as the thick membrane between the implied listener, a potential future wife and victim, and the actual reader, who sees right through this wealthy man's hunger to control and abuse. Conversations about a poem like this certainly help hammer the point home. But if we're being totally honest with you, a major reason we so desperately want our students to learn to distinguish between the writer and the speaker is because it's *soooooo* awkward when students read a classmate's poem and then say this poet is a "fool for love," "terrible to their friends," or an "unrepentant navel gazer." The speakers of our students' poems are often those things, but that doesn't mean the creators of those speakers are.

Poets often find that poems have a powerful effect when the membrane between the writer and the speaker is very thin, either narratively or emotionally, because that gives the reader a heady sense of intimacy with the words on the page. Poets experimenting with the possibilities in such a thin boundary may create speakers who enact their flaws or vulnerabilities on the page. They may tease the reader with hints that there may not really be a line between the poet and the speaker at all. Crafting and cultivating such a gray area creates exciting possibilities for a poet to amplify a sense of personal connection with the reader and to break down barriers that at times may make poetry feel intentionally obscure.

It is quite common for poets exploring the lyrical boundaries between themselves and their readers to look to Confessional poets as models. After all, Confessional poetry, which we discuss in greater detail in the previous chapter, is known for combining notes of sincerity and vulnerability, as well as intentional uses of first-person speakers, as a way to name, to heal from, and to resist various forms of oppression and trauma. But there are other lineages in poetry that provide examples of how you can bring your full self, your most secret self, misunderstood aspects of yourself, or yourself in solidarity with larger communities or ideas to the page. We look to The New York School to find a poetics of casual conversation, witty banter, and breezy confidences that might be used in poetry. We also look to experimental poets who note there are serious limitations to such first-person poetics, and instead create poetic language that attempts to hold a collective experience with multiplicities of voices or by disrupting easy notions about what is reasonable that certain everyday uses of language might provide.

The New York School

While there are many poets across time and place who have celebrated the poetic qualities of everyday speech, The New York School poets are a profoundly influential group of twentieth-century writers who transformed readers' expectations about the kinds of tones a poem could use. We now see that influence manifesting in the work of many contemporary poets working well beyond the boundaries of the fairly small group of people known as The New York School. First, though, let's establish that The New York School was not a school at all. It was just a group of writers and artists with close-knit and overlapping friendships and affinities. Literary historians and critics often refer to such loose networks of creative influencers as "a school." The New York School poets were friends and acquaintances both with each other and also with a group of visual artists known for abstract and experimental paintings and performance art, who shared a passion for the literary and visual art produced by the Surrealists a generation earlier.

These poets and artists did much of their most iconic work in the 1960s. Their work is characterized by a tone that seems both intelligent and off-the-cuff in its chattiness and use of nonchalant pop culture references. Frank O'Hara's "Lana Turner Has Collapsed" is considered one of the classic New York School poems. The poem begins with the speaker describing how he was rushing in a snowstorm to meet a friend when he happened to notice on the front page of a newspaper that Lana Turner, a well-known pop icon and Hollywood starlet of the time, had collapsed. O'Hara writes, suggesting a kind of parallel between the speaker's vulnerabilities and those of the actress, that:

> I have been to lots of parties
> and acted perfectly disgraceful
> but I never actually collapsed
> oh Lana Turner we love you get up.

Another classic New York School poem, John Ashbery's "The One Thing That Can Save America," treats one's personal life with a certain amount of breezy coyness in lines like "I know that I braid too much on my own / Snapped-off perceptions of things as they come to me. / They are private and always will be." (Go to our online companion to read these and other notable New York School poems in their entirety.)

Though their tone is decidedly off-the-cuff casual, it would be a mistake to dismiss poems like these as unserious or trite. There is a bold ambition embedded in this style. In his "Personism Manifesto," which was written with a winking ambivalence about the existence of so many self-satisfied and overly serious manifestos (like the ones we will talk about in the upcoming chapter on Surrealism), O'Hara says his Personist poetry "puts the poem squarely between the poet and the person, Lucky Pierre style, and the poem is correspondingly gratified. The poem is at last between two persons instead of two pages." This is a profound ideal expressed in playful, cheeky terms (with a sex joke to boot!), but we see in these lines a genuine and serious desire for authentic human connection via art propelling O'Hara's work and the works of many other poets influenced by his innovations.

Barbara Guest, for example, writes poems that frequently feature images from the domestic sphere, including caring for young children. In many of the Confessional poetries of roughly the same era, motherhood and domestic life are often depicted as a stifling realm with domestic imagery operating as metaphors for an oppressive patriarchy. Guest, though, was more often a part of New York School gatherings than she was the Confessional poetry scene. Her style features abrupt subject changes and interweaves the life of the mind with the mundane tasks of daily life in ways that are similar to those we see in poems by Ashbery or O'Hara. Consider these lines from "Eating Chocolate Ice Cream: Reading Mayakovsky:"

> I have written forty-eight, no forty-nine,
> no fifty-one poems.
> How many states are there?
> I cannot remember what is uniting America.
> It is then time for your nap.

In this poem, the speaker meditates on socialist philosophy, ideology, and art while going about the business of caring for her home and family. The poem's interest in philosophy and socialism—

> Yesterday we talked about Kant.
> Today let's think about Hegel.
> In another week we shall have reached Marx.

—also holds imagery of domestic labor, of cooking, washing, and caring for children.

> Life is a joy if one has industrious hands.
> Supper? Stew and well-cooked. Delicious.
> Well, perhaps just one more glass of milk.
> Nine o'clock! Bath time!

It is also worth noting how frequently Guest's poem interrupts itself. Like a phone call between two friends with the kids constantly interrupting to ask for snacks or other needs, the conversation loses the thread, picks it up further back, or jumps ahead abruptly. There is no time, the poem suggests, for crafty erudition or refined forms, only the urgent need to convey what ought to be said, a note of love, "I am waiting for you," along with hope for a tender revolution. "Tomorrow will be more real perhaps, than yesterday."

The New York School poets were also deeply influenced by Abstract Expressionist painting and Surrealism. Like those visual artists, they adopted the aesthetic stance that the emphasis of their work should be on the action of making, not the artifact on the page. For this reason, the poems often refer to their own making. Craig Morgan Teicher is a contemporary poet writing work that remains very much in the vein of the New York School. His first book, *Brenda Is in the Room*, is a book-length love poem dedicated to his then-fiancé, now-spouse, the poet Brenda Shaugnessy. That poem describes its own making as following guidelines set forth by the influential New York School poet A. R. Ammons. Teicher, like Ammons before him, writes the poem on a typewriter using a roll of cash register paper, about the width of a receipt you might receive today. The poem is meant to be diaristic, honest, and to capture even the most mundane experiences of the everyday. It borrows heavily from the Surrealistic method of automatic writing, where a writer attempts to chronicle thoughts exactly as they arise in the mind, with the aim of conveying an authentic portrait of human experience.

Though the poem we offer you in this book is a shorter one from a later collection, it illustrates many of these same qualities. The poem opens with a chatty confession about the very art form in which Teicher is working. "How tense it makes me, reading / poetry." His speaker describes this anxiety in greater detail, though also goes on a seeming tangent about a kind friend in school once paying for lunches, before asking the question the reader is surely starting to wonder about too: "So why did I choose poetry?" From this question, Teicher's speaker spins off into even more personal reveries about financial worries and grief over a mother's death, before returning in the end to the question about poetry. By this time that question has evolved into a much larger one about what it is a person should do with the life and mind they have, considering how very fragile both are. He describes realizing "my life / like all lives unfinished // And so I came to poetry." This final line ties the ending of the poem back to the question at the beginning and reveals how all the meandering thoughts and anecdotes, which seemed at times like digressions, were actually illustrating how poetry could hold fragmented memories of a childhood trauma that, when looked at together, create a sense of emotional understanding about how the present has come to be. By using an intentionally casual tone of voice, automatic writing techniques, and references to the making of the art from within,

Teicher can create a poem that is uniquely authentic and whose emotional impact is heightened by the sense of intimacy he has called forth across the distance of time and pages.

As you can see from Guest's poem, New York School poets were often quite political. Though they are best known for their attention to pop culture and ekphrastic writings in response to visual art, which can sometimes seem like work that strives for an apolitical tone, poets operating in this vein often demonstrate how political the imagination can be. Meanwhile, Teicher demonstrates that even when a poem jumps between subjects or meanders off on tangents, it can still be orbiting some of the most tender sites of human emotion.

Experimental Voices

The New York School poets' attention to pop culture and ekphrastic writings meant they were also influenced by the ways other artforms were blurring the space between makers and audiences. In the 1960s, during a heyday of New York School poetics, a style of performance art known as "Happenings" emerged in the US, as a kind of translation and extension of the Gutai movement among visual artists in 1950s Japan. Shiraga Kazuo created a piece called *Challenge to the Mud* by stripping half naked and rolling in a pile of mud. The artistry of that moment exists now in the form of photographs of the artist engaging in this playful work, as well as the impressions and patterns his body left in the earth. Happenings are improvisatory pieces that feature visual art elements, poetry, some bits of scripted text, and lots of calls for audience participation that could not be planned for or controlled. Yoko Ono created another of the oft-cited examples of a Happening with her work "Cut Piece," wherein she presented the audience with a pair of scissors and instructed the audience to cut away at the fabric she was draped in until she decided they should stop.

We can see this celebration of the act of making itself, as well as the power of a collaboration with an audience, flourishing in a variety of poetic directions. Some poets, like Teicher and Guest, have followed a thread of thought about voice and authenticity that lead them towards poems that emphasize an approachable tone of easy familiarity. Other poets have leaned into the elements of chance associated with improvisation, as well as the collaged and fragmentary effects of creative works developed through collaboration and conversation, sometimes rooted in the idea of public performance or drawing from the conventions of performance art.

Daniel Borzutsky's recent work, *Lake Michigan,* is a piece that uses voice in fascinating ways that are reminiscent of the experiments conducted by the Gutai artists or in Happenings. The long poem is framed as a work of performance art. Readers are meant to imagine some parts of the poem as lines as spoken by actors on a stage. Other parts of the poem present readers with collaged accounts of the Pinochet regime's secret and torturous interrogations in Chile. These are juxtaposed with reports of US Black Box sites and US immigration policies that often include detainment in prison-like environments and the separation of children from their parents or caregivers at the border.

> The beaches are filled with cages
>
> And the cages are filled with bodies
>
> And the bodies are filled with burdens
>
> And the burdens consume the bodies

These poems use the technique of collaging different voices together in a style reminiscent of The New York School and the Surrealists before them, as does Borzutzky's choice to use a form that evokes a performance.

> The men in uniform take the garbage away but they have a hard time distinguishing the garbage from the people so they scoop it all up and carry us into the next morning
>
> And in the next morning there is a confession
>
> I have put my burdens in the wrong body
>
> I have framed my burdens in the wrong language
>
> I have staked my burdens to the wrong nation

In many ways Borzutsky's work returns us to the Browning monologue "My Last Duchess" we alluded to at the beginning of this chapter. When we read Borzutsky's work we are not quite sure where the poet's authentic self can be found in the text. But unlike Browning, the poet's mask is not a performance of becoming someone other than himself. Rather, it is a gesture of solidarity—and complicity. In a poem about government torture that closely mirrors actual events of recent history, as well as those that are ongoing in this present moment, Borzutsky thins the membrane between self and others. Readers are made to feel very close to the fear and suffering the prisoners experience. They are also brought close to the detached cruelty of those inflicting the harm. None of us are these people, but many of us are or could become so vulnerable or give ourselves over as willing participants in systems of such cruelty, the poem suggests. This is the revelation born of Borzutsky's use of seemingly spontaneous, authentic, vulnerable lines of monologue and dialogue.

There are other crucial conversations around experimental poetry emerging from these lineages of influence, especially those experimental poetics sometimes referred to as the avant-garde, with which we think poets first entering conversations about contemporary poetry should be familiar. Some poets composing avant garde and performance art pieces under the influence of The New York School poets, painters, and performance artists developed projects whose stated intentions were to challenge racism and oppression. However, their execution of those projects often replicated the very systems they sought to critique. One significant example was Kenneth Goldsmith's public recitation of the autopsy report of Michael Brown, a teenager murdered by a police officer in Ferguson, MO. Another was Vanessa Place's creation of a Twitter account with an offensive picture of a "Mammy" caricature in the avatar position, that tweeted out lines from *Gone with the Wind*. Both works were widely criticized for reinscribing and reiterating the very racism the artists claimed to be critiquing, which is a problem we see emerging fairly commonly not only in poems written by students who are still learning, but also in the published pages of prestigious magazines.

The poet and essayist Cathy Park Hong has written about the ways many writers in the avant garde have failed to create artworks that fully reckon with or disrupt the individual or systemic workings of white supremacy. "To encounter the history of avant-garde poetry is to encounter a racist tradition," she writes in "Delusions of Whiteness in the Avant-Garde." She elaborates, writing "The avant-garde's 'delusion of whiteness' is the luxurious opinion that anyone can be 'post-identity' and can casually slip in and out of identities like a video game avatar, when there are those who are consistently harassed, surveilled, profiled, or deported for whom they are."

Debora Kuan's poem "Minority Assignment #2" provides one example (though many more can be found in our online companion) of a poem that embraces experimentation with everyday language as a way to provoke readers into a new relationship with their most basic assumptions about things like learning, relationships, and identity. In this poem, Kuan uses unexpected and surreal juxtapositions and imagery to imagine ways beyond the historical and contemporary traumas of racism. She is a poet who often makes allusions in her work to surrealist writers and practices, as well as to the words, stories, traditions, and art experienced in a Chinese American family. Throughout her series of "Minority Assignment" poems, she uses surrealist approaches to automatic writing and randomized word play to name and critique harmful and pervasive stereotypes. "We peep & spy & sleeper," she writes. "We exoticize our features." By also estranging biased language from its usual context, by turning nouns into verbs and juxtaposing images unexpectedly, Kuan also illustrates the senselessness of racist assumptions and of a dominant culture that constantly asks some people to explain and justify themselves. She also reclaims language that would objectify and instead uses it to create a poem where irregular syntax minimizes voices of oppression and amplifies the speaker's linguistic power and prowess.

More Experiments with the First Person Speaker and the Power of Connection

As we write this chapter on The New York School we have been mindful of, and want to direct your attention as writers to, the ways this movement in poetry was shaped in its early days by the writings of openly gay men, most notably John Ashbery and Frank O'Hara. During a time when they risked criminal prosecution, violence from police and citizens alike, being fired, losing their housing, and a host of other consequences, these poets were boldly transparent about who they were. To the degree that their poems risk notoriety by offering the most authentic voices they can bring to the page or offer alternative visions of gender to those being promulgated by hyper-masculine pop culture figures like John Wayne, their poems are deeply radical and political. But there is also so much more political work for poets to take up that the most canonized New York School work left untouched.

One of the endeavors we see poets undertaking with powerful effect is an exploration of how poetry can become an instrument of decolonial thought and expression. Can the English language ever really be decolonized? We don't know, but we see many contemporary Native American, First Nations, and Indigenous poets whose first language is English as a direct consequence of the violence of colonialism, using both translated and untranslated lines of their native languages in their poetry. This poetics becomes a way to express their individual fullness and complexity, while also preserving, vivifying, and passing forward those languages colonizers attempted to erase.

Layli Long Soldier is one poet who does this kind of work with the Dakota language in her work. We discuss her poem "38" in depth in the chapter "Docupoetics & Other Forms of Lyric Research." Other sample poems in this vein are listed in our online companion to this chapter. We've chosen to focus in this chapter on "*ê-kwêskît*—Turn-Around Woman" by Louise B. Halfe, whose Cree name is Sky Dancer. She is a survivor of the Blue Quills Residential School in Alberta, Canada, which was one of many such schools in the US and Canada designed for the express purpose of separating Native American and First Nations children from their families, their cultural heritage, and their native languages. Halfe is also one of the first poets working primarily in English who developed a poetics that would center restoration and reclamation of cultural heritage, who imagined poetry, even in the colonizing language of English, as a potential site of healing from the trauma of attempted genocide.

In "*ê-kwêskît*—Turn-Around Woman" she creates a speaker, perhaps a speaker very close to the poet herself. Turn-Around Woman, as the speaker refers to herself, insists, "I am not a saint. I am a crooked good." Through the poem she offers images of herself feeling pulled or divided:

These gifted mysterious people of long ago,
Kiyâs e-matâhtâwisiwak iyiniwak,
. . . They know the language,
the sleep, the dream, the laws . . .
I, Turn-Around, am not one of them.

She also writes, "I was taught by Old people. / An Indian Man, a White man. / An Indian Woman, a White Woman." The speaker frequently alludes to the different ways of understanding the world that the speaker carries inside herself, contradictions she may or may not have been able to fully reconcile over the course of her long and rich life. "In Rib Woman / stories are born. / The Old Man called it psychology. Me / I just dream it," she says.

The poem incorporates some key Cree spiritual and cultural teachings and figures, which are expanded on in great detail in later poems in *The Crooked Good,* the book-length collection in which this poem appears. Within this particular poem Halfe also interweaves a personal narrative of the speaker's life of struggle, which the poem suggests originates in how "The old ones navigated through my dreams. / Sometimes they dragged, scolded, cajoled, / cheered and celebrated. / I wanted to be with them."

In Halfe's work we can see how a poem provides a way to create an intimate space for a reader to really know a writer. That sense of "really knowing" someone can be stretched, as it is in this poem, to include not only personal history, but cultural traditions, stories, dreams, and languages. It is possible, Halfe shows us, to write poems from a deeply personal place that also speaks to collective griefs, memories, and hopes for a shared and connected future.

INVITATIONS TO REFLECT

Discuss Together

Readers bring a certain set of culturally coded expectations about poetry to any book they pick up or any performance space they walk into. Maybe they are expecting poems to be serious and meditative, emotionally fraught, or even overwrought. Maybe they are expecting poems to be rhythmically rich, replete with rhymes, and loaded with social and political import. What have you expected from poetry in the past and what do you expect from it now? In what ways do the poems discussed in this chapter live up to your past and present expectations? In what ways do they subvert those expectations? And, as a writer, in what ways do you want your own poetry to subvert expectations or create new ones for your readers? Consider how your tone, voice, and other elements of the speaker influence these goals.

For Further Study

Choose a collection you have loved for its rich voice—perhaps, as described here in reference to Teicher, its "intentionally casual tone of voice," perhaps its "automatic writing techniques," and its "references to the making of the art from within." (Another that comes to mind for us is Diane Seuss's *Frank Sonnets,* which alludes to O'Hara, and makes use of many of the same New York School techniques discussed here.) With your collection, see if you can trace its New York School origins or overlaps, and pay particular attention to its place in this lineage (for us, Seuss's "follows" O'Hara, by direct allusion, but also alludes to Plath—a confessional poet—and many other lineages).

Writing Exercises

1 **The Poem in the Telephone Lines**

Go through your phone and find a text message exchange that is at least 10 messages deep. Write a poem that begins and ends with quotes from these texts and also includes a food, a song, and an article of clothing somewhere in the middle.

2 **That Ekphrastic Life**

Go to an art gallery or thrift store with a friend. Take at least five pictures while you are there. Write a poem that describes one of those pictures and includes at least three quotes from a work of philosophy, political science, or art criticism that you find difficult but inspiring.

3 **Reading Mayakovsky and Eating Ice Cream and Everything Else that Happens**

Pick a day when you have many tasks on your to-do list—making a birthday cake, calling a parent, cleaning the bathroom, getting the oil changed in your car, etc. Every 15 minutes for 16 hours you must stop what you are doing and write a quick line of poetry. Then get back to the business at hand.

4 **Walk-Mulling with You**

Walk around your neighborhood thinking about the systems and forces and patterns that have shaped the place you live. Write a list of actions in which you saw your neighbors engage. Then write a list of 5 things about the future you are afraid of. Then make a list of 5 things you hope for. Weave these three lists together into one poem, elaborating and expanding and cutting as needed. Make the poem a direct address, a poem written like a letter or phone call to a "you," someone who has the power to save or destroy your life.

5 **Surrealist Estrangements**

With Debora Kuan's poem in mind, think about an "assignment" people with some degree of power try to give you to act in a certain way. First make a list of the behaviors or rules they expect. Then, estrange those rules by infusing each line with an unexpected verb and a disjunctive surrealist image.

4

Writing Out of Surrealism

A FEW POEMS TO START US OFF . . .

In this chapter, we offer a brief review of the late nineteenth-to-early-twentieth century origins of Surrealism, an artistic and literary zeitgeist with roots in French Symbolism and Romanian Dada, or nonsense, and stemming from resistance communities in Paris, New York, Madrid, and beyond. Visual, film, textile, and other artists, as well as poets, found themselves revolting against oppressive capitalist, dictator-oriented government regimes assuming power between the World Wars. In other chapters, in addition to those mentioned in the last one, you might consider Rebecca Tamás ("Interrogation"), Mita Mahato ("Extinction Limericks," but also much of her other work, and the use of collage), Kim Hyesoon ("All the Garbage of the World Unite"), and definitely Jorge Luis Borges ("Borges and I") to be Surrealist, especially in their use of stream of consciousness, strange dialogue, surprising, dream-like images, and the absurd to highlight hyperrealities and magnify the ways individual identity plays against the mainstream.

Gérard de Nerval, translated by Louis Simpson

Lines in Gold

Why not? Everything feels!
—Pythagoras

Man, do you think yours is the only soul?
Look around you. Everything that you see
Quivers with being. Though your thoughts are free,
One thing you do not think about, the whole.

Beasts have a mind. Respect it. Flowers too.
Look at one. Nature brought forth each petal.
There is a mystery that sleeps in metal.
"Everything feels!" and has power over you.

Be careful! The blind wall is spying on us.
Even matter is connected to a word . . .
Do not make it serve some unholy purpose.

A god in darkness often walks obscured.
As eyelids of a newborn infant open
A spirit wakes and gazes in the stone.

Marosa di Giorgio

[Untitled, trans. by Peter Boyle; Two Poems From *La falena* (*The Moth*)]

When I was an owl I observed everything with my hot and cold pupil; no being, no thing was lost on me. I floated above anyone walking by in the fields, my double cape open, my white legs half open; like a woman. And before I let out the petrifying scream, all fled to the gold mountain, to the mountain of shadows, saying: And that thing in mid-air like a star?

But also, I was a girl there in the house.

Mama kept the mystery to herself.

And looked at God, weeping.

* * *

They appeared, suddenly, like all the things in my life. Black, white, with silken shawls. In the middle of the field, the lake in the field, the house. Water birds gazing downwards, thoughtfully. Above tall claws. They looked like willows, like men, the most different sorts of things. We could see them through the windows and in the bedrooms the gossip went on. What did they predict? Rain? Wind? The coming summer, the winter beyond that?

One day, one came by himself, a black one. And violent people killed him. A girl saw the murder from far away. (Myself). And doesn't forget.

My life comes and goes.

Comes and goes.

And, always, there is a black bird that falls. And falls.

Eduardo Corral

Self Portrait with Tumbling and Lasso

I'm drumroll and voyeur.
    I'm watermark
and fable. I'm weaving
    the snarls
of a wolf through my hair
    like ribbons. At my feet
chisels

    and jigsaws. I'm
performing
    an autopsy on my shadow.
My rib cage a wall
    My heart
a crack in a wall,
    a foothold. I'm tumbling

upward:
    a French acrobat. I'm judder
and effigy.
    I'm pompadour
and splendid. I'm spinning
    on a spit, split
in half.

    An apple
in my mouth. I know
    what Eve
didn't know: a serpent
    is a fruit eaten to the core. I'm
a massacre
    of the dreamers,

a terra cotta soldier
    waiting for
his emperor's return.
    When I bow,
a black fish leaps
    from the small of my back.
I catch it.

I tear it apart. I fix
the scales
to my lips.
Every word I utter
is opalescent. I'm skinned
and Orphic.
I'm scarlet

and threshold. At my touch,
a piano
melts like a slab
of black ice. I'm
steam rising,
dissipating. I'm a ghost undressing.
I'm a cowboy

riding bareback.
My soul is
whirling
above my head like a lasso.
My right hand
a pistol. My left
automatic. I'm knocking

on every door.
I'm coming on strong,
like a missionary.
I'm kicking back
any legs, like a mule. I'm kicking up
my legs, like
a showgirl.

Zbigniew Herbert, translated from the Polish by Alyssa Valles

Hermes, Dog, and Star

Hermes is going along in the world. He meets a dog.

—I'm a god—Hermes introduces himself politely.

The dog sniffs his feet.

—I feel lonely. People betray the gods. But mortal animals without self-consciousness, that's what we want. In the evening after traveling all day we'll sit down under an oak. Then I'll tell you I feel old and want to die. It'll be a lie necessary to get you to lick my hands.

—Sure—the dog replies casually—I'll lick your hands. They're cold and they smell strange.

They go along and after a while they meet a star.

—I'm Hermes—the god says—and produces one of his most handsome faces.

—Would you by any chance feel like coming with us to the end of the world? I'll try to work it so that it's scary there and you have to lean your head on my arm.

—OK—says the star in a glassy voice. I don't care where I go. But your saying the end of the world is pure naivete. Sadly, there is no end of the World.

They go along. The dog, Hermes, and the star. Holding hands. Hermes thinks to himself: the next time he goes out looking for friends, he won't be so sincere.

Jose Hernandez Diaz

The West

The West has a seagull as President. The West bathes in the sun and the moonlight. The West skates and surfs and raps and cruises. The West flies a kite in spring. The West does not fear winter or Mexicans. The West eats a burrito for breakfast. The West has Korean BBQ for lunch. The West never forgives. Never forgets. The West will not go down without a fight. The West is strong. The West is light. The West can hold a thorn rose between her lips. The West, The West, The West.

DISCUSSION

Mina Loy wrote, in "Modern Poetry," that the genre was "prose bewitched, a music made of visual thoughts, the sound of an idea." We think this begins to get at the concept of writing out of Surrealism, and we'd add that it might be helpful to also consider the ways that, much like the senses in Loy's definition, in Surrealism the inanimate and animate blur . . .

Exquisite Collage Reading: Before you embark on the rest of this chapter, leaf through the textbook and lift language / phrases to create three to five "if" statements, and three to five unrelated "then" statements; cut them out and match them up randomly. For example: IF "the lyric 'they / them, she / her, he / him, ze / zou' is useful to crafting," then "How wide should the entrance to a bee hive be?" (lines taken from "Telling Secrets" and "Documentary Poetics" chapters, respectively). Note the fun leap that occurs, and how the seemingly unrelated clauses, when placed together, suggest revelation?! What you have constructed are called *conditionals*, one form of automatic writing that the Surrealists used—usually in pairs, with partners taking turns writing the "if," folding down the paper so the next person could not see, so that they penned the "then" portion without knowing how (or if!) it would connect. But, of course, like anything placed next to something else (what else is a metaphor?), it did. Conditionals make meaning or experiences via that juxtaposition, via the *experience of making*. Surrealists used such games—conditionals, syllogisms, questions and answers, and others—to open themselves to possibility, begin writing, and spark the unconscious.

Now, try reading this chapter out of our order (but into your own), by selecting a passage based on which epigraph you like:

. . .

13. "When she was born the wolf appeared."

—MAROSA DI GIORGIO

Reader: to learn more about the wolf, go to "Fur Cups & Saucers," section 13.

. . .

C. "Our brains are dulled by the incurable mania of wanting to make the unknown known, classifiable."

—ANDRÉ BRETON, THE FIRST MANIFESTO OF SURREALISM

&

"I never read him."

—LEONORA CARRINGTON TO HER NIECE, SPEAKING OF BRETON'S MANIFESTOES

Reader: If you like C, go to Global and Intersectional Implications.

. . .

IV. "Scientific knowledge enumerates, measures, classifies, and kills . . . [it] is a lion without antelopes and without zebras."

—AIMÉ CÉSAIRE, "POETRY AND KNOWLEDGE"

Reader: if you are interested in *IV.*, begin immediately below this.

*

IV. Non-sense and the Ecosystem of Surrealism

If Surrealism were a *cento*—Latin for patchwork, a cento being poetry's more intentional game of Exquisite Corpse, linguistic or visual associative collage-making—it might patch together Dali's melting clocks, Meret Oppenheim's fur cup and saucer, an assortment of chance and collaborative experiences, transcribed dream sequences, Remedios Varo's owl-woman—with the heart of a violin—filtering starlight to paint a bird. Found objects! Juxtaposition! Joseph Cornell's shadow boxes flocked with words and feathers. René Magritte's not-a-pipe, or an apple where a face should be, black hat floating above the head. And, of course, Man Ray's evocative *L'étoile de mer*, a starfish in a jar, the promise of heat and the body's salt, but strained through glass and chemical . . . and music, faintly, from another room, dissonant but somehow familiar, your mind making associative leaps between this and something you are quite sure you *almost* remember.

Indeed, you might picture these things when you think of Surrealism, a term that has, since its post-World War I, Modernist / avant-garde origins, been also co-opted by capitalism and marketed on dorm room posters and other commercial goods. Many early Surrealists would have been furious about this, fighting as they were to subvert mainstream and oppressive thought patterns, but today it is possible that it is, in fact, mainstream culture that introduced you to Surrealism. However, looking back a hundred years, you'll see that the seeds of this movement are in the wild disruption of the status quo, through strange combinations of the reality of image and hyper-reality of imagination—or dream—and associative leaps that create the Surreal, a concept not coined but given a name in 1917 by French poet and playwright Guillame Apollinaire, and later described by the self-dubbed "Father of Surrealism" André Breton in his first Manifesto (1924) as "Psychic automatism in its pure state, by which one proposes to express—verbally, by means of the written word, or in any other manner—the actual functioning of thought. Dictated by thought, in the absence of any control exercised by reason, exempt from any aesthetic or moral concern." Not exactly the stuff of textbooks, eh? This is going to make Surrealism difficult to define.

13. Fur Cups & Saucers

Political and personal, valuing the intersection of cultures, identities, beliefs and practices that collectively defy definition, Surrealism cannot be contained in its cities or artistic circles of origin. In her introduction to *Surrealist Women: An International Anthology* (1998), Penelope Rosemont writes that Surrealism "has neither dogma nor catechism," that it "most emphatically does *not* signify unreality, or a denial of the real, or a 'refusal to accept reality.' It insists, rather, on *more* reality, a higher reality." Combining poetry and then-new Freudian psychoanalytic theory, the Surrealists' written conclusions based on their trance-speaking create a kind of ars poetica—both poetic theory and art of poetry. They attempt to bring to the surface the unexpected and divergent patterns of thought that live in our subconscious. Rosemont explains:

> Surrealism begins with the recognition that the real . . . includes many diverse elements that are ordinarily repressed or suppressed in exploitative, inegalitarian societies . . . Far from being a mode of irrationalist escapism, surrealism is an immeasurably expanded awareness.
>
> The social diffusion of this radical awareness is what the first surrealists called the surrealist revolution (which was also the title they gave their journal, *La Revolution surréaliste*). Their chosen method for its realization was the affirmation of the Marvelous—the production of disquietingly antirational images that disrupt positivist and other restrictive ways of thinking and being, thereby provoking all who behold them to come to grips with their own "inner reality" and its relation to the external world.
>
> Affirmation of the Marvelous, which is also the negation of all that rationalizes misery, is the key to all forms of surrealist research, also known as the "practice of poetry." For surrealists, poetry is always discovery, risk, revelation, adventure, an activity of the mind, a method of

> knowledge leading to revolutionary solutions to the fundamental problems of life. Poetry is therefore the opposite of "literature"—a term which, in surrealist discourse, signifies a benumbing distraction that serves only the needs of repression and conformity.

Poetry—an expressive / inventive process that includes, in addition to writing, means of production such as visuals and film, psychoanalysis, and dreams—according to Rosemont, Césaire, Loy, and others, *may be the key* to releasing poets and artists, and by extension all of us, from oppressive forces. In fact, this is what the Surrealists sought—a freedom of the mind, both conscious and unconscious, and political liberation from fascist forces, many of which threatened not just artists' lives, but anyone who existed outside the mainstream reigns of power in most European countries at the turn of the century (and beyond!).

C. Global and Intersecting Implications

What began as seeds in various global communities responding to post-World War I political unrest, became a collection of artists and writers gathering for salons in Paris, where they took refuge from Nazi or other fascist occupations of their home cities. Bridging from the Romantic / imitation of nature plus imagination, the Dada "nonsense" movement of Romanian Tristan Tzara (who referred to himself as "Papa Dada"), the intensity of the French Symbolists, and the Freudian study of the conscious and unconscious, id, ego, and superego, into something new—defined and redefined by Breton in his Surrealist Manifestos, and finally sprung out of by many initial adherents, Surrealists fled later to New York and Mexico City, where their influence rippled and spread.

Surrealist women, in particular, asserted the need for less capitalist, more eco-friendly dealings with the earth and its inhabitants, and moreover, approached community and collaboration with feminist-adjacent practices. While many of the original self-proclaimed Surrealist men in France objectified women as "mediums" or muses, it is perhaps the more politically engaged and radically progressive Surrealist work that lasts today. In our "Poetics of Liberation" chapter we'll talk more about Surrealism's role in the art of global liberation movements. In this chapter we'd like to do a gloss on some of the women Surrealists, who were overlooked in their own time but have become some of the most enduringly influential poets from that era—such as Mina Loy and Marosa di Giorgio—as well as the artistic friendship among Remedios Varos and Leonora Carrington, both visual artists and writers who, together with Hungarian photographer Kati Horna, worked in a collective in Mexico City after fleeing Fascism in Spain and England.

In their writings and artwork, these women continued to influence one another not through galvanizing any overly wrought manifestos or sets of rules for one another, but through collaborative and permission-giving magic, working for decades parallel to, but also divorced from, the efforts and effects of Surrealism in other parts of the world. Perhaps relying more deeply on occult and divinatory poetics, and certainly on her own stint in a sanatorium, Carrington eventually penned a novel, *The Hearing Trumpet*, that among other things, calls back to earliest societies' temple goddesses and the sublime power of female forms to conquer masculinity and return the earth, via a magical, human-created apocalypse, to its less civilized, more animal / hybrid-animal-human, more intriguing state. Early on in the novel, Carrington's protagonist Marian makes several incisive jabs at America and the widespread evils of capitalism and institutions; later, she boils and eats herself alive, becoming through the ritual reborn. The repeated presence of a close friend, Carmella, is based on real-life Remedios Varo—with several characteristics that mirror the women's friendship and characters, including Varo's letters to strangers and the smoking of cigars (both of which Carmella engages in, in the book). The lively details of their exchanges on the page feel like the kind of assignment we give our students—to eavesdrop on and / or record a real-life conversation and then turn it into fiction or poetry. The fantastical and wild leaps of the book are what we imagine might happen if such conversations went the way of our imaginations, instead of being confined by the realities of man-made societies. In many ways, the lasting weirdness of this specific collaboration outlasts the political moment of Surrealism's codifying salons in Paris and lands itself squarely as a kind of code for poetic, visionary friendships.

There is a story of artist and writer Leonora Carrington later in life. At tea, Carrington tells her niece of how she once sat in the audience of one of Breton's public lectures, listening only half-attentively to his presentation. Her niece was impressed by the affiliation to Breton and his famous manifestos, but Carrington, to correct the awe, leaned over and admitted conspiratorially and dismissively: "I never read them."

This, to us, defines in many ways the dominant attitude of writing out of this movement—that anything deemed a "rule" should be questioned, subdued, or ignored. At the same time, each person should pen a manifesto (but perhaps the kind that only applies to the self, unimposing on others' lives). And cover something in fur. And surprise themselves, drawing up out of the subconscious the unexpected and weird.

Surrealist poetry seems, then, to suggest the best of what poetry does—expand realities and push limits, creatively and philosophically. It also suggests a generous spirit of collaboration with other artists in and out of one's own discipline. Most of all, it is about exploring those deep recesses of imagination, "without any irritable reaching after fact and reason," as Breton says in one of those manifestos a surrealist free spirit may or may not take to heart. It is certainly un-rubricable, immeasurable by outcomes and quantitative assessments. Teachers: Please don't try. Or if you must, try to make one that defies its own pedagogical imperatives.

Further Arcs and Mysteries of Ancestry

No one knows whether the story of French Symbolist Gérard de Nerval walking a pet lobster on a blue silk leash through Paris, to the opera, is true or not true. We do know that Nerval was excessively strange and playful; that he once "rescued" a lobster from sea nets; that he used to leave animals as messages for his friends; that the Moon Card of a tarot deck shows a lobster climbing out of the ocean; that Nerval said of the shelled animal:

> I have a liking for lobsters. They are peaceful, serious creatures. They know the secrets of the sea, they don't bark, and they don't gobble up your monadic privacy like dogs do.

So, walking the lobster may be a metaphor for many other things, such as Nerval's affiliation for relying upon the marvelous as an antidote to the regular, or to his belief that inanimate objects, animals, all non-human things, still held vibrations of life.

Regardless, one can see early splinters of Surrealism in Nerval's late nineteenth-century sonnet "Lines in Gold." Opening with an epigraph from Pythagoras, *Why not! Everything feels!,* Nerval's speaker gives direction, telling the listener: "Look around you. Everything that you see / Quivers with being" (2–3). Inhabiting the distinctly Romantic voice of the Enlightenment poet, and also commanding the voicy lyric that preceded this, the poem tells us "Beasts have a mind. Respect it. Flowers too. Look at one" (5–6), but then follows with a rhyme of "petal" and "metal" (in the French, an image-rhyme; in the translation shared here, also sonic rhyme), moving from the natural to the human-forged, suddenly getting weird(er): "Nature brought forth each petal. / There is a mystery that sleeps in metal. / 'Everything feels!' and has power over you" (6–8). This prefaces what happens next—the typical volta moves us from reverence of the natural world to a near-paranoia, as the poem hinges here into the admonition: "Be careful! The blind wall is spying on us" (9). *What???* Here we get the literal transition from the Romantic to dark symbolism, on the precipice of the Surreal.

Later would come Pablo Neruda, Federico García Lorca, Antonio Machado, and César Vallejo, followed by Jerome Rothenberg, Robert Bly's, and James Wright's ideas about Deep Image. Since we'll talk about all of that in the next chapter, here we'll focus on some contemporary poets writing in the tradition. One of our favorites is Eduardo Corral, who works in ekphrasis, elegy, received and invented forms, all the while moving between languages, in this case Spanish and English, to write poems of Mexico–US border politics, family lineage, queerness, class and status. Corral's work is often elegy and ode combined (What elegy isn't an ode? What ode isn't elegiac?), full of associative leaps and homages to artists, political leaders, and Harlem Renaissance poets who also influenced so many Surrealists of one hundred years ago and today.

Writes contemporary poet, teacher, and scholar Carl Phillips in his introduction to Corral's *Slow Lightning*: "In these poems, a cage implies all the rest that lies outside it; any frame frames a window through which to see the other possibilities unfolding" (xi). Like a poem! The containers of Corral's poems are porous—as is his speaker—inhabiting both sense and nonsense, as in his "Self-Portrait with Tumbling and Lasso," in which that speaker claims:

I'm watermark
and fable. I'm weaving
the snarls
of a wolf through my hair
like ribbon. (2–6)

Can you hear the Nerval in that? Everything *feeling, having power* over us? The influence lingers in a self claiming to be fable, as the wolf snarls through one's hair, the ribbon that may as well be leading a lobster to the opera. And in Corral's elegiac "After Bei Dao / After Jean Valentine" (a contemporary Chinese author and New York poet, respectively), this blur of sense and identity, listing and narrative brings us:

Fingers are rooting inside a violin to pull out

The last scraps of birdsong

A gold wheel spinning in your mind

Like insomnia (11–14)

That last bit—the sleeplessness and the overlap of natural and human-made, brought into the body to become simile—is reminiscent not just of the two writers to which the title pays tribute but also Surrealists like Phillipe Soupault, whose repetition, as in his poem "Georgia," often created a chant (you can find his poem via our online companion). In Corral, that repetition is subtler, but makes a beautiful, embroidered line, "rooting," "spinning," with the actions creating parallels then between what enacts: "fingers" and a "gold wheel," each, then, gaining agency. Everything is feeling! Everything is a mystery, sleeping in metal.

Or, perhaps, doing the things dogs and stars do. In Polish poet Zbigniew Herbert's prose poem "Hermes, Dog, and Star," the wild movements of dream dialogue merge with a linguistic play, with reversals of words assisting with associative leaps, as in the natural reversal of "god" to "dog" one might expect in a joke:

Hermes is going along in the world. He meets a dog.

—I'm a god—Hermes introduces himself politely.

> The dog sniffs his feet.
>
> —I feel lonely. People betray the gods. But mortal animals without self-consciousness, that's what we want.

So, Hermes goes on, working too hard intellectually to convince the dog to lick his hands. Of course, the dog complies easily: "Sure . . . I'll lick your hands. They're cold and they smell strange."

Eventually the pair meet a star, and Hermes tries to convince the star to accompany them to the end of the world; the star suggests that's actually impossible, but agrees to accompany them anyway. The poem reads like a fable, except without any moral, as playful, but without any meaning. A star agreeing to travel to the end of the world with an animal and godlike companion? Sure, since the god is the guardian of travelers. Why not! Or perhaps the meaning is lost to us only because we haven't spent enough time in the subconscious, where dreams and worlds are made and unmade.

Contemporary Mexican American poet Jose Hernandez Diaz has certainly spent time in that space, and his work falls within the Surrealist lineage, though his tone is more directly political. Diaz's prose poem "The West" draws—like Herbert—from the easy, everyday rhythms of prose. Syntax and conventional grammar allow for both momentum and a conversational pause; and the anaphoric repetition of "The West," because it stabilizes and makes familiar the subject, offers permission for more destabilizing and dreamy leaps:

> The West has a seagull as President. The West bathes in the sun and the moonlight. The West skates and surfs and raps and cruises. The West flies a kite in spring. The West does not fear winter or Mexicans. The West eats a burrito for breakfast. The West has Korean BBQ for lunch.

You can hear that "West" being both *America as a whole* and *a Californian* specifically, but The West is also, perhaps, a British child who "flies a kite in spring." And, "The West" reaches even into religious texts, ones which some find comforting while others find rife with oppression—such as 1 Corinthians, verse 13, where "love never fails." In Diaz's work, the message feels more sinister: "The West never forgets." In lines relying both on mimesis and internal rhyme, both traditions of The West, Diaz tells us "The West will not go down without a fight. The West is strong. The West is light." Further, rhyming "light" and "fight" suggests the West's fight *might be* light—Diaz creates a kind of image-to-concept transport from the parallel made with that sonic echo. What else could or would the West do? Pretty much anything, in Diaz's work—appropriating traditional foods, for better or worse, by "eat[ing] a burrito for breakfast" and "Korean BBQ for lunch." Boundaries dissolve, cultures dissolve; meaning, perhaps, dissolves. This brief and powerful poem suggests the West, both a capital noun and a time-space concept, contains all possible realities. Much like a Surrealist poet or poem. But West-er.

Ways to inhabit and write out of Surrealism, we suggest, are to document your dreams, play some collaborative games, wrangle repetition until it surprises you, visit museums around the world, and engage in the works of Surrealist-inspired visual and literary artists.

INVITATIONS TO REFLECT

Discuss Together

People will often describe something shocking, incredible, or overwhelming as "surreal." Although it can be tempting for people who love words to get a little pedantic about definitions, let's not fret over the fact that language morphs with time and widespread usage. Instead, consider how the surreal poems at the beginning of this chapter are surreal in a different way from how this word is commonly used today. In what ways has your understanding of Surrealism changed by reading this chapter?

For Further Study

Have you had moments in your life where you've encountered the Surreal, whether on dorm room posters, lunch boxes, or in a museum or avant garde novel? (Write down some of the images you recall, in language, and save them for a later exercise—perhaps when you need to enliven a flat poem.) Are there Surrealist traditions you'd like to research and learn more about? Which book or film or collected works of art, in any discipline, interest you? Choose a work situated in the Surrealist lineage and study it for how it engages with hyper-reality, juxtaposition, collage-making, etc., in form and subject. What moves does the author or artist or director make that you note as distinctly influenced by the Surreal? What do they add to the lineage? In addition to those poets and collections referenced in this chapter (all of which we recommend checking out), here are some other examples to get you started: Ocean Vuong's *Night Sky with Exit Wounds*, Bianca Stone's *Poetry Comics From the Book of Hours,* Charles Simic's *Dime-Store Alchemy,* Bat for Lashes' music video for "What's a Girl to Do," Max Ernst's collage novel, *Une Semaine De Bonte,* Magritte's painting *The Son of Man.*

Writing Exercises

1 **CENTO Means PATCHWORK [& Other Collage]**

One of our favorite introductory activities, which we feel is also good for advanced poets, is to create an "abstract" made up by cento (a form of collage, "cento" means "100" in Italian, and is a poetic style in which the author simply borrows and then pastes together into some semblance of "order" 100 lines from other poets). For yours, choose lines (anywhere from 20-100) from a text that you cannot "make sense" of, as a window into that text. Choose a theory essay or textbook chapter (Perhaps one of ours? We're not precious!) and lift phrases and lines, collaging them together into a "poem." If you're feeling extremely Surrealist, get yourself a pair of scissors and actually cut up the text before reassembling. If you don't want to deface the actual book, make a photocopy of the pages from which you intend to work. Or, go buy some books that are already disintegrating, at a thrift store or yard sale. This would also work well for another way to collage, in which you take visuals from old textbooks—like "found" poets do—and overlay text. Visual poets Mita Mahato (whose "Extinction Limericks" you encountered in Sound, Shape, and Space), Kathryn Smith, Nance Van Winckel, Sarah Sloat, and others practice this technique. Look them up for more examples.

2 **Papa Dada and His Paper Bag**

Tristan Tzara used to choose a newspaper article the length of a poem he wanted to write, cut it up into individual words, and place them all into a paper bag, drawing them out one by one and recording them in that order. Alternately, use an online word randomizer. "The poem will be like you," he instructs those willing to try.

3 **Exquisite Corpse and Variations on EC (Collaborations)**

- Conditionals from Poem-Trash: Go back to your conditionals that you made early in the chapter and try again to construct some new ones by looking through your own poem-scraps to lift language for new ones. Then, turn these into a poem. Feel free to include one or more made up of our lines; you can just add an epigraph that says "with a conditional from *Advanced Poetry: A Writer's Guide and Anthology*" or something along those lines. We give you permission.
- Classic Exquisite Corpse: Play a traditional game of EC by gathering two or more friends together and passing a piece of paper. Begin by writing a line, folding down the paper, passing it so the next person cannot see that line; they will write a line and pass the paper. Continue in a circle until you've filled the page; unfold and read aloud.

- Definitions or Questions and Answers: Just like the last game, this is about concealing and revealing. One person writes a question, folds down the paper, then passes it to another, who writes an answer without seeing the question. You can do this with two or more players, then mine the created text for poem-ideas.

4 **Invent a New System / Order, or Natural Manifesto**

"Poetic knowledge," writes Aimé Césaire, "is born in the great silence of scientific knowledge." He doesn't mean that the natural world has to be quiet. Rather, utilizing the conscious and unconscious, working against racist taxonomies, we might create a new order—something akin to what the natural world suggests. Considering Césaire's claims, re-personalize the self among others, inventing a cosmology that centers the natural world rather than moving away from it, and re-personalizes humans in the process.

5 **"How Wide Should the Entrance to a Beehive Be?" [Automatic Writing]**

Engage in the purest form of automatic writing by simply putting a question, epigraph, or some other single line at the top of your page, and then writing, without worrying what you are thinking or whether it makes sense, for 10 minutes straight. The line above (from another chapter in this text) might be used as a prompt, or you can snag any question asked in this text, or any line from a poem you enjoy. Having fun and letting yourself be weird is the primary requirement.

6 **Document your Dreams! / Dream Diary**

As many surrealists did and many writers still do, make a practice to write down your dreams as soon as you wake. If you cannot remember whole sequences, simply jot down any images, phrases, or ideas that you recall. Use these later in places where your poems sag or need energy, or simply write the dream out as a prose poem. Embellish as the poem demands.

5

Duende, Deep Image, & The Poetics of Spells

A FEW POEMS TO START US OFF . . .

In this chapter, we trace the poetic lineage of duende / *dwende—from Spanish, Filipino, and other global ancestries—through a poetics known as Deep Image via American translators' renditions, to contemporary feminist spells. We also suggest those spells' roots may trace back to similar spirits of the land as Federico Garcia Lorca's duende, born out of either poverty or magical / Surrealist trichomes, and sometimes both.*

Josefina de la Torre

[Untitled, from Poemas de la Isla, *translated by Carlos Reyes]*

On which of these pathways
will I find your shadow?
Where will I find the track
of your unknown going?
I walk, eyes lowered,
counting the pebbles,
Condemning to prisons
of eyelids and heartbeats
all of the grey outlines
which the sun draws in the dirt
and every white curve
that air forms on the earth.
I don't know which road
or which path it will be.

*

Night's mane,
lost horse of dawn.
Fine and lustrous hair,
of long transparencies,
shivering skin.
What hidden dream along the white shores
violent and silent
galloping of the dawn!
Sleeping pools of water,
flexible haunches of the whole night.
Weary vigilance—
unsleeping wind—
weary humidity . . .
What hidden dream under the white shores
and how solemn, the motionless
galloping of the dawn!

*

The recently scrubbed sky
is swept clean of clouds.
The moon, alone, in the background,
opens from time to time.
I make my way through the sky
walking and walking
and enter the white moon
which opens from time to time.

James Wright

Milkweed

While I stood here, in the open, lost in myself,
I must have looked a long time
Down the corn rows, beyond grass,
The small house,
White walls, animals lumbering toward the barn.
I look down now. It is all changed.
Whatever it was I lost, whatever I wept for
Was a wild, gentle thing, the small dark eyes
Loving me in secret.
It is here. At a touch of my hand,
The air fills with delicate creatures
From the other world.

Diane Seuss

[I Dreamed I Had To Find My Way From the City Where I Live Now]

I dreamed I had to find my way from the city where I live now
to the place I call my hometown, I had to ride a bike and night
was falling and to make things worse there had been flooding,
there was a flood, why in dreams do streams escape their borders,
why must I backtrack to keep myself from drowning, the alternate path
was dark and then I had to pee, squat on the side of the road among
the cattails and puzzlegrass, and lost my pants in the process, lost them
in the dark, there'd been a flood, I was wandering without pants between
the land of my earliest days and what I now call home, then came a man
in a truck, just my luck a man with a truck, a knife, and a dream, it was
a knife that could cut an ear of corn from its stalk, many ears from many
stalks, he saw that the road was dark, he saw the shadows of stalks
in the moonlight, and then he robbed me of my dream, it became his
dream,
and like Lorca in "Rider's Song" I never made it back to the motherland.

Brigit Pegeen Kelly

Song

Listen: there was a goat's head hanging by ropes in a tree.
All night it hung there and sang. And those who heard it
Felt a hurt in their hearts and thought they were hearing
The song of a night bird. They sat up in their beds, and then
They lay back down again. In the night wind, the goat's head
Swayed back and forth, and from far off it shone faintly
The way the moonlight shone on the train track miles away
Beside which the goat's headless body lay. Some boys
Had hacked its head off. It was harder work than they had imagined.
The goat cried like a man and struggled hard. But they
Finished the job. They hung the bleeding head by the school
And then ran off into the darkness that seems to hide everything.
The head hung in the tree. The body lay by the tracks.
The head called to the body. The body to the head.
They missed each other. The missing grew large between them,
Until it pulled the heart right out of the body, until
The drawn heart flew toward the head, flew as a bird flies
Back to its cage and the familiar perch from which it trills.
Then the heart sang in the head, softly at first and then louder,
Sang long and low until the morning light came up over
The school and over the tree, and then the singing stopped . . .
The goat had belonged to a small girl. She named
The goat Broken Thorn Sweet Blackberry, named it after
The night's bush of stars, because the goat's silky hair
Was dark as well water, because it had eyes like wild fruit.
The girl lived near a high railroad track. At night
She heard the trains passing, the sweet sound of the train's horn
Pouring softly over her bed, and each morning she woke
To give the bleating goat his pail of warm milk. She sang
Him songs about girls with ropes and cooks in boats.
She brushed him with a stiff brush. She dreamed daily
That he grew bigger, and he did. She thought her dreaming
Made it so. But one night the girl didn't hear the train's horn,
And the next morning she woke to an empty yard. The goat
Was gone. Everything looked strange. It was as if a storm
Had passed through while she slept, wind and stones, rain
Stripping the branches of fruit. She knew that someone
Had stolen the goat and that he had come to harm. She called
To him. All morning and into the afternoon, she called

And called. She walked and walked. In her chest a bad feeling
Like the feeling of the stones gouging the soft undersides
Of her bare feet. Then somebody found the goat's body
By the high tracks, the flies already filling their soft bottles
At the goat's torn neck. Then somebody found the head
Hanging in a tree by the school. They hurried to take
These things away so that the girl would not see them.
They hurried to raise money to buy the girl another goat.
They hurried to find the boys who had done this, to hear
Them say it was a joke, a joke, it was nothing but a joke . . . .
But listen: here is the point. The boys thought to have
Their fun and be done with it. It was harder work than they
Had imagined, this silly sacrifice, but they finished the job,
Whistling as they washed their large hands in the dark.
What they didn't know was that the goat's head was already
Singing behind them in the tree. What they didn't know
Was that the goat's head would go on singing, just for them,
Long after the ropes were down, and that they would learn to listen,
Pail after pail, stroke after patient stroke. They would
Wake in the night thinking they heard the wind in the trees
Or a night bird, but their hearts beating harder. There
Would be a whistle, a hum, a high murmur, and, at last, a song,
The low song a lost boy sings remembering his mother's call.
Not a cruel song, no, no, not cruel at all. This song
Is sweet. It is sweet. The heart dies of this sweetness.

Jennifer Givhan

Desert Duende

After Emily

loaded she says. loaded.
but locked. she doesn't wonder
at the cage. the click. the barrel.
stock. stop. unhinge. she is spark-exhausted.
she barricades. mines
the spine. heart. cacti. bleeds.
no one explains when. to die.
no one has to. nature. of thirst.
instinct. blinking back
extinction. near the brink.
always. the brick. the oven.
near loaded. not shot.
the rains meant to come.
she wanders. pecking livers.
mouthwashing dust. speckling
silt. end trails. rattles.
bullhorns. bullets. bullshit.
unloaded. sand-skirts. she kicks
herself. bricks come. later. and fast.
she never held a. gun. she
glistens. metal sun-spit. cacti rungs.
she tugs. triggers. ignites.

Rachelle Cruz

Self-Portrait as Blood

If there is a river more ecstatic than this
simmering between fingers,
black-red as night parting through the reeds,
then let me gnaw my mother's finger
into the bell of her silence.

If there is a river more powerful than this,
pray that it flows through the magic of return.
Silt loosened by the heart's surge
and carried into the chambers of my wilderness.

If there is a river more present than this,
teach me how to unfurl dawn with my hands,
to stroke honey-mouthed generations
with this wild, wild water.

DISCUSSION

If you're a DIY home crafter or artistic upcycler, maybe you like to collect those paint color palettes from hardware stores, to string garlands of them for your kitchen nook or shingles for your miniature houses. Or perhaps you find it intriguing to read the descriptive, metaphoric forest and field names each company gives their greens, to stand before the range of them and critique their strange and insulting origins. Long before those ombre walls of hues, back in 1814, German mineralogist Abraham Gottlob Werner attempted to classify and name each color in the visible spectrum. His color-names sound enough like the spirits stirred in the blood that one might mistake them—such is the richness of hue in deep image and duende poetics.

See for yourself. Can you guess which of the following phrases come from Werner's *Nomenclature of Colors*, and which are excerpts from poems driven by duende or deep image?

(a) A cloister, a silence / Closing around a blossom of fire
(b) Red Spots of the Lygaeus Apterus Fly / Red on the golden Rennette Apple
(c) Ripe Coalmar Pear, Irish Pitcher Apple / Brimstone Butterfly
(d) Green vein in her throat green wing in my mouth / green thorn in my eye
(e) I had a beehive / inside my heart, / and from my old bitterness / the gold bees / were contriving white combs / and sweet honey
(f) High colored sulphur / Head of Golden Pheasant / Canterbury Bell, Campanula Persicifolia
(g) Opening with their sharp gold wings / The purple and crimson wounds of the flowers

Well, maybe you can discern them, because *you* are a poet, but don't they *all* sound like verse? Or dream? If you'd like to know:

(a) is James Wright / translation of Vajello, from "The Jewel";
(b) is the Animal and Vegetable descriptions of "Hyacinth Red," No. 83 in *Werner's Nomenclature*;
(c) is Vegetable description of "Siskin Green," No. 61 and Animal description of "Asparagus Green," No. 58;
(d) is Natalie Diaz, from "In the Desire Field;"
(e) is Antonio Machado, from Barnstone's translation of "last night while I was sleeping;"

(f) is Mineral description of "Gamboge Yellow," No. 66, Animal description of "Kings Yellow," No. 67, & Vegetable description of "Campanula Purple," No. 39;

(g) is Brigit Pegeen Kelly, from "Divining the Field."

All the poetic lines here come from the lineages of duende and deep image, two poetic styles infused with color names, minerals, fauna, and flora, and in which the poets often recognize properties of life that appear in the waking world—alive in the nomenclature of colors and other documentation of phenomena: one way of gathering ingredients.

A Little on Lorca and Ingredient-gathering Friendships

Spanish poet, playwright, and theater director Federico García Lorca famously said that you "must awaken the duende in the remotest mansions of the blood." He also noted that the land where he lived—and wrote—was "all thistles and terminal stones," an image that evokes poverty, landscape, and death, and transports us to something thrumming with the echo of a guitar chord or bullfight, the hum that hangs in the air long after the last strum or thunder of hoof and flick of cape, crimson and rippling, or the flamenco spirit that comes jutting into one's legs during the trance-like, passionate dance.

Lorca grew up in Southern Spain, where flamenco and bullfights threaded into the community fabric. Considered to be part of the "Generation of '27," a group of poets who brought Surrealism and symbolism to Spain between the World Wars (and during Spain's own Civil War), Lorca was openly queer and a political activist, two facets of his identity that led to his persecution by the fascist Franco regime, who murdered Lorca in the street in 1936. During his lifetime, Lorca befriended and championed a range of artists, poets, and grassroots politicians, and together with his peers, helped lead a movement of cultural salons and intellectual studies, as well as linking Madrid and New York in lectures and poetics. Perhaps best known for *Poet in New York* and his lecture-turned-essay, "Play and Theory of the Duende," on *cante jondo,* or deep song, Lorca was also heavily influenced by his cohort at Residencia de Estudiantes, a school and residence in Madrid that welcomed and housed many Surrealists and avant-garde artists, including Lorca, painter Salvador Dali, filmmaker Luis Buñuel, and others whose personalities reflected the deep spirit of Spanish culture, such as Lorca's good friend Emilio Prados, who Lorca called *el cazador de nubes*, or "The Cloud Hunter," as he would lean out the window with a mirror, trying to catch the clouds.

Prados published some of Lorca's early poems in *Litoral,* a magazine of poems and drawings, and generally gathered all the activists' essays and elegies. He also filled his dorm walls with portraits of Walt Whitman and Lorca, who Prados saw as his most intimate friend. Prados' literary efforts mirror those of Lorca, merging in his poetry impulses of the avant-garde, the natural world, his own Andalusian / Arabic roots—driving him to identify deeply with the subconscious otherness of Surrealism. If you are hungry for more epistolary poetry after reading M.L. Smoker's response to Richard Hugo (in our earlier chapter on epistolary and the lyric "I," which certainly overlaps in many ways with duende poetics!), you'll really dig this, too: we mention Prados because of Lorca's correspondence with him—Lorca saved 26 postcards, letters, and poems from his friend, and spent time with Prados in his working of *El Jardin*, a manuscript about the garden, the "lyrical body through which walking we can arrive at the heart of the night."

Unlike many Surrealist painters or their Symbolist forebears, Lorca and other Spanish poets were concerned with some narrative cohesion, even if the cognitive and imagistic leaps they made relied upon a semblance of dream mythos and mysterious magic. Given their persecution and marginalization, it is no wonder they identified with ancient spell-like forces; it is also no wonder they sought with such fervor the duende their work is known to carry.

A Brief History of the Duende

In popular Spanish culture, a duende is a house spirit that wreaks havoc and mischief on the domestic scenario, wrecking rooms and breaking dishes, a nuisance at best and at worst, a demon. Originating in the term "*dueño de casa*," which translates roughly as "master of the house," the duende in Spanish folklore has relatives in Filipino (dwende) and Latin American traditions, often appearing as mythical, hidden creatures who possess strange magic. In Federico Garcia Lorca's 1933 lecture "Theory and Play of the Duende," which we suggest you read in tandem with this chapter, Lorca talked of dancers, musicians, visual artists and other performers who can harness and call forth the duende, "a power, not a work; . . . a struggle, not a thought," and quoting Goethe—a mystical naturalist and philosopher—who defines it as "A mysterious power which everyone senses and no philosopher explains." Lorca doesn't see himself as a philosopher, but rather an artist, articulating the praxis of art, much like how the garden may lead us to the heart of night. The duende, writes Lorca, is, "in sum, the spirit of the earth, the same duende that scorched the heart of Nietzche, who looked for its external forms on the Rialto Bridge and in the music of Bizet, without ever finding it and without knowing that the duende he was pursuing had leaped straight from the Greek mysteries to the dancers of Cádiz or the beheaded, Dionysian scream of Silvero's siguiriya." Dionysian, as in, Dionysus, the god of wine / grape harvest, the orchard, the garden. Something *from the earth, not the intellectual mind.* Lorca makes a distinction between the duende and the angel or muse, who "guide" and "dictate" respectively, and who come from without—as in, *outside* the body, as opposed to the duende, coming from within the house of the body, or "through the soles of the feet." Most of all, Lorca makes clear that the duende is not a philosophy or an intellectual experience, but rather, those dark sounds / feelings that emerge from the blood, something we recognize but cannot name, something with which the poet wrestles, inside the self, where the emotion lives—the ineffable driving force that commands our creations. It is also likely what commanded his friend, Emilio Prados, to throw his diary off the cliffs of Coastal Spain when he fled Madrid, fearing imminent murder. On his journey, Prados carried in his pocket an anthology of 39 activist poets, half of whom were murdered shortly after. Like many Surrealists, Prados escaped to Mexico, where he lived until his death in 1962.

Living Metaphor: A Form and a Radius of Action

Lorca wrote that "In order to live, a metaphor needs two elements: a form, and a radius of action. A central nucleus and the perspective surrounding it. The nucleus opens like the flower that startles us by its strangeness; but within the radius of light we learn the name of the flower, and we get to know its perfume."

We think of Lorca's form as the image or figurative language that carries the concept, and the radius of action as how the metaphor moves in the poem. The startling occurs when we are transformed or transferred through the process so that we are able to experience it synesthetically and feel its embodiment viscerally—a relationship with image that transports us, as if by magic, what we first felt in art and then spent the rest of our lives attempting to find again and recreate.

For those of you who have spent your lives searching for this duende, in thistles and terminal stones, in dreams and the blood of dead animals, in the texts you took to read in the fields of your county or the cobbled alleys of your town, scribbling dark stirrings you are not sure how to share, this chapter is for you.

But it is not something your professors or writing mentors can transfer or even teach to you by theory—it is not something you experience because of fame or proximity to success; it is easier found, perhaps, in solitude, or at least in energy that comes from the forces of solitude. Lorca begins "A Poet in New York" by saying, "Whenever I speak before a large group, I always think I must have taken the wrong door." You may recognize the shy power of the introvert here, who can perform but will not do so without darkness. In this same lecture, Lorca told his audience: "I have come . . . not to give you honey . . . but sand or hemlock or salt water." Hemlock—what Socrates consumed to cause his own death—and salt water, which you cannot drink! Those poets who possess the duende are strange and called to ancestral, animal magic—think of Eduardo Corral's speaker in our last chapter, weaving "the snarls / of a wolf through [his hair] / like ribbon," or like the iconic poem, "Song," by Brigit Pegeen Kelly, in which a severed goat head calls to its body:

> Listen: there was a goat's head hanging by ropes in a tree.
> All night it hung there and sang. And those who heard it
> Felt a hurt in their hearts and thought they were hearing
> The song of a night bird.

Like Corral and Kelly, poets who "have duende" often make use of dreamlike imagination, physical caesura (where leaps can be made), fragments, and imagistic zoom, and they sidle up to the Surreal, as these impulses influenced their development. To trace such contemporary poets' threads more clearly back to Lorca and the Spanish tradition, let's look at translation, the diaspora of duende, and the transfer into deep image.

Duende, James Wright, and Deep Image

We can't talk about Deep Image without talking about James Wright. If you know, you know. If you don't, please put this book down and go read "A Blessing," which you can find online, linked via our companion site or just as easily via a simple search—you can even find Wright reading it to you, and all manner of obnoxious free analysis and other clickbait, but we highly suggest just enjoying the poem—perhaps saying it aloud to yourself; the rhythms of natural speech are lovely. (We aren't including the poem because, frankly, permissions are expensive, and we can't afford them for every poem we wish to share with you!)

Okay, now that you've read "A Blessing" and probably "Lying in a Hammock in William Duffy's Farm in Pine Island Minnesota" and maybe his famous football poem, "Autumn Begins in Martins Ferry, Ohio," (which may have been in your high school anthologies), you might like to know how Wright arrived at mysterious images and famous last lines. Wright, a student of traditional verse, used to compose in near-formal rhythms, even received forms; he moved away from this through time. In the mid-20th century, working on his translations of Spanish poets Antonio Machado, César Vallejo (yes, as your eager geek guides, we suggest you go look these up, too!), and Federico García Lorca (whom you already know!), Wright became heavily influenced by the spirit and struggle of duende. Paired with collaborative letters and conversations, the Spanish poets' work made for "a radical shift in forms" for Wright—the shift Lorca writes about—as the duende awakens new images and pathways in the central marrow of a poet's bones, and puts a name to the wild melancholy so many of us are born feeling, unable to define.

In Wright's work, the turn to duende often occurs after a narrative beginning in everyday experiences. On a road trip through Minnesota with his friend (the poet Robert Bly), Wright famously stops to visit two ponies by the side of the road, and this happenstance becomes an intuitive unfolding of Lorca's metaphor flower. Wright's biographer, Jonathan Blunk, explains how the famous enjambed lines of Wright's "A Blessing," "break / into blossom," were an echo of lines Wright had translated, in his journal, from Antonio Machado: "On the naked earth of the road / The hour breaks into blossom." But, we think, Wright did more than simply translate the language of image; what we see in Wright's translation is the "break / into blossom" taking on new *radius of action,* through the poetic line: Wright's version operates on the precept that the moment the speaker steps away from his car and the highway and instead communes with animals, he is brought closer to his own animal form, and the revelation of "Suddenly I realize / That if I stepped out of my body I would break / Into blossom" operates on the *hinge image*—an image suspended across a line—and its two image -concepts: if he stepped out of his body he would *break!*; if he stepped out of his body, *he would become flowers*. There is the return to the earth's ingredients! The form is the flower we see, via imagination, at the poem's closing; it is what the reader gets to realize along with the speaker in the poem, though it is never stated or described; it happens only in our minds. In this case, the radius of action is the realization, the imagined state of breaking into blossom, after interacting with animals—the roadside ponies—*who transported that speaker to his most alive self.*

Translating Machado, and with him the culture of the Andalusian romantic, Wright brings an imagistic, imaginative and participatory transport to American poetry. Wright's syntax and line usage as he moved away from strictly British received traditions, and into Spanish and other received traditions, transformed his writing, and offered those writing in the English language a new kind of poetics—that of the duende-earth merged with deep image.

While we're nerding out, we suggest you check out the biography, *James Wright: A Life in Poetry*, by Jonathan Blunk, in which Blunk also reveals how Wright's syntax in "The Jewel" borrows directly from César Vallejo's poem, "Espergesia." A classic case of poetic translation infusing itself into the translator's mind, only the last two lines of Wright's tiny poem are originals: "When I stand upright in the wind, / My bones turn to dark emeralds." Everything that precedes traces the evolution of the lineage: That cave, that blossom of fire, is where perhaps the duende lives for both Vallejo and, as translator, Wright.

Wright and his contemporaries may have popularized the duende via their use of the related deep image, but the origins of this lineage stem from a wider geographic and cultural net, moving from traditions of the land, to duende, to deep image, in that order.

The Poetics of Deep Image and the Shadow Self

A brief history lesson: the term *deep image* was coined by critics Jerome Rothenberg and Robert Kelly in the 1960s, developed by poet and scholar Robert Bly, and applied to mid-century American poets such as Galway Kinnell, James Wright, and in the late 1980s, Brigit Pegeen Kelly. Notes The Poetry Foundation, "The new group of deep-image poets was often narrative, focusing on allowing concrete images and experiences to generate poetic meaning." Generally, one does not have to look far to note other poets referencing this ancestry directly: there is an online literary journal, *duende*, which publishes works that arrive in the 21st century still carrying echoes of this lineage, such as Ariel Francisco's "Reading James Wright on the L Train" (linked via our online companion); and former US Poet Laureate, Tracy K. Smith, named her second poetry collection *duende* (2007). In Diane Seuss's *frank: sonnets* (2021), one poem, included here in our chapter anthology, ends "like Lorca in 'Rider's Song' I never made it back to the motherland." These works reference the concepts, and also use deep image poetics to transport a reader.

In deep image poetry, as noted, narrative lies in the *image*—not necessarily in conventional story arc. And the image is more than just "direct presentation of the thing;" it is the concrete image by which we might access the territory of the abstract emotion, the *felt* reality, but also of the subconscious mind—it should transport us into that subconscious experience, it should evoke something beyond, perhaps, what we experience with our senses alone. Something otherworldly, or at least requiring us to participate in the meaning-making.

To explore further how this works in a poem, let's look again at James Wright's "Milkweed," which relies on the botanical / lepidoptera knowledge that the monarch butterfly eats only the flowers of the milkweed plant (a botanist or spell caster's knowledge, perhaps). The poem begins pretty straightforward, with a speaker on a farm, but where we go later is a surprise:

> I look down now. It is all changed.
> Whatever it was I lost, whatever I wept for
> Was a wild, gentle thing, the small dark eyes
> Loving me in secret.
> It is here. At a touch of my hand,
> The air fills with delicate creatures
> From the other world.

Those delicate creatures—"whatever it was [the speaker] lost, whatever [he] wept for / was a wild, gentle thing, the small dark eyes / Loving [him] in secret"—those creatures are the memories, or whatever deep things he lost in himself. But they are ALSO the butterflies, which he rouses into the air "at a touch of [his] hand." Here they are, transported through the "milkweed" / sustenance of this poem—the deep image, the felt feeling—into "delicate creatures / from the other world." In *Twentieth Century Pleasures,* in his essay, "James Wright," poet Robert Hass remarks on how Wright "tries to see what can be made to happen by saying beautiful things, by repeating his talismanic nouns and adjectives of the discovery of the inner world." These many talismanic nouns and adjectives offer us a personal world that is also political (something you remember from the earlier chapter, "Telling Secrets" discussions on intimacy and confession, or will see in later chapters' discussion of embodiment)—they refer to the body politic via the body, its moving through the world. This use of the body and its sensory machinations, paired with the chemicals of the brain, and the leaps of the psyche, is where we hook, too, into poetic theory.

In Robert Bly's explanation of deep image, he compares the poem to an animal, saying that the body of the animal moves around rhythmically and with some "psychic energy." There's the monarch!—the poem is the milkweed, the longing of the psyche is that delicate creature we reach through image. Wright communicates this through the extended conceit that transports us; *we* fly up from the flowers.

This is achieved, Bly might argue, through Jungian archetypal symbols. According to twentieth-century psychologist Carl Jung, "A symbol does not define or explain; it points beyond itself to a meaning that is darkly divined yet still beyond our grasp, and cannot be adequately expressed in the familiar words of our language." These symbols come to us through the collective consciousness, into the unconscious, and rise up in us to influence thought. For Bly, and for Wright, we move between these worlds. What a poet knows through everyday logic, reason, and narrative may not be enough—but what we access through imagination, through image, to the deep unconscious and back to consciousness again—that is poetry. The symbols become a way of reaching back through time and tradition, through fairy tale logic and—dare we say?—magic.

This movement is ancestral—deep image leaps into Jungian symbol, into the shadow. How do we give poets permission to play with these leaps, these layers of self, these layers even of possibility? Enter the Shadow Self. Referring to Dorianne Laux and Kim Addonizio's chapter, "The Shadow," from their book, *The Poet's Companion: A Guide to the Pleasures of Writing Poetry,* we often encourage new poets, in our classes, to complete exercises in exploring their "shadows," creating "doubles," second selves, which possess some pseudonym related to their names (much like Borges does in "Borges and I," from the chapter, "Telling Secrets"). These second selves offer budding writers a way to depart from surface narrative into subconscious "darkness"—their shadow selves often commit acts of romantic bravery, of symbolic violence, of dream logic, that their "real" selves might be afraid to engage. These shadow selves allow the poets permission to diverge from and therefore endorse the making of the self on the page, to travel by image rather than story, to explore a deep consciousness that may be more alive to thistles and terminal stones, to the awakening of duende "in the remote mansions of the blood."

One poet who did this matter-of-factly both in verse and in her acting career was Josefina de la Torre, one of Lorca's mentees who sought political asylum in Madrid during the Spanish Civil War. Unable to return to her home in Gran Canaria, de la Torre lived in Madrid and was involved—long after many of her contemporaries' deaths or departures—in literary pursuits, as well as acting and singing (including playing Maria Von Trapp in a Spanish production of a musical on the Von Trapp family!). No doubt she found asylum in such doubles on stage, as well as in exploring her "shadow" self on the page, both directly and indirectly. In one poem, her speaker asks, "On which of these pathways / will I find your shadow?" and, in another, her work becomes talismanic with the, "Night's mane, lost horse of dawn." This nearly feels like deep image already—the night as a moving animal. Yet another has the speaker relating, as if possessed by unearthly magic, that the sky is "swept clean of clouds," and the moon opening, as that speaker confesses, chant like:

> I make my way through the sky
> walking and walking
> and enter the white moon
> which opens from time to time.

The hint of the witch or sorceress as a pedestrian of the sky, entering the "moon / which opens" (for her, it seems!) is both precursor to and invocational of the magic handed down by the Spanish (Andalusian) and island traditions.

Contemporary Feminist Renditions of Image as the Poetics of Spells

Another way of thinking about this lineage is by tracing how Lorca's "sand or hemlock or salt water" merges in practice with the poetics of spells, charms that enthrall many would-be-word-witches (casters and receivers) with their healing and / or hexing, magical disruptive powers.

Sound a lot like duende? We think so, too—there is an intersection here that derives back through the received Lorca / Vallejo / Machado / Wright + Jungian tradition to earlier cultural powers: those house-spirits as companions of the women who cast them out or lived among them: powerful women, domestic or community figures who certainly held magical reigns, who cast spells and made elixirs by necessity.

Within the range of today's spell-casting poets (witches, midwives, and more)—those whose stations necessitate magic—we witness an arrival. A spell requires ingredients: up from the earth, through those foot-soles or the roots of plants, the skeletons of animals—plus musical invocation / repetition, evocation of insight or consciousness, given to or borrowed from the familiar flora and fauna, and mysterious forces, moving through the animal of the metaphor or the movement of dream; this feels very much like how duende and deep image arrive in praxis. Imagist H.D.'s indeterminate-voiced "Oread" (which you can read online) or many of the Surrealist women's poems illustrate that the voice of such a spell is intimate, conspiratorial, & invocational. Both now and in the past, the poetics of spells includes texts that function by image plus language—such as the visual poetics of Mita Mahato (whose extinction limericks you may remember from the chapter "Sound, Shape, and Space") or Gabrielle Bates (whose "From the Circus" can be found linked via our online companion)—and it includes those team efforts that merge two or more disciplines, such as poet Bianca Stone's collaborations with classicist poet-scholar Anne Carson, or Frances Cannon's visual reviews. The layering of discipline is one way of continuing a spell.

Spells also appear syntactically, such as in Jennifer Givhan's "Desert Duende," from her first collection, *Landscape with Headless Mama*. The poem opens with the third-person character locked and loaded, presumably in a room (such as Emily Dickinson's, for whom the poem is dedicated) or the *room of the desert,* possibly in possession of a gun, and the speaker-narrator telling us "she doesn't wonder / at the cage. the click. the barrel. / stock. stop. unhinge. she is spark-exhausted." *We* might wonder at the mystery of the rhetorical context / narrative, but the poem moves so quickly into its spell-like lines that we find ourselves not caring about meaning or origin so much as sound and image. "Desert Duende" might as well be the arc of a poem's magic, through the duende, deep image, charm-making tradition, those thistle-like cacti, and stone-like brick, dust, bullets, sand. In syntax paused by periods but not any other punctuation (much like Dickinson employed dashes), enjambed for the "shotgun effect" of the line break against those short sentences, Givhan creates a spell-paced list of grammatical phrases, ingredients added one by one, with the physical stop of the period chiming a staccato rhythm mid- and end-line. Rhymes, such as "mines / the spine," are carried over enjambed syntax, and some of the thoughts are interrupted then continued, as in "no one explains when. to die.," which could have been unpunctuated for logic but is offered as chant-like music; or the thoughts are cut off halfway and never finished, forcing the reader to imagine the rest of that idea, as in "no one has to. nature. of thirst. / instinct." In these interrupted-and-abandoned sentences, it is as if the ability to think has been arrested by trauma and also picked up by instinct. The inner echoes of vowel rhyme corroborate: "instinct. blinking back / extinction. near the brink." Those soft 'i' sounds, 'n's, and 'k' clacks create parallels of *instinct, blinking, extinction,* and *brink*, suggesting they all blend for the gun-toting desert protagonist (and / or for the American poet in her Amherst room). At the end of this act—as Anton Chekov might have said—the loaded gun must go off, and we witness that it is the human self, not the gun, that flames into life:

> she never held a. gun. she
> glistens. metal sun-spit. cacti rungs.
> she tugs. triggers. ignites

At the end, the girl holding the gun becomes flamenco, poison, cure, fire—she leaps into something mythical, like a spell. Jennifer Givhan's power to conjure also conjures us, gives us back to the land as the ruler of what comes through our feet.

Can we cast such spells, too, relying on these deep traditions to guide our solo pursuits? Let's practice with an invitation to reflect and a few prompts to get that hemoglobin traveling, that duende coming up through us.

INVITATIONS TO REFLECT

Discuss Together

Duende, deep imagery, and spells are all poetic styles that center imagery and draw their sense of meaning from associative logic. Unlike more commonly discussed forms of logic, which are based on principles of cause and effect or the scientific method, associative logic is the logic of dreams. What feelings and ideas do you associate with the sight of blood or the moon or an egg yolk? Certain images are so archetypal, so rooted in folklore, lullabies, fairy tales, and nursery rhymes, even across disparate cultures, that we have similar responses to the images. Poets working in these traditions pay close attention to their own associations with images and also to the ways others respond to them as well. Look back at the poems at the opening of this chapter. How do those poems use the power of shared subconscious associations and the logic of dreams to draw readers into and through poems that are driven by imagery?

For Further Study

Choose a book in the traditional lineage of spells, deep image, and / or duende, and study it for how it engages with the struggle of duende, the concept of deep image, and the influence of spells, etc. in form and / or subject. What literary moves does the author make? What do they add to the spellscape of poetics? In addition to those poets and collections referenced in this chapter, and those in "Poetics of Liberation" and "Sound, Shape, & Space: Received and Invented Forms," which also share spells, here are some other examples to get you started: H.D., *Sea Rose;* Galway Kinnel, *Body Rags*; Li Young Lee, *Rose;* Evie Shockley, *The Bone Goddess;* Brigit Pegeen Kelly, *The Orchard* or *Song*; Sara Eliza Johnson, *Bone Map*; Jennifer Givhan, *Protection Spell;* Rachelle Cruz, *God's Will for Monsters;* Kiki Petrosino, *Witch Wife;* Rachel McKibben, *Blud;* Bianca Stone, *Poetry Comics From the Book of Hours*; Natalie Diaz, *Postcolonial Love Poem.*

Writing Exercises

1 *Dueño de Casa*

Think of what spirits rule your house—your body / house (the "remotest mansions of the blood"), your spatial house, your land / house (later, in our chapter "Writing the Field," merge this with our discussion of ecotone!). For many, these house spirits are ancestral and named, as Rachelle Cruz's aswang in her collection, *God's Will for Monsters,* which takes as its central character the Filipino aswang, a shapeshifting evil being that Cruz reclaims as a positive and playful force, giving it various agencies. In her preceding chapbook, *Self Portrait as Rumor and Blood,* Cruz commands:

> If there is a river more powerful than this,
> pray that it flows through the magic of return.
> Silt loosened by the heart's surge
> and carried into the chambers of my wilderness.

That silt, that wilderness, is the magic of the housemaster. Interrogate your own monsters and list images that relate. Then, put them into a poem that relies more on those images than on story. Bonus for writing the poem in the voice of your spirit.

2 *Ekphrasis: Exhibit Tour or Museum Guide*

Visit the Prado Museum online: Goya, Bosch, Caravaggio, Valázquez; or remember / rely upon notes from a museum visit when you stood before paintings from this or other eras that recall darkness. Using principles of ekphrasis (Greek for "description," ekphrasis is any art that responds to / deepens a conversation with other art), write from the voice of the painter, or a character within the painting, allowing the Jungian shadow to dominate your images and control your poem's direction. Or, allow yourself to be the voice of a painter or their character, and walk us through the museum, room by room, offering us your take on the art from a character's view.

3 *Dream Sequence / Deep Image*

For a week, wake up each morning and record images from your dreams, the strange, the deep and the blurry. At the end of the week, use all of these in a poem that relies on sequencing them but also on some other kind of cohesion. Try writing it with physical caesura (also known as negative space), allowing the reader to imagine how those leaps work to create experience.

4 *Rim of the Wound*

The duende, it is said, prefers the "rim of the wound," and poets have written from this place—as well as from its purpled bruise or blazing crater—for thousands of years. What "wounds" would you be willing to revisit in verse? Make a list in your journal, and then come up with a corresponding visual for each. (For inspiration, read Anne Carson's *Autobiography of Red,* noting all the "red" imagery that coincides with Geryon's story.) Make attendant, detailed notes of images that each visual contains, things related by association and leap. Then, write from the rim of that visual (wound) . . . with awareness of it but not quite going to the center. Include as many of your sensory images as you can fit into the poem. Be as concrete as possible.

5 *Casting a Spell*

Janie Elizabeth Miller describes her micro-collection, *Book of (Eco) Spells,* as "a poet's guide to art & action in a time of global environmental & social crisis." What follows are two excerpts (you can find the rest online). What do you notice about the following: tone, syntax, use of verbs? How are these spells?

Spell 1

Sitting in a field of spongy grass under a flight pattern, cross your legs and gaze to the sky drinking in gasoline. Image / ine attaching gasoline cells to lung cells, lung cells to spirit non-cells, then coloring the spirit ashen. Write a haiku titled "tar body" in which you invoke the nature of assimilation.

Spell 2

In an ancient graveyard recently bulldozed for a suburban neighborhood development, place both palms upon the dirt that is also the cells of a stranger, 6 squirrels, 27 songbirds, 127 dragonflies & 2 dinosaurs. Image / ine time as gesture, a phantom wind beyond the senses. Translate this song beyond knowing into an elegy for animacy.

Using these as both model and direction, complete a brief poem of three to four lines—a haiku or "translation of song"—which follows her commands but is also a new creation.

6

The Poetics of Liberation

A FEW POEMS TO START US OFF . . .

In this chapter we'll introduce you to poems written to comfort the afflicted and afflict the comfortable. We'll look at poems that seek to topple hegemonies and galvanize revolutions. Here are five poems we'll discuss in greater detail in this chapter. We encourage you to read them first and develop your own interpretations before diving into our analysis of them.

Monica A. Hand

Black is Beautiful

Me and D in our crushed-velvet jackets blue-jeans high heels. We are going to New York City to see Nina Simone at the Apollo. We're taking the path train across the river then the subway uptown. D knows her way around. She goes to FIT. I've been to the Apollo many times before but this is the first time on my own. Just me and D. We are going to see Nina Simone. At the Apollo. Our seats are way up in the balcony. The orchestra section is full of white people. Nina is singing Mississippi Goddam. Me and D we look at each other and nod. Nina plays the piano a long time as if she forgets we are there. But we are. Nina goes Holy Roller African all in one wave of her hands ragtime to classical and back again. We are in her groove our seats rocking with our bodies. Our young female bodies, big Afros and big dreams. The balcony is a smoky black sway. The orchestra white. Someone fidgets. Another one coughs. Nina stops. Quiet. Her voice a swift typhoon. You could hear their hearts hesitate. Stop. Nina chuckles then returns to her song. Mississippi Goddam. It's different now. Bruised. Me and D we look at each other and nod. We are at the Apollo. It's Nina Simone.

Laura Hershey

In the Way

Could you move, the waitress says,
politely of course,
you're in the way.
A common request, my trusted wheelchair just
an impediment, an obstacle to the busy,
a clumsy roadblock I haul with me down every road
and when parked
an interruption
or at least a slowing down
of the life I only
wish to be part of; a piece of surplus furniture
in the already crowded rooms
of restaurants, bars, theaters.

Usually
I accommodate,
backing into corners
turning sideways
angling my wheels
to leave a clear path
asking, politely of course,
Is that better?

I get in the way
without trying.
I apologize
excuse myself
and move out of the way.

But not today.
Today I listen
to a small, recalcitrant voice inside
that insists:
Such power
should not be wasted.

If I alone can be so much
and so often in the way,
if I can create such worry among waitpersons

such consternation in concert halls
such alarm in the aisles
of grocery stores
just imagine the aggravation a dozen
or two dozen
or three hundred
people using wheelchairs can cause people
who would rather not see our needs
or hear our demands
or acknowledge our rights!
Just imagine!

Better yet, see me now!
See me block this doorway, plant my wheels firm,
see me lock my brakes!
No, I tell some bureaucrat
who wants to get into his office
so he can make decisions about my future.
No, I will not turn
I will not move over
I will not get out of your way
not until the police order me to, under threat of arrest
and maybe not even then!

In the way
in the way all day,
I woman this barricade which is mine
whenever I need it,
this roadblock I haul with me down every road,
this wall I can construct at will,
and be happily in the way with,
and say no with,
and plaster with scrawled signs about freedom,
and add to the bigger walls growing
around whole buildings, around whole city blocks.
I can turn back
customers, employees, delivery people, even cops.
I can keep the usually powerful
in or out of their offices.

I can be in the way
in the way
I can be in the way
my way.

Roy G. Guzmán

Queerodactyl

Bones classified as those of a seafarer. Nimble
limbs that commanded pressure, searched
after water.
                    For now we'll say this languid metaphor
of blood is inconclusive; that it is unimaginable
for the body to be opened twenty times in a row
without a parliament of owls
                                        hooting inexhaustibly
throughout the night. & what of the recognition
of one's voice as it's issued from an unused tunnel—
a martyr searching for salvation in no-man's-land?
How unfaithful
                            the echo must be its source, to the
metallic whisper in a cave of handprints, songs of
resistance, a vulture ingesting a carrion bird midflight.
A crime scene sketch artist renders the image
of an asteroid as it makes contact with the ocean
that is the body.
                            From where the falling star buries
its head into the earthy bosom, a photogenic tsunami
erupts. Tragedy
                            is where undefined county lines
congregate, where woods abut gravel roads. When
your body was dumped a pregnant doe leapt. Her eyes
beamed. Her hooves recited a pink aurora.

Naomi Shihab Nye

A Palestinian Might Say

What?
You don't feel at home in your country,
almost overnight?
All the simple things
you cared about,
maybe took for granted . . .
you feel
insulted, invisible?
Almost as if you're not there?
But you're there.
Where before you mingled freely . . .
appreciated people who weren't
just like you . . .
divisions grow stronger.
That's what "chosen" and "unchosen" will do.
(Just keep your eyes on your houses and gardens.
Keep your eyes on that tree in bloom.)
Yes, a wall. Ours came later but . . .
who talks about how sad the land looks,
marked by a massive wall?
That's not a normal shadow.
It's something else looming over your lives.

Kenji C. Liu

Warding Spell Against Trump v. Hawaii :: 585 US ___ (2018)

Materials needed:

Pure salt

Fresh pine cones, bark, and needles

Fennel stalk

Red wine

Paper and pencil

Matches

1. At first light, journey. Collect cones, bark, and needles from single pine. Then, in circle of salt, distribute needles and bark equally between four directions.

> Note: Korematsu 是松 "this pine tree," 是 "this" = ancient compound of 早 "early" (sun + first) + 止 (orig.) "foot" or 正 "upright" (a nail + foot) = (orig.) "upright sun," but now = "this" or "this be right or correct," and 松 "pine tree" composed of 木 "tree" + 公 "public" (opposite + private) or possibly 公 "public" (to distribute + object) = (orig.) "equal communal division of resources."

2. In circle at noon, pour red wine into bowl. In mortar, crush cones to dust. Stir into wine with fennel stalk. Do not drink.

> Note: Trump, unexplained variant of triumph, Latin triumphus = hymn in honor of Bacchus, Greek Dionysus, god of wine and ritual madness—the god who comes from outside = a cult foreign god from Asia or Ethiopia—holds a phallic thyrsus = staff of fennel and tipped with a pine cone = also a weapon.

3. Throughout afternoon, pencil and paper. Write rune ᛋ (Sowilō) 17 million times, then cross each out with rune ᛁ (Isaz). As sun sets, burn all. Stir ashes into wine with fennel stalk. Do not drink.

> Note: Immigration and Customs Enforcement (ICE) = ice = Anglo-Saxon rune = īs = Proto-Germanic rune = Isaz, runic alphabet crucial in 19th–20th century German occultism, Anglo-Saxon rune Sigel or Proto-Germanic rune Sowilō = sun, incorporated into Nazi SS insignia by Reichsführer Himmler, architect of mass genocide, kidnapped

> "racially valuable" children, deported residents of annexed territories as slave labor.

4. As sun rises again, sprinkle contents of bowl around pine tree while shouting 585 times: SERVE THE PEOPLE SERVE THE PEOPLE SHINE SHINE SHINE. Let earth drink.

> Note: Roberts = derived from Germanic hrod and beraht = bright renown, and proto-Germanic hropiz and berhtaz, and proto-Indo-European kreH to shout and berHg to shine, British surname reflecting servile status, servant or son of.

5. Keep as life raft: salt circle. And fennel stalk, to digest the coming years.

DISCUSSION

In our lives as poets, we have sometimes heard people describe a subset of poetry as "political poetry," often with a tone or cringe that suggests they don't like it or consider it somehow less than. Sometimes they will elaborate and say they dislike work that seems polemical. This kind of conversation among poets has become less common in recent years. When the subject comes up, we often hear the reply (and have replied ourselves too) that all poetry, like so much else in our lives, is inherently political. Imagining you can choose whether to engage in a civil rights struggle or other political questions is a sign to us that the comforts of privilege have allowed a person to remain ignorant to how much the power and capital they've been granted influences their world view.

This is not to say there is something inherently privileged about writing a poem about a flower that doesn't explicitly reference ongoing wars or other political issues. Quite the contrary—as you can see in the "Writing in the Field" chapter in this very textbook, a hallmark of ecopoetics is a deeply political approach to writing about the natural world. Lots of poets write elegies and odes and other appreciations of flowers, knowing well that there are political implications to expressing love for the non-human world in a time of climate crisis. A credo of feminist thought is that the personal is political. Often confessional poems, many of which center domestic situations in a seemingly apolitical way, do the political work making women's perspectives, which historically were relegated to the home not the literary salon, central to the art. Or consider how many of the New York School poets referred openly to their lives as gay men in a time when living out of the closet could lead to arrest and prosecution, as well as other forms of persecution. As you can see, we reject the idea that there is or could be an apolitical poetry, but we do see distinct formal and stylistic choices in poems that are designed to bolster the goals of a particular movement and we'd like to highlight both the theory and the craft that inform such choices.

Liberatory poetics conceive of and respond to ideas about audience in distinct ways. Consider, for example, Assata Shakur's lines, which are often recited in a call-and-response fashion, at Black Lives Matter rallies and protests. "It is our duty to fight for our freedom. / It is our duty to win. / We must love each other and support each other. / We have nothing to lose but our chains." The lines make elegant use of repetition. They also make use of rhythmic cadences, which allow a large audience to recite them clearly in unison. The lines convey their message in a plainspoken, clear manner, without allusive imagery or metaphors, instead emphasizing the importance of conveying a precise message people can refer to for guidance in a chaotic situation or in which they can find a clarity of purpose. This poem is unique in how fully it has transcended the page and become part of a ritualized public performance, making it as practical as it is lyric. But there are many other ways poetry can become intertwined with movements for social justice and otherwise influence how people come to feel and be free.

The Liberatory Poetics of Surrealism

You've already read about how Surrealism emerged from a fascination with what were then new theories in psychology about an unconscious mind, as well as artistic attempts to recover from psychic trauma of world war, and an aesthetic fascination with dreamscapes. But Surrealism also has a history of operating as a mode of revolutionary imagination, with deeply political underpinnings. André Breton, author of the Surrealist manifestos, famously became a passionate Marxist, going so far as to excommunicate artists and writers whose political imaginations were not sufficiently radical in his estimation. While many of the original white French men who had participated in the early days of Surrealist experimentation grumbled, rolled their eyes, or felt betrayed and devastated by Breton's imperious demands for a certain kind of left-wing political conformity, internationally Surrealism evolved into an explicitly political movement. Later stages of Surrealism were defined by a yearning to liberate the human imagination from the kinds of intellectual and creative practices that had made the genocides and enslavements of the Colonial era thinkable. Throughout South America, the Caribbean, and in Eastern European Soviet bloc countries, Surrealism's liberatory poetics invigorated art, literature, and politics.

The impact of Surrealism on Aimé Césaire, a Black poet from the Caribbean island Martinique, which had once been a French colony, was particularly profound. He credited Surrealist methods, along with influential Black intellectual and writer Frantz Fanon's use of Freudian psychoanalytic theories, as a way to unpack the traumatic effects of racism, slavery, and colonization. Césaire went on to become a key figure in the development of a literary Pan-African movement known in French as Le Négritude. Césaire said: "Surrealism provided me with what I had been confusedly searching for . . . we have been branded by Cartesian philosophy, by French rhetoric; but if we break with all that, if we plumb the depths, then what we will find is fundamentally black." Suzanne Césaire, an eminent critic who was also married to Aimé, described the points of connection between Surrealist and Post-Colonial thought in "Surrealism and Us: 1943." She writes,

> Our surrealism will supply this rising people with a punch from its very depths. Our surrealism will enable us to finally transcend the sordid antinomies of the present: white / blacks, Europeans / Africans, civilized / savages—at last rediscovering the magic power of the *mahoulis*, drawn directly from living sources. Colonial ideology will be purified in the welder's blue flame. We shall recover our value as metal, our cutting edge of steel, our unprecedented communions.

You can see this twinned lineage of surrealism and political consciousness informing many of the poets working today. Many of Roy G. Guzmán's poems use elements of surrealism alongside practical plainspokenness and docupoetic techniques to describe the experiences of their family in Honduras during a period of political crisis. They also use these techniques to evoke some of their experiences as a child migrant crossing borders under harrowing circumstances. In a series of poems called "Queerodactyl," Guzmán uses a surreal image of a human-pterodactyl hybrid as a way to convey how it feels to be a person with multiple identities, none of which fit into easy binaries. How can a poet describe being queer and Honduran and American and having a non-binary gender? How to convey the experience of being a person who carries memories of being a child migrant and who even now must find ways to navigate the boundary lines policed by bureaucratic forms and procedures? Where traditional rhetoric creates identity categories and boxes to check, surrealism allows for nuance, complexity, beauty, and delight.

> For now we'll say this languid metaphor
> of blood is inconclusive; that it is unimaginable
> for the body to be opened twenty times in a row
> without a parliament of owls

For a poet who also wants to name and confront the constant threats of violence, the almost absurd horror of lynchings of people with queer identities, or the many needless deaths in the desert borderlands, surrealism also offers a way of writing these truths without simply reiterating the trauma in those stories. Guzmán uses notes of surrealism to create moments where readers can grieve while protecting their tenderness and humanity. "When / your body was dumped a pregnant doe leapt. Her eyes / beamed. Her hooves recited a pink aurora," they write.

The Surrealists succeeded in bringing a deep sense of interconnectedness into the daily lives of people through their artistic practices in so many ways. Who doesn't love the shock of surprise and delight that goes along with their playful antics like the time Gérard de Nerval (supposedly) walked his pet lobster on a leash through the streets of Paris? But their dreamlike methods were meant to accomplish more than mere weirdness—they were designed to interrupt the mechanized compliance of people unthinkingly fulfilling their function in oppressive hegemonic systems. Another compelling example of how poetry can have very real-world consequences can be found in the life and work of Surrealist poet and Nazi Resister, Robert Desnos.

The way the accounts go, Desnos had been captured by Nazis while he was participating in missions for the French Resistance and was being held in a concentration camp. At this point in the war, people called from their barracks into a truck knew very well they were being taken to their deaths. Desnos and the others whose names had been called waited to be ordered onto such a truck. But suddenly he jumped from his place in line, grabbed a condemned man's hand, and began to read his palm. Back in his youth, in days of peace and making art, Desnos had been famous among the writers for giving the most poetic palm readings.

Now he says, "Oh" to a man who, like him, expects to die in moments, "I see you have a very long lifeline. And you are going to have three children." According to the essayist Susan Griffin, in this moment Desnos "is exuberant. And his excitement is contagious. First one man, then another, offers up his hand, and the prediction is for longevity, more children, abundant joy. As Desnos reads more palms, not only does the mood of the prisoners change but that of the guards too." As we know, the Nazis would later claim they were only following orders. Their minds and will had been overtaken, they said, by the power of a Fascist vision of the world. But on this day, Desnos reminded them they could be something else and gave them the courage to break ranks for a moment. All the men, along with Desnos, were sent back into the barracks to live a little longer. According to Griffin, "Desnos has saved his own life and the lives of others by using his imagination."

The Black Arts Movement

But let's not get too fixated on the Surrealists—there are, after all, many ways that poetry has and can be crafted to fulfill aesthetic and political goals. At the center of many conversations about poetics, liberation, or the intersection of poetry and activism, you will find the Black Arts Movement. In his 1968 essay, "The Black Arts Movement," Larry Neal described this new approach to art-making as the "aesthetic and spiritual sister of the Black power concept." Rob Karenya added in his description of the movement that "Black Art must expose the enemy, praise the people, and support the revolution."

BAM is closely associated with Amiri Baraka, who first published under the name LeRoi Jones when he was a young poet in New York writing works that are sometimes associated with the New York School. Baraka founded a Black Arts Repertory Theater and School in Harlem that became a model for similar spaces that opened around the country over the next decade. Because these performance spaces were so central to creating and nurturing the Black Arts Movement, poets and playwrights were key figures in the creation of a movement that prioritized close ties to community groups and issues, as well as the development of nationally distributed magazines and presses, not to mention live performances of poetry.

In *New Thoughts on the Black Arts Movement*, Cherise A. Pollard describes the poetry of the Black Arts Movement as being loosely defined, with lots of stylistic variation, but notes there was a general agreement that "art should be used to galvanize the black masses to revolt against their white capitalist oppressors" and also that it "celebrated the African origins of the Black community, championed black urban culture, critiqued Western aesthetics, and encouraged the production and reception of black arts by black people." You can see these ideals in the work of Gwendolyn Brooks, who wrote poems celebrating Black life and Black communities, but who also undertook more practical endeavors like creating new presses to be a platform for writers ignored by the major presses who refused time and again to publish non-white authors.

There are so many poets we could point to whose work illustrates the influence of the Black Arts Movement on contemporary literature and you can find a sizable list to read in our online companion to this chapter. Monica A. Hand's poetry collection *me and Nina* is particularly interesting to consider in this context, because the book chronicles an adolescence in the wake of BAM's innovations and transformations, while also embracing poetics and thematics of Womanist poets like Pat Parker, Alice Walker, and Audre Lorde. In Hand's "Upward Bound," the speaker describes joining a program where:

> They talk about Revolution about change. They are Black and they are proud. . . We journalize, write poetry, draw and film our neighborhoods, stage Lorraine Hansberry's *To Be Young Gifted and Black*. Each flat nose girl is Nina Simone singing from her gut—angry then sad then proud.

This poem, like others in the book, also surfaces additional complexities, pointing to girls and women carrying the secrets of how they have been abused, or, in this poem, the ways narratives about race can be overly simplistic. "I write a poem about living in the projects even though I really live in a three-family house on Ninth Avenue. D makes a pretty dashiki from a *Vogue* pattern."

Throughout the collection, though, Hand traces with affection and admiration the influence of Black artists like the musician Nina Simone and the poet Lucille Clifton with poems written to and about them. In Hand's work we can see how tracing one's poetic lineage is not only a way of inspiring and educating oneself, but it can also be a political act. By situating her work as part of a legacy, Hand resists erasure and whitewashing. Instead, her work imagines poetry that exists as part of the work of building nurturing, multi-generational communities, which is quite a contrast to many traditional European and white American narratives that imagine writers as solitary geniuses endlessly obliterating the past to make something entirely new.

Though some scholars have described the Black Arts Movement as short-lived, dating only from about 1960–1970, others assert it was an extension of the Harlem Renaissance, making it part of a decades-long flourishing of Black art in the US Many writers today point to the Black Arts Movement as a source of inspiration for their own efforts to create literary organizations that would nurture writers with identities that have been historically marginalized by publishers and Academica (Cave Canem, Kundiman, Canto

Mundo, and Asian American Writers Workshop among them). BAM also critiqued the Eurocentric focus of many English literature curricula in many university English departments and inspired the creation of ethnic literature classes in those same departments. If you are reading this textbook for a class in an English department right now, it is likely that your department has made (or refused despite significant pressure to make) significant changes to the coursework involved in pursuing an English major. These reforms were inspired by intellectuals involved in the Black Arts Movement. Beyond that, BAM was a major influence on the development of hip hop and 1990s era spoken word poetry like that emerging from the Nuyorican poets and other poetry slams that proliferated then and since.

Accessibility and Liberation

There is no shortage of poets participating in activist movements we could point to for further consideration of what it means to write with a liberatory poetics at the heart of your work. Some of the works we find particularly insightful, though, are those that emerged from poets whose writings were shaped by their activist engagement in the struggle to pass the Americans with Disabilities Act, as well as subsequent struggles to protect and enhance the legal protections included in that law.

We allude to Laura Hershey's writings in the chapter "Writing the Body," but want to direct your attention more closely to her work here. Many of Hershey's poems first appeared in pamphlets, broadsides, or newsletters as part of her work as a disability rights activist. Unlike poets writing for publication in literary magazines or with an eye towards placing their book with a literary press, poets writing to galvanize and recruit members of a movement have a different relationship to their audience. They are also likely imagining different possibilities for how their work will be received by that audience. While speaking to and wanting to impress lovers of poetry is a particular kind of pleasure and challenge for poets, liberatory poems often strive for accessibility in terms of their meaning and form. Poets working in these traditions often prioritize being understood by and inspiring to a broad public.

Earlier in this chapter we wanted to flag for you the ways the phrase "political poetry" has sometimes been used in problematically disparaging ways, so you will be prepared to interpret and respond to various conversations in poetry that you may enter in the coming years. Similarly, we want to unpack the word "accessible," which is another adjective often used to describe poems, sometimes as a gentle insult meant to imply that the poem is shallow or easy. We want to invite you to think about this word more deeply than that, to remember how accessible also means that people who use wheelchairs, are assisted by sign language interpreters, or benefit from other accommodations are able to access poetry readings, conferences, and workshops. For many poets, "accessible" is a word that means "you are welcome here, you are wanted here, and you are able to be here."

Laura Hershey's poem, "In the Way," opens with a fairly straightforward narrative —a waitress asks the speaker, "*Could you move,*" and the speaker, annoyed at how common the request is, not to mention the ways such requests highlight how pervasively inaccessible so many ableist spaces are, explains how she usually responds.

> I accommodate,
> backing into corners
> turning sideways
> angling my wheels to leave a clear path
> asking, politely of course,
> *Is that better?*

But then the poem turns towards a new tone, one of opposition.

> Today I listen
> to a small, recalcitrant voice inside
> that insists:
> *Such power*
> *should not be wasted.*

The speaker begins to notice how much power she has to create worry, consternation, alarm if she were to refuse to move. This is when the poem carries readers into a new narrative moment, the moment when the speaker, like Hershey herself once did, participates in nonviolent direct action by refusing to move.

> No, I tell some bureaucrat
> who wants to get into his office
> so he can make decisions about my future.
> No, I will not turn
> I will not move over
> I will not get out of your way

The poem begins to repeat phrases like "I will" and "I will not" and "in the way," building towards a defiant crescendo expressed by the speaker and likely felt in readers who may find themselves stirring to join her barricade, to say in solidarity with those last, so-chantable lines,

> I can be in the way
> in the way
> I can be in the way
> *my* way.

Poetic Liberation through a Community-Building Practice

As poets you have the imaginative capacity to bring the memory of those people the dominant culture has tried to erase back to life in the minds of your readers. You also have the ability to imagine alternate histories and futures that give readers a glimpse of justice, a glimpse that might just be the spark that can keep them going. With this spark of imagination, this glimpse of what is true or possible, people can accomplish a lot. Never forget how poetry can become an essential part of creatively pragmatic undertakings. Consider, for example, Naomi Shihab Nye's "A Palestinian Might Say." The poem describes in clear and evocative language the physical and psychological suffering of Palestinian people. "Where before you mingled freely . . . / appreciated people who weren't / just like you . . . / divisions grow stronger." The poem also emphasizes the patterns of othering, division, isolation, and confinement. Even as the poem describes the situation Palestinian people presently face, Nye, a Palestinian American writer, chooses images and language, such as the recurring references to a wall, to simultaneously critique the clamoring in the US to build walls to keep immigrants out and bolster a white supremacist narrative about who does and does not belong in the country. She writes, "Who talks about how sad the land looks, / marked by a massive wall? / That's not a normal shadow. / It's something else looming over your lives."

One effect of this poem is to galvanize its readers into action, to push back against the encroaching shadows of fascist leadership that dreams of walls and separations of people. But this poem also does something in addition to sounding an alarm. The poem, like all the poems in Nye's collection *The Tiny Journalist,* is inspired by and alludes to the video journalism of Janna Jihad Ayyad, who began collecting footage of anti-occupation protests on her mother's smartphone when she was just seven years old. By celebrating and amplifying the profound impact those videos by the "Youngest Journalist in Palestine" had, the poems do more than teach readers how to see suffering and cruelty with the clarity of a child's eye-view. They also give readers an example and the encouragement to speak what they know to be true.

For poets who engage directly with a liberatory poetics, there can be no meaningful boundary between the personal and the political, because a society where power is derived through othering renders apolitical individualism a delusion in which only the privileged elite can indulge. Nye describes who must attend to the relationship between the personal and political, and who is encouraged to ignore such intertwining, when she writes, "That's what "chosen" and "unchosen" will do. / (Just keep your eyes on your houses and gardens. / Keep your eyes on that tree in bloom.)" Nye's poem shows how an understanding of the political implications of othering can inspire a poetics of solidarity that manifests in her work as attention to shared struggles.

Kenji C. Liu's work as a poet and editor is another example of how poetry can become an embodiment of liberatory imagination. In 2018, shortly after the US Supreme Court upheld a travel ban instituted by the Trump administration on immigrants from majority-Muslim nations, Liu put out a "call for contributions of magic spells in response to SCOTUS' Trump v. Hawaii decision and the incarceration of children and families in ICE concentration camps." The result was a feature of fourteen poems published by *Unmargin* magazine, "Incantations: The SCOTUS Decision in Trump v. Hawaii."

Poems like those in this feature, including Liu's own "Warding Spell Against Trump v. Hawaii :: 585 US ___ (2018)," are examples of a kind of poem described as an "occasional" poem. The term occasional refers to how they are written in response to a particular occasion. Poems composed and read at inaugurations are examples of this, as are epithalamiums (a traditional poetic form written to be read at weddings). Though less celebratory, poems that respond to atrocities and tragedies are also considered occasional poems. Great occasional poems speak in meaningful ways to their moment, but also have depths that resonate beyond a single moment in time.

This ability to contextualize the present moment historically is one of the reasons Liu's poem remains so resonant. The lyrical translation notes of certain Japanese words that mean "this be right or correct" or "equal communal division of resources" calls to mind for readers the US history of immigration—both the presence of many immigrant communities currently living in the US, as well as the shameful history of xenophobia expressed in the Chinese Exclusion Act, which prevented people from many Asian nations from immigrating to the US, as well as the Japanese internment camps during World War II. The etymological chain in this poem that links ICE to Nazi paraphernalia draws a kind of timeline that reminds readers how these legal decisions are not only rooted in past atrocities but also have the power to call forth future ones.

This poem's presence in Liu's larger editorial project also illustrates how a poetics of liberation is not about an individual poet's ego. The goal of writing in this tradition is not to create a poem that serves as a monument to the ages, though we celebrate how enduring Liu's poem is. Instead, in a poetics of liberation, the poetry serves as one of the ways a community of people come together to celebrate, to revel, and, when necessary, to organize and resist. In this paradigm, the poet is not a singular genius but a person who knows how to bring communities together through art-making occasions. While we know well that the audience for poetry can be perceived to be quite small, we also know that poetry is unique in its power to move people. We have known poems to give protestors courage, give communities an anchor, even awake in Nazis a moment of mercy. This is the kind of poetry we yearn to see more of in print and in the streets.

INVITATIONS TO REFLECT

Discuss Together

What makes poetry powerful? Describe how your own approach to writing poetry locates its power in the page or in reaching beyond that printed form. Then describe how you see the poems in this chapter relating to, reaching after, summoning, or critiquing various forms of power.

For Further Study

By now you are likely beginning to think of how your work sits at the intersection of many poetic lineages. As one example, think about how Kenji C. Liu's "Warding Spell Against Trump v. Hawaii :: 585 US ___ (2018)" belongs to the Poetics of Liberation, the Poetics of Spells, Ecopoetics (we'll discuss this later, in our Writing in the Field chapter), and Documentary Poetics (in that chapter, we'll talk more about lyric imagining). Lui's poem merges a range of influences to advocate for intersecting justices: social, racial, environmental, personal, political. Choose another poem from this chapter and try to identify potential lineages. Then, do this with your own work. Write down some of these, and save your notes for writing an artist statement, which we will invite you to do in the second part of this textbook.

Writing Exercises

1 **Ode to an Icon**

With Monica A. Hand's poems to Nina Simone in mind, write a poem of appreciation to a musician, artist, writer, pop icon, or other public figure who helped you figure out how to be more fully yourself when you were a teenager.

2 **The Real Monsters**

With Roy G. Guzmán's poems in mind, write a portrait of yourself as a mythic creature. Be honest about the complex ways the animal of yourself might be tender, vulnerable, violent, or threatened.

3 **In the Way**

Write a list poem in which you say what you will do and what you will not. Move between everyday domestic items and larger communal or political situations.

4 **The Urgent Occasion**

Write a letter to a government official about an issue that matters to you and affects your life. Then erase, compress, expand or translate that letter into an occasional poem that responds to the historical moment you find yourself in.

5 **A Child's Eye View**

Where there are human rights crises, there are children documenting suffering and hope. You can see the drawings made by Jewish children in the Terzín Ghetto during the Holocaust by going to the website of the Jewish Museum in Prague. The Academy of American Pediatrics released drawings made by detained migrant children at the US border in 2019, the same year Naomi Shihab Nye's *The Tiny Journalist* was released. Though an exhibit of Palestinian children's art was taken down by the Oakland Museum of Children's Art, these drawings are widely available online. Look at some or all of these images to remind yourself how much and how clearly children see the world around them.

Then take out some markers or crayons and draw, as you would have when you were a child, a moment when you were first introduced to the concept of race, your own maybe, or that of a classmate or a parent. By drawing like a child, you can focus your attention not on what was said or what you thought, but on physical details—what looks you saw on people's faces or what was happening out the window at that moment. These details will help you write a poem later.

The next step is to write the poem. Your poem could be descriptive, a poem that tells the truth about the moment you've drawn, in keeping with the style of Naomi Shihab Nye. You can also write a poem with an alternate ending or previously unimagined future, in the spirit of Aracelis Girmay's ideal city. You are an adult and a poet now—you can write in a window where there was a wall, transform a locked door into a horse you can ride away on, if you wish it someone cruel can collapse as a fish on the floor or watch in shock as butterflies instead of words fly out of their mouths. You can also write exactly what happened and know that, as a writer, you are the one who decides what parts of that moment matter and what, of everything that might have been said, was really true.

7

Writing the Body

A FEW POEMS TO START US OFF . . .

One of the exciting conversations we see contemporary poets having in their work is about what it means to have a body, to be a body, to have a sense of self that transcends or feels separate from the body, to navigate a community of bodies via your own. A lot of these poets are drawing on multi-disciplinary conversations that include theorists, philosophers, activists, and other artists and intellectuals. In this chapter we introduce you to embodied poetics, queer poetics, and disability poetics, as well as craft questions around the subjects of metaphor and genre-blurring forms, which are just some of the areas of conversation that make writing on the theme of the body so intellectually, emotionally, and imaginatively rich.

Debjani Chatterjee

What I Did Today

Today I blew up the Northern General—again;
bulldozed the waiting room in Hell
where I had sat all morning in a silly gown;
I strangled the arrogant GP who knew so little
but pretended to know it all;
my itching hands throttled the oncologists:
the indifferent one who swanned off on holiday,
forgetful of referring me for a Hickman Line
under anesthesia at a half-decent hospital,
and the one who lost my consent form and thrust me
into a nightmare place of endless screams;
I fought the boffin butcher who drilled holes in me;
and finally I exterminated
every homicidal side-kick masquerading
as an angel of mercy . . .
All these things and more I did today.
In violent days and everlasting nights,
I've lost count of the times I have done these things . . .

Bruce Snider

Frutti di Mare

Alone, finally, me and you
together, first time in a long week.
We stand in the kitchen cutting
chunks of halibut, fresh crab meat.
Pressing hard, I cleave a stubborn
clam, slice my finger. *More*,
my blood seems to say, *more*
across onions, the counter, while you
grab paper towels, stubbornly
staunch the flow, my knees gone weak.
Hours later, red permeates
the make-shift bandage, the cut
gaping as an ER doctor cuts
sterile thread to sew it up. *No more*
knives for you, he says. I meet
his spectacled eyes, then yours.
We laugh. How many weeks?
you ask. Pain? Infection? your stubborn
worried voice less stubborn
in this light. Home again, you clean cutlery
say the grass needs mowed this week,
then stand sorting bills and more
while I, looking up at you,
think about that day, years ago, we met,
remembering our young selves, their unmet
needs—raw, impulsive, newborn—
hungry for our bodies, for a me and you.
Now, on the sofa, unsexy, my cut
hand elevated on a pillow, I ask for more
ice and can see the weeks
ahead of laundry, quarrel, devotion, weeks
of living where we meet
what we are and more,
this day and daily-ness reborn
in me and the map of stitches on my cut
finger that points to you.

Ama Codjoe

On Seeing and Being Seen

I don't like being photographed. When we kissed
at a wedding, the night grew long and luminous.
You unhooked my bra. *A photograph*
passes for proof, Sontag says, *that a given thing*
has happened. Or you leaned back to watch
as I eased the straps from my shoulders.
Hooks and eyes. Right now, my breasts
are too tender to be touched. *Their breasts*
were horrifying, Elizabeth Bishop writes. Tell her
someone wanted to touch them. I am touching
the photograph of my last seduction. It is as slick
as a magazine page, as dark as a street
darkened by rain. When I want to remember
something beautiful, instead of taking
a photograph, I close my eyes.
Tonight, I am alone in my tenderness.
There is nothing in my hand except a certain
grasping. In my mind's eye, I am
stroking your hair with damp fingertips. This is exactly
how it happened. On the lit-up hotel bed,
I remember thinking, My body is a lens
I can look through with my mind.

Meg Day

10 AM Is When You Come to Me

In some other life, I can hear you
breathing: a pale sound like running
fingers through tangled hair. I dreamt
again of swimming in the quarry
& surfaced here when you called for me
in a voice only my sleeping self could
know. Now the dapple of the aspen
respires on the wall & the shades cut
its song a staff of light. Leave me—
that me—in bed with the woman
who said all the sounds for pleasure
were made with vowels I couldn't
hear. Keep me instead with this small sun
that sips at the sky blue hem of our sheets
then dips & reappears: a drowsy penny
in the belt of Venus, your aureole nodding
slow & copper as it bobs against cotton
in cornflower or clay. What a waste
the groan of the mattress must be
when you backstroke into me & pull
the night up over our heads. Your eyes
are two moons I float beneath & my lungs
fill with a wet hum your hips return.
It's Sunday—or so you say with both hands
on my chest—& hot breath is the only hymn
whose refrain we can recall. And then you
reach for me like I could've been another
man. You make me sing without a sound.

CA Conrad

(Soma)tic 5: Storm SOAKED Bread

—for Julian Brolaski

Sit outside under shelter of a doorway, pavilion, or umbrella on a park bench, but somewhere outside where you can easily touch, smell, taste, FEEL the storm. Lean your face into the weather, face pointed UP to the sky, stay there for a bit with eyes closed while water fills the wells of your eyes. Come back into the shelter properly baptized in the beauty of pure elements and be quiet and still for a few minutes. Take some preliminary notes about your surroundings. Try not to engage with others who might run to your shelter for cover. If they insist on talking MOVE somewhere else; you are a poet with a storm to digest, this isn't time for small talk! You are not running from the storm, you are opening to it, you are IN IT! Stick a bare arm or foot into the storm, let your skin take in a meditative measure of wind and rain. If you are someone who RAN from storms in the past take time to examine the joys of the experience. Remind yourself you are a human being who is approximately 80 percent water SO WHAT'S THE HARM OF A FEW DROPS ON THE OUTSIDE!? Right? YES! Pause, hold your breath for a count of 4, then write with a FURY and without thinking, just let it FLOW OUT OF YOU, write, write, WRITE!

Set an empty cup in the storm, hold a slice of bread in the storm. Then put a little salt and pepper on your storm soaked bread, maybe some oregano and garlic. With deliberate SLOOOWNESS chew your storm bread and drink the storm captured in your cup. Slowly. So, slowly, please, with, a, slowness, that, is, foreign, to, you. THINK the whole slow time of chewing and drinking how this water has been in a cycle for MILLIONS OF YEARS, falling to earth, quenching horses, elephants, lizards, dinosaurs, humans. They pissed, they died, their water evaporated and gathered again into clouds to drizzle down AND STORM DOWN into rivers, puddles, aqueducts, and ancient cupped hands. Humans who LOVED, who are long dead, humans who thieved, raped, murdered, were generous, playful, disappointed, fearful, annoyed and adored one another, each of them dying in their own way, their water going back to the sky, coming back down to your bread, your lips, your stomach, to feed your sinew, your brain, your living, beautiful day. Take your notes POET, IT IS YOUR MOMENT to be totally aware, completely aware!

One Day I Will Step from the Beauty Parlor and Enlist in the Frequency of Starlings

my favorite morning
is not caring if
blood on sheets
is yours or mine

a machine in
your station
rides me
tracks to snacks
snacks to tracks

I feel very fortunate
to know magic is real
and poetry is real
you can see it in the writing
a belief in one is missing

a mouse eating
the dead
cat our
longed-for
malfunction

I was born
in Topeka
otherwise
they would have
never let me in

they circle away holding this place
opening opening opening OPENING UP
I grope the tree down its root

if truth soothes
soothing was
not truth's goal

my goal
is to do what
produces
memory
as gentle
as vicious
can

one promise: when
I get to the bottom I'll
accelerate deeper
my small pile
of poems
surprising
everyone along the
open wound
"was there a
death" they ask
"a merger" I say

everyone paying attention
enjoy your visit
everyone else
good luck

Cameron Awkward-Rich

[Black Feeling]

. . .

& after that, even the whirring of your head goes quiet. Even your breath. No sound. Someone in workshop says something like, in Italian, stanza means room. Don't roll your eyes. Here you are in the room. Here you are with things, but no names for things.

. . .

You've been in this city for weeks now & no one knows your name. No one except the man at the bus stop with his tallboy. His paper bag. When he asks, you tell him you work at the university, you teach. He was a cop, 'til someone died & he found the bottle. Or, the drink came first & then the falling off this umber world. In this moment, you're a man to him. Some kind of boy genius philosopher, who knows? There is something neither one of you can say. You're circling like animals, like prey.

. . .

The truth is, most black folk look at you & see a woman. White people look at you & see a reckless boy. Either way, there you are in the room with your body.

. . .

Everywhere, the bus names a kind of underworld. The man lives there, but you are just a passenger. He clears a space, says sit. You can't sit. He looks at you with so much gratitude you think you'll die.

. . .

You have to understand that there are many rooms. Each of them operates by other laws. Here, once you name a thing, you can't take it back. It has its own life now, one that moves along without concern for you. At first, you go around talking to the trees & for just a moment they turn to face you.

. . .

By the time the bus arrives the light has gone & the man is holding out his hand. You take it, not expecting to be thrown against him. Against him, you are years ago, a frantic girl alone. The man is on his knees. You are a boy holding up his brother. The man is on his knees. Either way, there you are in the room with your body. Your one, wet face.

[O

god of the loophole

god of the veil

god of the break

the fugitive

in endless flight]

Somewhere, there's a room where things go to lose their names. A rose becomes [ ]. A daughter becomes [ ]. Her son [ ].

. . .

Unlocking your apartment, you realize you never caught his name. He just looked at you & saw a door. He can't walk back through but there you were. An image racing on the other side.

DISCUSSION

If you were an acting student in a workshop with Jacques Lecoq, your first assignment would be to perform with an entirely neutral face mask. Then you would advance through various expressive masks—happy, tragic, angry. Your last lesson would involve the most sophisticated mask of all—a clown's nose.

We dismiss clowns as mere jokes at our peril. The art of clowning is the art of understanding the body as a source of pleasure and strength, even as it is also the site of our precarious vulnerabilities. Lecoq celebrated the gifts of control, restraint, insight, and honesty that only the greatest of clowns possess. In this chapter we have similar praise for those poets who place their own bodies at the center of their work.

Lecoq is best known for developing a theory of embodied poetics, by which art is created from within an understanding that thinking and behavior are the product of the whole human organism, not the brain alone. Moreover, the brain and the body are situated in and engaged with the surrounding environment. This approach to art-making pushes back against traditional notions about the "life of the mind" and rejects the ways many in Academia and the literary arts have historically tended to deny the relevance of the body altogether. The idea that the mind and body are separate and the mind always overrules the body is one of the core principles of the Enlightenment-era thinking that led to the creation of the set of intellectual practices we often refer to as the scientific method. It is an epistemological system, a set of assumptions about what we know and how we know it, rooted in many different kinds of privilege. After all, it takes quite a lot of power and luck to live a life where you never or seldom have to think about what your body needs and never feel how your mind responds to the pressures of hunger, stress, or pain. Lecoq's approach to performance art has been a revelation for artists in many disciplines because of how his methods acknowledge the crucial role of the body in acts of creation and expression.

While Lecoq designed his theories with actors in mind, there are parallel investigations in poetry into what it means to write with awareness of how our words emerge from our full bodies, which exist in relationship to other bodies. In her essay, "Getting Comfortable," the poet and disability rights activist Laura Hershey (whose work you also see in the chapter "The Poetics of Liberation") describes the process of preparing, in collaboration and conversation with a care attendant, her body to write. She explains,

> The process of getting comfortable demands a certain style, both explicatory and poetic: You see, this is the way I want it. This is what I mean. Not quite that far. Left, not right. Pull a little further. Push again.

> A careful calculation of timing, tune and tempo. This is my language: explication, correction, repetition.

By describing these steps, she critiques ableist erasures and assumptions about disabled art-making. The description also poses a pointed challenge to Enlightenment notions of mind-body duality, "If I leave behind my body to write, what (how) does the reader read? Can a reader read a mind without having a body to read?"

Debjani Chatterjee takes a similar approach in her poem, "What I Did Today," which describes the small humiliations that go along with having such a vulnerable body—there is the physical pain, yes, but there is also the condescension and dismissal from the doctors. With itching hands and other unmedicated pains from cancer treatments, "I had sat all morning in a silly gown," the speaker tells readers. This poem is rooted in that kind of attention to the way the body feels in these moments, but Chatterjee also lets her imagination run wild, indulging in acts of vengeance and cries for justice that can only happen in the mind. "I strangled the arrogant GP who knew so little / but pretended to know it all," she writes. "I exterminated / every homicidal side-kick masquerading / as an angel of mercy . . ." Her imagination is able to engage in completely free play, in part because she grounds the poem so carefully and thoroughly in material reality.

Pleasure, Pain, and the Source of Feeling

Not every writer is so alert to the bodies their readers will use to read a poem or to how their own bodies are engaged with their minds during the act of composing a poem. Some writers have their minds totally fixed on ideas like "free play of the imagination" and forget the meat of themselves altogether. But writers whose work is rooted in the loamy flesh must ask themselves questions akin to those a great clown must ask—How do you control your limbs so perfectly they seem to fall and flail as you tumble with precision? What is the choreography of steps you take, striding with top hat and cane into a somersault that lands you flat on your back? What shrug of the shoulder or outstretched arm will reveal the notes of fear or grief behind that veil of face paint and the red nose? When, the clown is always asking themselves, should I hold on tight and when should I let it all unfurl? These are not questions about punchlines or who to make the butt of the joke; those parts of clowning are the surface veneer of more essential questions about how to cope with these bodies that falter and fail even as they carry us and others through.

We're drawn to "Frutti de Mare" as a poem that exemplifies embodied poetics because of the ways it renders both death and love in a tragicomic mode that centers the physical sensations of a body in pain, in desire, and in the calm acceptance of mortality and other vulnerabilities. First, readers are shown the pleasures of good food and good company.

Alone, finally, me and you
together, first time in a long week.
We stand in the kitchen cutting
chunks of halibut, fresh crab meat.

Then comes the pain of the cut finger and the vulnerability the small injury brings out in the speaker.

More,
my blood seems to say, *more*
across onions, the counter, while you
grab paper towels, stubbornly
staunch the flow, my knees gone weak.

The discussion of knives with the doctor reminds the speaker of a youth when he had more reckless passions and urges, when he and his lover are "remembering our young selves, their unmet / needs—raw, impulsive, newborn— / hungry for our bodies, for a me and you." But in this moment the speaker is content to be a body on a chair, negotiating all the domestic tedium of a life together, the injured finger pointing towards some abstract notion of love and togetherness that is only imaginable because of these embodied experiences of stitches and bandages, lawn mowers and laundry, a comfort of familiarity that only deepens after so much time has passed.

Like Snider's poem, Meg Day's "10 AM Is When You Come to Me" is also rooted in the erotic. Unlike love poems, which exalt a concept or a feeling, erotic poetry resists such mind-body dichotomies. Emotions emerge from physical sensations and material circumstances. Many of the poets who are most notable for bringing their bodies fully onto the page are also those who have bodies that, in this moment in history, are most likely to be remarked upon, dismissed, erased, or othered. Such lived experiences perhaps bring writers into deep awareness of themselves not only as thinking and feeling beings, but also situated in and engaged with other such beings, many of whom seem to be trying to impose their subjectivities on the world writ large. This particular poem is just one example of how both disability poetics and queer theory might influence a writer's approach to a poem about the erotic.

Day, who is deaf and genderqueer, begins the poem as the speaker wakes from a dream. "In some other life, I can hear you / breathing." But the poem resists ableist tropes of longing to be fixed, and pivots away from such harmful and all-too-pervasive storylines. "Leave me—that me—" Day writes, "in bed with the woman / who said all the sounds for pleasure / were made with vowels I couldn't / hear." Day then turns the readers' attention to the lush array of senses to which this speaker has access—

> Your eyes
> are two moons I float beneath & my lungs
> fill with a wet hum your hips return.
> . . . . You make me sing without a sound.

The poem is a sexy celebration of the body, but in keeping with the principles of embodied poetics, the poem is also attentive to how the mind is engaged with both the body and the lover and the pervasive problematic narratives from the broader culture about who they are in relation to each other. The former lover who implies the speaker is missing some crucial aspect of pleasure in the form of vowels signifies a host of other ableist assumptions and microaggressions delivered in a similar vein. The kind of ecstatic experience Day offers readers through such vivid descriptions requires struggle and rejection of those forces that would schism such a moment. Here we can notice how writing about the body and its erotic capacities is not just an act of pleasure, but one of politics as well.

Ama Codjoe's "On Seeing and Being Seen" is another poem that addresses erotic longing from an intersectional perspective. This poem centers on lesbian desire and also reclaims beauty and desirability from the racist and Eurocentric aesthetics that are so pervasive in many poetic traditions. Codjoe quotes from Elizabeth Bishop's poem "In the Waiting Room," where a child picks up an issue of *National Geographic*, a publication already notorious for othering and objectifying the bodies of Black and Brown women. Bishop goes on to describe the child's revulsion. We wish we could say the purpose of this poem by Bishop is to critique such racism, but the truth is that the poem accepts, embraces, and advances such misogynoir. Codjoe's poem, on the other hand, names the harm in Bishop's poem and the beauty standards on which it rests. And then Codjoe uses the occasion of erotic longing to offer a counternarrative—that such breasts as those the speaker has and those the speaker desires on other bodies are beautiful and loved. The poem ends with a celebration of how body and spirit are intertwined, with each having the potential to beautify the other. She writes, capturing everything we've tried to say here about embodied poetics in a single elegant line: "My body is a lens / I can look through with my mind."

What a Metaphor Is to a Body

Writing from within a full and complex awareness of one's body certainly involves attending to the sensations of having a body, but it also involves attending to the experiences of others and valuing their perceptions about their bodies and the world. Blindness, deafness, mental illness, and other forms of disability are frequently used as metaphors in literature. But such metaphors fail to account for how those disabilities are real, material ways many people experience the world. When a writer uses blindness as a metaphor, they erase the realities of all those people who experience the world with and through their blindness, for whom blindness is not about lacking, but rather a partial description of the sensory system they use to know their minds, their bodies, their world. And the same can be said of any other disability, of any other body a person uses to think and be and know. Sheila Black, one of the major theorists working on disability poetics, describes a fundamental principle of disability poetics as "the process of making normalcy and ableism visible and thereby highlighting their strangeness, which makes disability poetry inherently a poetry of liberation / revolution."

But let's step back for a moment and linger a bit over what a metaphor is. After all, one of the very exciting conversations that has crossed from disability theories and activism into poetics and literary craft is this conversation about metaphor. In figurative language we often refer to tenors and vehicles. We discuss this a little in the chapter "Telling Secrets," but to review, the tenor is the thing—or concept—being described, and the vehicle is the figurative language you use to describe it—to transport our thinking about it from abstract to concrete. In a line like "Justice is blind," justice would be the tenor, blindness would be the vehicle—but it is a vehicle, in this case, that relies on assumptions about blindness having negative connotations. Additionally, in many metaphors, the tenor is presented as the more real part of the equation, while the vehicle is reduced to mere decoration. This balance doesn't always sit well with writers, especially those who have become aware of what it is to have one's experiences or even one's very body treated as somehow less real than those of others. After all, blindness is far more real than justice, but it is all too rare for blindness to take the role of tenor in literature, to be depicted as the primary way of experiencing the world. Instead, it is constantly forced into the role of being a vehicle, and even worse, being a vehicle used to describe a lack or a loss. Using language in this way is ableist, and such metaphors are so pervasive in English that it takes many writers quite a lot of time and practice to notice and remove figures of speech that rely on stereotypes and cliches of disability (like those related blindness, deafness, mobility issues, or neurological difference) from their lexicon.

These critiques of metaphor don't just point to ways the craft of poetry has the potential to oppress and erase. They also carry in them proposals for embodied poetics and approaches to craft that are exhilarating in their potential to more fully depict the experience of being human. Black sees disability poetics as an intellectual orientation that doesn't so much make old, tired metaphors off limits as it brings writers into more nuanced, vigorous engagement with what complex truths our bodies and our language can express together. Black says, "because disability deals so directly with many of the soft, inchoate, under-expressed parts of being alive in the world, it is a rich ground for thinking about this project of being human in genuinely new ways."

CA Conrad's (soma)tic poetry is a particularly fascinating example of what kinds of radical, visionary possibilities emerge when writers think deeply about how the words on a page are rooted in the bodies that called them into being, as well as those that received them through acts of reading or listening. Conrad's poetics involve first creating a ritual, the purpose of which is to create a different kind of investment in and awareness of the everyday. For example, in "(Soma)tic 5: Storm SOAKED Bread," Conrad instructs readers to sit "somewhere outside where you can easily touch, smell, taste, FEEL the storm." After more detailed discussion of what it means to be a poet open to a rainstorm, Conrad then asks readers to "Set an empty cup in the storm, hold a slice of bread in the storm. Then put a little salt and pepper on your storm soaked bread, maybe some oregano and garlic. With deliberate SLOOOWNESS chew your storm bread and drink the storm captured in your cup."

While Conrad's (soma)tic instructions often read as poems in their own right, these rituals usually include space for taking notes on sensory details and perceptions, which Conrad later crafts into poems. Upon completing this (soma)tic, Conrad composed the poem, "One Day I Will Step from the Beauty Parlor and Enlist in the Frequency of Starlings," which ends with the lines, "everyone paying attention / enjoy your visit / everyone else / good luck." This method of experiencing poetry requires constant awareness of a person creating this language from a very particular set of embodied circumstances.

A practice of attending to the precise circumstances of how one feels and thinks within their body often becomes a springboard towards surprising and evocative language. In the essay "On Intersectional Queer Poetics," Julie R. Enzer writes, "Naming our realities, giving language to our bodies and how they move through the world, builds power individually and collectively." Tony Titchkosky's essay "Life with Dead Metaphors" echoes this theme, positing disability poetics as another site of liberatory imagination, writing, "To regard metaphor as a place where we nurture the capacity to let new understandings arise is also a way to orient to the call in disability studies." Eli Clare writes in "Stolen Bodies, Reclaimed Bodies: Disability and Queerness" that "The work of refiguring the world is often framed as the work of changing the material, external conditions of our oppression. But just as certainly, our bodies—or more accurately, what we believe about our bodies—need to change so that they don't become storage sites, traps, for the very oppression we want to eradicate." Poets who embrace the key principles of mind, body, and understanding of their social circumstances prepare themselves to imagine beyond simplistic cis, heteronormative, ableist, and other stultifying conventions.

Genre / Gender Blur

In addition to naming and celebrating the ways ideas emerging from conversations among theorists in the field of Critical Disability Studies can enrich one's poetics, we also want to linger over the significant impact Queer theories about gender as a spectrum, rather than a binary, have had had on the way poets conceive of their craft and use of forms in recent years. The description of gender as a spectrum has been translated by many contemporary writers who now speak about genre in parallel terms. Considering *genre* and *gender* share the root word for *genus*, which is a type or class of noun, it makes sense that reorienting one set of categories (gender) could have implications for other rigid categories (like literary genres). A cascade of blurrings emerging from the field of Queer Theory has altered many assumptions among poets about what a poem can be in ways we can only describe as exhilarating.

Genre-blurring work is that which resists easy categorization as a poem. Perhaps it's a prose poem that is as much fairy tale as it is music. Or perhaps the piece has many of the qualities of an essay—research, prose passages, arguments—but it also makes associative leaps and uses the pause created by the field of the page to structure ideas and invite the reader to participate in experience-making. Perhaps the piece erases, fragments, or juxtaposes texts in ways that resist categorization. In any work where the resistance to classification is as much a part of its meaning as the form it happens to take, that work can be thought of as genre-blurred, or what you might sometimes hear called "hybrid."

Cameron Awkward-Rich's poem is one interesting example of how a genre-blurring form, with elements of both prose and poetry, can be the perfect mode for conveying the experience of feeling oneself move between and beyond cis-gender categories. It is also the perfect form for expressing frustration when others try to slot you into such categories against your will. "The truth is, most black folk look at you & see a woman. White people look at you & see a reckless boy. Either way, there you are in the room with your body." This poem also illustrates how the racist urge to create categories, classes, and castes is also one that can be resisted by refusing such definitions and demarcations.

In this poem genre-blur is not just a form, it is an aesthetic gesture of freedom and resistance. Awkward-Rich writes, "Here, once you name a thing, you can't take it back." So it is an extraordinary gesture when the poem introduces brackets with gaps that refuse to name things, that refuse to burden tenors with vehicles and instead let them be entirely themselves. "A rose becomes [ ]. A daughter becomes [ ]. Her son [ ]." Such writing also becomes a way to encourage or insist readers practice more fluid ways of thinking. By creating circumstances wherein a reader cannot rely on familiar categories, writers practicing genre-blur direct the readers' attentions to other more open ways of perceiving, understanding, and organizing their experiences of the world.

INVITATIONS TO REFLECT

Discuss Together

In this chapter we introduced you to the idea of "embodied poetics" and we highlighted some of the ways metaphorical thinking slips over a line into stereotyping. Revisit Cameron Awkward-Rich's poem "[Black Feeling]" reproduced at the front of this chapter and describe what kinds of traps and what kinds of liberation the poet tries to find in metaphors, in language, and in the experiences held in brackets that seem to have no language. Then, think about how you might reconsider the influence of this chapter's ideas on your own poetry.

For Further Study

Find an essay, journal, or anthology that delves into embodied poetics and / or the concept of genre blur and hybridity, such as those listed in our online companion by Gabrielle Calvocoressi, Kazim Ali, Oliver Baez Bendorf, Eileen Myles, Jos Charles, and more. Study their ideas and consider how your work, or a work you are currently reading, may or may not be informed by this lineage. What other lineages intersect?

Writing Exercises

1 **The Impossibly Real**

With CA Conrad's (soma)tic approach to creating rituals in mind, along with Debjani Chatterjee's technique of launching a fantasy from an embodied experience of discomfort, write a poem that begins with a description of your body in a moment of intense physical sensations. Then describe your body doing something it is not physically capable of—Flying? Growing a long tail? Becoming invisible? Warping through space? Keep writing to discover how your speaker's experience changes as the seemingly impossible becomes real and tangible.

2 **Preparing to Write**

Write your own descriptive meditation on how you prepare to write, inspired by Laura Hershey's reflection on her process. For every four lines of concrete, descriptive detail, add one line of commentary on politics or power that influence your material circumstances in some way.

3 **The Fullness of the Moment**

Write a poem about an intimate encounter that includes something you would like to stop thinking about or worrying over.

4 **Saying the Unsayable**

Write a poem about an experience you can't describe in words, using parentheses, brackets, ellipses, or indentations so that your silences on the page can carry that ineffable meaning.

5 **The Mime, the Clown, the Poet**

An exercise inspired by Jacques Lecoq: Before an audience, or in complete privacy, mime a time you felt intense physical sensations. Next, metaphorically or literally put on the red nose of the clown and act out the experience again with a clown's slapstick mayhem. Finally, write a description of the experience. You may wish to allude to how it felt to mime or clown it, but you don't have to.

8

The Racial Imaginary

A FEW POEMS TO START US OFF . . .

In this chapter we reflect on how ideas about race and experiences with racism might shape a poet's vision of the world, relationship to imaginative possibilities, and approach to the poetic craft. We look at authors who chart paths for what writers, who devote their lives and spirits to the possibilities of imagination, might do about the harmful fantasies white supremacy and colonialism impose on people. We approach this chapter knowing that race is a social construct, but racism is real and causes real harm. This chapter explores how artists might name and respond to the harms of racism, and we hope these sample poems will give you some ideas about how to write poems that do the same. And, as always, we hope this chapter will serve as an introduction to lineages of poets who can become ongoing inspirations to you as a writer.

Roger Reeves

In a Brief, Animated World: The Marriage of Anne of Denmark to James of Scotland, 1589

Nature always begins with resistance—
The small congregation of ants refusing
To allow the femur bone of the fox
To rest, meatless, the heavy head of flies
In January straying from the graves
Which are the corners of this house—
The four Negroes at Queen Anne's wedding
Dancing in the snow, naked, before her
Carriage, the creak of carriage wheels
Counting out steps—1-2-3-Turn-Jump-
Turn—their arms wide as goose wings,
Bow, then a breaking at the waist,
Mucus spills from their mouths onto—
And before a guest from Oslo can point
To the blood-tinged saliva, the wagon wheels
Gather every stitch of spit, grind,
Then smear—the body, if allowed,
Will dance even as it is ruined—a mule
Collapsing in a furrow it's just hewed—
The sway and undulation of the famished—
There are no straight lines but unto death—
Four men turning circles in the snow—
The arch of their toes calling Anne to lean
Forward, admire the work of the unshod
Sinking below all this white. She thinks:
In a brief, animated world, this would not be
Agony. The leg of her fox stole slips
From her shoulders and points to the men
Shivering in their last plié. Yes, she thinks,
But agony is sometimes necessary.

Aracelis Girmay

& When We Woke

It rained all night. It did not rain.
I strapped my life to a buoy—& sent it out.
& was hoping for a city whose people sing
from their windows or rooftops,
about the beauty of their children
& their children's eyes, & the color of the fields
when it is dusk. & was hoping for a city
as free as the rain, whose people roam
wherever they want, free as any real, free thing is free.
Joyful. Green. & was hoping
for a city of 100 old women whose bones
are thick & big in their worker hands
beautiful as old doors. & when we woke,
dear reader, we'd landed in a city of 100 old women
telling their daughters things. & when we turned
to walk away, because we did not think we were citizens
of this strange & holy place, you & I, the hundred old
women said, No, No! You are one of us! We are your
mothers! You! You! Too! Come & listen to our secrets.
We are telling every person with a face!
& they stood us in a line facing the sea,
(because that is the direction we came from)
& behind us there was another line of women
& another, & we sang songs. & we filled the songs
with our mothers' names. & we filled the songs
with trees for our mothers to stand under,
& good water for our mothers to drink. & we filled

the songs with beds for our mothers to lay down in
& rest. We filled the songs with rest. & good food
for our mothers to eat. We made them a place
in our singing, & we faced the sea.
We are still making them a place
in our singing. Do you understand?
We make them a place where they can walk freely,
untouched by knives or the police who patrol
the borders of countries like little & fake hatred-gods
who patrol the land though the land says, I go on
& on, so far, you lose your eye on me.
We make our mothers a place in our singing & our place
does not have a flag or, even, one language.
Do you understand? We sing like this for days,
standing in lines & lines & lines, facing the sea.
The sea knows what to do. We sing like this for days
until our throats are torn with singing. Do you understand?
We must build houses for our mothers in our poems. I am not sure,
but think, This is my wisest song.

Jaswinder Bolina

Partisan Poem

You're not the hero of this story.

You're what odor rankles
the dog into snarling, what clang

in the ductwork beggars the kid
into pleading for a nightlight

against sleep, against her dreams
of violence. You're the dread

in the cellar, the bed wetted,
what sets the adrenals leaking

their frantic mojo, what footfalls
down an alleyway force the hand

into its pocket in search of keys
to weave between the fingers.

You're what makes the fist,
what startles the breath out of me.

You spectre in the swamp gas,
you spider in a slipper, you snake

into my sleeping bag like an overcoat
pouncing from its hook into a corner

of my eye when I enter the house
in an off light, my familiar torqued

sinister, my prairie home made
alien, and you as the pupa birthed

from an acid bath in steaming
nurseries of your landing craft,

you as invading army and secret
police berating me I'm wrong

about your best intentions, and all you
ever seem to tell me is I'm wrong

when all it ever seems to me is
the one thing worse than a good man

with a bad idea is a bad man
with a great idea, and I might be wrong,

but you are so abundant, so burdened,
so bloated with the very best ideas.

Leanne Betasamosake Simpson

this accident of being lost

listen for the hesitant beat
sit at the edge of the woods
shape shift around the defense
ban the word *should*

follow the bluebird
past the smoke & contraband
my frightened lower back
a witness on unkept-promise land

hide under mindimooyenh's skirt
wrap swamp tea around your chest
fill your empty with smoked meat
vomit this fucking mess

weave spruce into your fix
forget missed shots & mean boys
tie these seven pieces of heart
use whiskey as your decoys

play by the skin of old teeth
the ritual of giving thanks
laughing hearts & feeding fires
compasses & riverbanks

i'm just going to sit here past late
the stars don't care at what cost
you breathe while i whisper a song
"this accident of being lost"

Tess Taylor

Downhill White Supremacists March on Sacramento

High in the Sierra
green summer aspen

whisper to the lake.
The snowpack glitters.

Over the passes
Winnebago thunder

 out of the wide red flats of Nevada.

Huge crooked knuckles,
the dark screes loom.

Deep in the roadbeds,
the bones of the Irish

& Chinese workers
whose lives were pitted

against one another
to drive down & down

the price of their labor
—who shattered their bodies

 dynamiting these crossings—

blaze in their graves.

DISCUSSION

Given that poetry has a deep history of being used as both a vehicle for personal expression and as a method for speaking truth to power, it is not surprising that some of the most groundbreaking conversations about identity, privilege, stereotypes, and bias are happening in lyric form. In this chapter we will talk about how poets craft work that critiques and dreams, names and heals.

Our thinking here, along with the title of the chapter which we chose as an homage, has been deeply influenced by *The Racial Imaginary: Writers on Race in the Life of the Mind*, an influential volume of essays edited by Claudia Rankine, Beth Lofreda, and Cap Max King. (You can find links to some of these essays via our online companion.) In that collection, the editors and contributors wanted to push back on an old narrative dominating certain powerful literary circles, a narrative which suggests that creative writing somehow can or should be a universalizing depiction of the human experience and that such "universal" literature can be achieved by erasing race from writing altogether. Black, Indigenous, and Brown writers, among others, have, of course, long known and been saying that it is not possible to reflect the realities of their lived experience without contending with the ways their race and the forces of racism impact their lives, and thus their literary imaginations. They've also tried to direct white writers' attentions to the fact that they also have a racial identity, despite the ways that white supremacist narratives try to insist that that whiteness isn't a race, it's just the default or "normal." But it has taken a very long time for publishers and editors, the majority of whom have been, and still are white people, to begin to hear this message.

In their introduction to the anthology Lofreda and Rankine write,

> To argue that the imagination is or can be somehow free of race—that it is the one region of self or experience that is free of race—and that I have a right to imagine whoever I want, and that it damages or deforms my art to set limits on my imagination—acts as if the imagination is not part of me, is not created by the same web of history and culture that made me.

We can point to a host of poets who have found inspiration in the work of examining those webs of history and culture that shaped them. And in short order we will. But first, we'd like to point out that one of the paradoxes of writing about race is that there is no credible scientific or biological theory of race—it's an invention of white European imaginations seeking some kind of justification for their desire to grow wealth and power through colonization and enslavement. But please don't misunderstand—just because some people with monstrous imaginations advanced a bogus theory in the fifteenth and sixteenth centuries that variations in skin tone correspond to different degrees of humanity doesn't mean that theory doesn't affect our world or our experiences today. Any person reading this text who is thinking right now about saying "I don't see race" would do well to sit tight for a while and keep reading. The fact that race is a culturally constructed ideology doesn't change the fact that it still, unfortunately, has a lot of power.

Telling and Re-Telling the History of Racism

Roger Reeves's poetry collection, *King Me*, features many poems set in historical situations or places where the presence of enslaved people and all the tortures and cruelties that went along with the practice of slavery are often erased, cropped out, or conveniently forgotten. In his poems he tells more complex histories, which are painful to hear but also necessary to know to create different futures. In the poem "In a Brief, Animated World: The Marriage of Anne of Denmark to James of Scotland, 1589," he describes the racist and violent theatrics involved in a royal wedding. We also want to note for you that Roger Reeves is himself Black, which we think is important to know going into a poem that uses archaic language about race and describes racist violence. Knowing that the author and imagined speaker of the poem has suffered as a consequence of these historical events impacts how we might understand and interpret the words on the page.

> The four Negroes at Queen Anne's wedding
> Dancing in the snow, naked, before her
> Carriage, the creak of carriage wheels
> Counting out steps—*1-2-3 Turn-Jump-*
> *Turn*—their arms wide as goose wings.

This scene, which the monarchs and their emissaries must have choreographed with an idea of beauty in mind, is consistent with so much of the other art commissioned by elites of this time. It was a demonstration of white power conveyed through the dehumanization and othering of Black people's bodies. It was also a performance that disregarded pain in search of craft elements like four-point symmetry or the marked color contrast of Black skin against white snow. Which is one example of the reasons why we regard with suspicion any discussion of craft that elevates above all else ideas about form.

These parts of history are often glossed over, for many reasons, one of which is that some influential people don't like the way such stories awaken their sense of guilt or shame. Another reason is that such influential people can no longer imagine themselves or the world around them in the comfortable way they prefer if they are forced to confront how such realities are built on a foundation of constant, relentless brutality across centuries. That brutality is even hard to accept when it is disguised as part of a culture's highest ideals, like love, family, or beauty.

> Four men turning circles in the snow—
> The arch of their toes calling Anne to lean
> Forward, admire the work of the unshod
> Sinking below all this white. She thinks:
> *In a brief, animated world, this would not be*
> *Agony.*

As we read these lines, we think about how this poem recreates that historical moment in our own mind's eye, and makes readers see the terrible dance all over again. The poem recreates the moment of "the men / shivering in their last plié." But unlike the cavalier shrug of Anne, holding the leg of her fox stole as she thinks to herself, "*Agony is sometimes necessary*," this poem suggests agony is sometimes necessary, not to please wealthy and powerful people as a form of entertainment, certainly not to prove some theory about who does or does not have the right, but to make honest, restorative, just imagination possible.

Reeves's poem does a lot of painful, but necessary work naming and diagnosing the historical circumstances that brought us to this moment. The poem is also an example of the work his poetry does to fill in the gaps created by the erasures and whitewashing of Eurocentrism and white supremacy. These are important imaginative undertakings, but also traumatic poems to read, most especially for our students who have identities directly impacted by the present legacies of such history. So, we'd like to take a closer look at Aracelis Girmay's poem "& When We Woke" as an example of how a poet can also grapple with racist trauma with an eye towards healing.

Girmay's poem opens with a gesture of both despair and hope. The speaker "strapped my life to a buoy—& sent it out, / & I was hoping for a city whose people sing." The poem goes on to list more details of that hope, including descriptions of beautiful Brown-skinned children and people roaming free in a world of green. The emphasis on the beauty of the color brown, the celebration of workers' hands, and the allusion to fields highlight for readers that the speaker's dream of an ideal city sits in contrast to the horrors of slavery.

The poem then pivots to how the 100-year-old women of this city teach their daughters to sing facing the sea ("because that is the direction we came from"). This image of singing to the sea is a reminder of how the trauma and grief of slavery is carried across generations. The people who died in that ocean crossing the Middle Passage and those who died in bondage after—how can such loss be reckoned with? For Girmay, the answer lies in this song of healing and hope, where poems like this one remember those lost lives and call them forth again as glimmers of love and beauty. "& filled the songs / without mothers' names & we filled the songs / with trees for our mothers to stand under, / & good water for our mothers to drink . . ." This visionary imagination goes on for many more lines, illustrating the power of a writer's imagination. A poet can not only document the truth about the past but can also call a new future into being. The poem ends with an invitation to readers to join her in this work of transformative visioning. "Do you understand?" Girmay writes. "We must build houses for our mothers in our poems. / I am not sure, / but I think, This is my wisest song."

Race and the Relationships between Author, Speaker, and Reader

A key way we see the racial imaginary affecting the craft and poetics of many writers is in how they seek to navigate the complex interplay between the poet, the speaker of the poem, and a diverse audience of readers (for more on the relationships between these, see the earlier chapter, "Telling Secrets."). These elements can present a writer with difficult questions and choices. Jaswinder Bolina's "Partisan Poem" is one that investigates the potential and limitations of rhetoric, discourse, and the ways we can attempt to persuade and move each other. Bolina is a poet whose work often explores themes like immigrant experiences (especially the pressure to assimilate), racist ideologies manifesting in government policies, as well as a host of other philosophical issues around the question of being human in an age of rapid technological expansion and global climate change. In most of his poems he merges surrealist flights of fancy with a New York School-inspired witty, urbane tone. He's a poet who keeps readers on their toes, never letting us settle into easy assumptions about the speaker's place in the world or their own.

We think "Partisan Poem" is particularly interesting to look at in a conversation about the relationship between the poet, speaker, and implied audience, because he is so attentive to how a racial imaginary on all parts shapes those dynamics. The poem is written as a direct address, or apostrophe, to a "you." It is composed of a litany of impressively ingenious insults.

> You're what odor rankles
> the dog into snarling, what clang
> in the ductwork beggars the kid
> into pleading for a nightlight
> against sleep, against her dreams
> of violence. You're the dread
> in the cellar, the bed wetted . . .

The title, "Partisan Poem," suggests the speaker might be a political partisan, someone participating in the hostile and divisive rhetoric. One could read this poem as an indictment against such vitriol by pointing out the laughable absurdity of such rhetoric via a series of poetically sick burns. But that reading is a little too simple; it elides moments of genuine authenticity and the assumptions Bolina is playing upon about the relationships between writer, speaker, and reader.

Lines like "You're what makes the fist, / what startles the breath out of me" remind readers that while there have not been waves of Punjabi-Americans beating people up in alleys, there absolutely has been a significant rise in violent hate crimes directed against people with skin tones like Bolina's and that increase has been in concert with the return of undisguised hate speech from politicians at their podiums. In a gesture of solidarity and a spirit of shared struggle, the poem has lines that call to mind the threats of violence women of all racial backgrounds, though to different degrees, live with in a patriarchal society where men who are credibly accused of sexual assault are nevertheless allowed to assume positions of enormous power. You are, the poem accuses,

> what footfalls
> down an alleyway force the hand
> into its pocket in search of keys
> to weave between the fingers.

The poem also evokes the way anti-immigrant, racist rhetoric makes people feel unwelcome in their own countries: "my prairie home made / alien." It also acknowledges the looming specter of "secret / police berating me." Those of you reading this textbook who remember the radio show *A Prairie Home Companion* may appreciate the way this line critiques the show host and poet Garrison Keillor's vision of an imaginary all-white, all-Lutheran, entirely safe, and utterly wholesome community of English majors. The line reminds us of how frightening it can be for someone of a different race, religion, or ethnicity to enter such communities.

So, who is the audience for this poem? We would suggest that this poem is successful in part because of how many layers of audience Bolina speaks to. There's the "you," who is perhaps Donald Trump himself, but also any white supremacist or Eurocentric supporter of an aspiring autocrat or dictator who might encounter the poem. But we also notice that for some readers there is such pleasure in the speaker's acidic wit that we think the poem is also written for an audience of people who know what it's like to live in terror of the political opposition and who are galvanized by the acknowledgment the poem makes of their own frustration and rage. We also think the poem is calling forth their capacity for gentleness, despite so much reasonable fear and fury, with that title. Bolina anticipates an audience of readers who can be tempered by the reminder that indulging in too much partisan rhetoric is potentially toxic and unproductive, even if it is a cathartic release.

Because Bolina is so aware not only of who he is, but also how others see him, as well as who others are and how he can see them so clearly, he's able to offer readers this multi-layered experience of themselves. Readers of this poem are asked to understand themselves as the potential recipients of insults, as potential slingers of insults, and ultimately as people trapped in the imperfect, muddled complexity of a society wherein "the one thing worse than a good man // with a bad idea is a bad man / with a great idea." The speaker acknowledges, as good-hearted and humble people do, that "I might be wrong." But despite the admission of fallibility, it is clear the speaker has lived through enough and paid attention enough to end the poem on a note of certainty readers need to hear, laced with a cynical irony he trusts they will be able to understand. This final note is the assertion that cocksure con men trying to run the show are truly "so abundant, so burdened / so bloated with the very best ideas."

We've heard too many stories about poets being told in workshops or by editors that they are either saying too much about their race or not doing enough to educate their readers, who the critics either assume must be white or who they seem to think matter more than readers with other backgrounds. In his essay, "Color Coded," Bolina described such an experience he had, saying,

> Firsthand experience of racism is the kind of thing a poet probably ought to write about. But the first time I wrote a poem about it, a white poet lamented that I was merely outing the obvious, only reiterating something he, I, and many other readers of poetry already knew was wrong. As notable anti-Semite Ezra Pound declared long ago, the artist's central task is to *make it new*. The white poet's complaint was that, though my poem may have been well-written, even publishable, it hadn't made racism new.

By centering an imagined audience of readers who have experienced racist threats and violence Bolina creates an artistic space where he can delve into, complicate, and elevate the questions that he most wants to ask and answer in his work. He is able to create a poetic intimacy with readers who are moved by poetry's capacities to reassure that we are not alone in our daily experiences of life's difficulties, both mundane (like whether or how to temper one's political rhetoric) or extraordinary (how to be and feel safe again after a political leader has told the nation "people like you are not welcome in your own country"). As Rankine says, "A writer's imagination is also the place where a racial imaginary—conceived before she came into being yet deeply lodged in her own mind—takes up its residence. And the disentangling and harnessing of these things is the writer's endless and unfinishable but not fruitless task." Many of our students have carried the burdensome voices of strangers, TV shows, movies, friends, ads on the bus, and so many more products of our cultures that tell them they are something they are not. We've seen how our students are compelled to carry a racialized stereotype of themselves in their minds alongside their vision of themselves as the person they actually are. Poems like Bolina's don't make racism new, but they do offer a new vision of how one can hold fast to a sense of reality in the face of racism's distortions.

Leanne Betasamosake Simpson's poem "this accident of being lost" is another example of thinking about the relationship between writer and reader. In this work, though, she imagines a relationship between speaker and reader that is predicated on an already-existing shared understanding. She ignores what is sometimes called "the white gaze" and creates a poem that operates in conversation with the rituals and teachings of the First Nations communities of which she is a member, without any compunction to explain to settler colonialist readers who a mindimooyenh is, how swamp tea might heal, or other details in the poem that will surely resonate differently with Michi Saagiig Nishnaabeg and other Indigenous readers. We notice that this poem moves between images of connection with land and traditions that the speaker does not feel the need to explicate—"follow the bluebird / past the smoke & contraband"—and images of threats and violence on colonized land that the speaker does not feel require any justification—"my frightened lower back / a witness on unkept-promise land."

One of the reasons we are attentive to the lyrical freedom Simpson asserts in this poem, by offering lines and images without explication or translation, is because she writes elsewhere about the toll constant attention to readers who occupy an oppressive presence in one's life can take. In the short story "Plight" from the same collection, which is also called *The Accident of Being Lost*, she describes a group of First Nations friends, living in a liberal city neighborhood, strategizing about how to ensure they are able to engage without harassment in traditional practices and ceremonies associated with the maple syrup harvest. She writes in this story:

> We know how to do this so they'll be into it. Hand out the flyers first. Have a community meeting. Ask permission. Listen to their paternalistic bullshit and feedback. Let them have influence. Let them bask in the plight of the Native people so they can feel self-righteous. Make them feel better, and when reconciliation comes up at the next dinner party, they can hold us up as the solution and brag to their real friends about our plight. I proofread the flyer one more time because everyone knows white people hate typos.

As teachers and poets who have benefited from whiteness and settler colonialism, we don't pretend to know firsthand how it feels to live and write with so many layers of oppressive voices standing between what one yearns to say and what one can imagine editors, publishers, classmates, and teachers being capable of understanding. But we want to point anyone reading this textbook, especially those poets trying to imagine lyrical ways out of rhetorical double binds, towards those writers who find their voices on the page by imaging an audience of readers who already know the expressions, languages, traditions, foods, and habits that are integral parts of their daily lives. Some writers find the imaginative freedom they need to create by writing with an audience of readers in mind who are longing to read literature that knows them well. The Nobel-prize-winning novelist, Toni Morrison, often spoke of eschewing the white gaze in a way that made her writing feel open, instead of constrained. "I'm writing for black people," she said in an interview with *The Guardian*, "in the same way that Tolstoy was not writing for me, a 14-year-old coloured girl from Lorain, Ohio. I don't have to apologise or consider myself limited because I don't [write about white people]—which is not absolutely true, there are lots of white people in my books. The point is not having the white critic sit on your shoulder and approve it." While we can't promise there won't be editors, agents, and others who will pressure you to focus your revisions on how white people especially will interpret your work, you can turn to writers like Morrison and Simpson to find reassurance and examples of how to write for an audience of readers with whom you can imagine cultivating an authentic and intimate relationship of shared understanding. And just as Tolstoy's work spoke deeply to a young Toni Morrison and Leanne Betasamosake's work speaks deeply to us, you can have confidence that other readers will also find powerful resonances in your honest depiction of human experiences, even if, perhaps especially if, they aren't being catered to like spoiled children.

That Art of Looking Inward

We consider the act of reflecting on one's own racial identity to be a profoundly productive one that can help a writer more fully understand their own voice and their interpretations of the events and situations they describe on the page; it also helps writers think about how readers might respond to their work. But we also want to caution that we often see new writers, particularly new white writers who have seldom been asked to notice or contemplate their own racial identity, reach for persona poems to engage with their questions about race. While we aren't inclined to ever tell an artist that a certain approach is off-limits or against the rules, we do want to draw your attention to the all-too-common move wherein a writer creates a persona poem from the perspective of an identity with which they have no lived experience. So often these kinds of poems use dialects that read as insulting rather than authentic or are laced with stereotypical and cliched images the writer was too ignorant to recognize as stereotypes. Other times it is blatantly obvious that the writer is taking a twisted pleasure in imagining themselves into the body and mind of a person who a racist, sexist, or otherwise hegemonic society has told them they are permitted to dominate in other respects. Using one's imagination in this way can painfully mirror the operations of colonization and slavery.

To write any poem, but especially a persona poem, you must be prepared to be ruthlessly honest with yourself about your intentions, appropriations, and implicit biases. You must also make a profound commitment to research, deep reading, and deep listening. In her book, *Appropriate: A Provocation*, about the poetics of imagining other people's lives, perspectives, and experiences, Paisley Rekdal suggests, in an essay that takes the form of a letter to her students:

> while we all have identities, few of us are prepared to unravel the Gordian knot of social realities, history, and fantasy that constitute a self and its attendant ideas of race, ethnicity, gender, sexuality, or even physical or mental ability, let alone discuss what an accurate representation of any of these selves might look like on the page. And the more you and I think about identity, the more we might discover that cultural appropriation is less a question of "staying in one's lane," as one of your classmates put it, than an evolving conversation we must have around privilege and aesthetic fashion in literary practice.

Rekdal encourages young and new writers to pay close attention to discourse, and reflect on their own system of developing ethics, as they move forward. Tess Taylor is such a poet who models the kind of honest self-interrogation we love to see. Rather than indulging in power-hungry fantasies of imagining she can know what it is like to move through a racist society as a person with an historically marginalized racial identity, she attempts to fully see the nature of her white privilege and to use her position to more thoughtfully understand the inner workings of racism perpetuated by white people. In an essay she contributed to *The Racial Imaginary* anthology, Taylor says that "My wish as a writer about my own racial experience is to unsettle the kind of position of invisibility that whiteness so often assumes; to become uncomfortable in my own skin, to distrust what I'm told about who I am, or even to distrust what I can see. This discomfort, even a little, reminds me (even a little) not to take all the privilege I get every day from my own skin for granted." In the book, *Rift Zone*, Taylor investigates literal and metaphorical fault lines to tell a personal and collective history of settler colonialism, racism, segregation, and desecration of the land. Taylor focusses on the circumstance in her home state of California, but her excavation of white people's silence around racism and genocide, as well as the work of self-reflection, interrogation, and acknowledgment of privilege and complicity, resonate beyond those state lines.

In "Downhill White Supremacists March on Sacramento," she balances an idyllic, escapist view up into the summer aspens of the Sierras against a vision below where

> deep in the roadbeds,
> the bones of the Irish
> & Chinese workers
> whose lives were pitted

against one another
to drive down & down
the price of their labor.

The poem contends with the ways racist theories adapt to maintain white supremacist power. This image of the march illustrates clearly how often those who might otherwise find class solidarity with marginalized peoples instead choose to seek out a measure of race privilege in exchange for participating in the project of racialized othering and oppression. Such groups often do the work of policing these categories of difference, which is what readers see the white supremacist marchers in this poem doing.

This poem, like many others in *Rift Zone*, draws on a variety of scholarly disciplines to understand a moment. Living, as her speakers do, on fault lines while awaiting the next fire season, Taylor attends to the millennia of memory in the redwoods, to the eons in the rock, as part of a story that stretches into the more recent history, the centuries of extraction capitalism that have created certain grooves of thinking into which white supremacists now slip all too easily. Then she returns to the present moment where one can see a way into the future—the speaker turns her head from the scene of protests in the road towards the glitter of snowpack beyond the lake, which is one direction that road can lead, while in the other direction,

—who shattered their bodies

  dynamiting these crossings—

blaze in their graves.

Taylor's is an important voice in an emerging body of work from white poets excavating the histories of whiteness and privilege, who seek to understand precisely how these ideas were first created and then maintained through willful ignorance by those who benefitted from them. Her work provides excellent examples of how one might participate in the project of decolonization and liberation without culturally appropriating or enacting a white savior complex.

We'd love to see anyone reading this textbook consider how to infuse their poetic projects with such self-reflective honesty as Taylor's, such confidence and conviction as Simpson's, such careful consideration of how history creates the present as we see in Reeves's work, the healing potential of imagination in poems like Girmay's, and such imaginative leaps into other ways of being and knowing as we see in Bolina's.

INVITATIONS TO REFLECT

Discuss Together

Who are your ideal readers and what kind of relationship with them do you want your poems to nurture? What assumptions about you as the writer or themselves as readers would you like to reinforce or unsettle? What complicities do you want to hold yourself accountable for? How do the poems in this chapter help you imagine ways to implement these aspirations for your writing?

For Further Study

Consider your favorite contemporary poetry collections. In what ways do they engage with the racial imaginary? How do these ways also intersect with other lineages you've read about in this textbook, and how do those intersections complicate self-reflexivity, imaginative leaps, or other choices regarding rhetorical positioning of authors, speakers, and listeners? Try mapping these relationships as we do in earlier chapters, and then adding those nuances to your larger poetic lineage maps (see assignment in index).

Writing Exercises

1 The Invective

Bolina wrote an invective, a litany of insults. There is a fairly impressive literary tradition of such forms; oral traditions in West Africa and Scotland, as well as those among Black communities in the American South, to name a few, elevate the exchange of insults to a literary form. Try your own hand at it, but please, for the sake of your workshop community, pick a public figure, not a private citizen your classmates might know or meet some day. Like Bolina, be sure self-awareness and self-critique become a major subtext, or even the main thrust, of the poem.

2 Mapping, Naming, Remembering

Choose a statue, park, building, garden, or any other public monument that prominently features the name of some significant historical figure in your community. Research the history of that figure, as well as the history of that location. We recommend referring to sites like MappingPrejudice.umn.edu or DecolonialAtlas.wordpress.com to be sure you are getting a complete picture. Then, write a poem that tells the story of what that monument means to you and others in the community where you live.

3 Finding All the Threads You Weave

Try to notice the ways your everyday experiences are shaped by larger political forces. To write this poem you will first need to spend a day noticing. Create two columns in a notebook. Once an hour, stop and write on one side the things you are doing—eating a bagel, riding the subway, washing the dishes. In the other column write any and all news of the outside world you've heard—maybe the headlines on the radio or someone on the bus talking on the phone about their application for a green card or a petition someone shares on social media. For those of you who find your everyday activities bring you into painful awareness of political forces—maybe your list itemizes constant deflecting of microaggressions or hours of tedious paperwork necessary to safeguard your status in the country where you live—you might find it more productive to keep a separate column where you list the moments when you felt free or joyful or struck by something truly beautiful. Then write a poem that weaves all these facets of the world you experience and move through.

4 Building Houses for Our Mothers

With Aracelis Girmay's poem in mind, write a poem that is a vision of the world you want to live in. Make a list of what tendernesses and joys you want to call into being for others. Include in that list the memories of what the people in this future have overcome and how. Include the names of those who would otherwise have been forgotten. Like Girmay, make your poem a song by using repetition of images and syntax. Imbue your list with incantatory qualities through such repetition.

5 **The Collective Voice**

The call-and-response form is an ancient poetic form rooted in an oral tradition. It is often seen in ritual acts like church services, as well as public gatherings like rallies or sports events. Write a poem that makes use of the potential beauty of such repetition, as well as the power of many voices joining together in the same lines.

9

Writing in the Field

A FEW POEMS TO START US OFF . . .

In this chapter, we look at several lineages of ecopoetics, which is one way of referring to the poetry-branch of nature writing. You are likely familiar with religious devotionals and other odes that celebrate nature, and such pastoral views of farms and rural life that romanticize landscape. Too, there are biblical psalms, Indigenous creation stories and songs, and a long tradition of love poems across cultures that mirror or parallel human experiences with those of animal and plant creatures. We love these harmonic depictions of life on earth; in fact, ignoring these positive relationships undermines our role in that greater ecosystem. But too often, such nature poetry forgets to acknowledge the tensions between humanity and the rest of the natural world, including the many effects of capitalism, including ongoing colonization, resource extraction, garbage, and climate change. In this section, we aim to share all of these approaches to writing "in the field"—those that are celebratory and perhaps symbiotic, as well as those that acknowledge gender and race dynamics, such as the antipastoral; those that acknowledge environmental degradation, such as the necropastoral; and those that highlight gender and other forms of injustice, both merging and disrupting received uses of language and metaphor on the field of the page.

Vievee Francis

Another Antipastoral

I want to put down what the mountain has awakened.

My mouthful of grass.
My curious tale. I want to stand still but find myself moved patch by patch.
There's a bleat in my throat. Words fail me here. Can you understand? I sink to
my knees tired or not. I now know the ragweed from the goldenrod, and the blinding
beauty of green. Don't you see? I am shedding my skins. I am a paper hive, a wolf spider,
the creeping ivy, the ache of a birch, a heifer, a doe. I have fallen from my dream
of progress: the clear-cut glass, the potted and balconied tree, the lemon-waxed
wood over a marbled pillar, into my own nocturne. The lullabies I had forgotten.
How could I know what slept inside? What would rend my fantasies to cud and up
from this belly's wet straw-strewn field—

these soundings.

Jos Charles

From *FEELD*

i

thees wite skirtes / & orang
sweters / i wont / inn the feedynge marte /
wile mye vegetable partes bloome /
inn the commen waye / a grackel
inn the guarden rooste / the tall
wymon wasching handes /
or eyeing turnups
/ the sadened powres wee rub / so economicalie /
inn 1 virsion off thynges /
alarum is mye nayme
/ unkempt & handeld
i am hors /
i am sadeld / i am a brokn hors

Gerard Manley Hopkins

The Windhover

To Christ our Lord

I caught this morning morning's minion, king-
  dom of daylight's dauphin, dapple-dawn-drawn Falcon, in his riding
  Of the rolling level underneath him steady air, and striding
High there, how he rung upon the rein of a wimpling wing
In his ecstasy! then off, off forth on swing,
  As a skate's heel sweeps smooth on a bow-bend: the hurl and gliding
  Rebuffed the big wind. My heart in hiding
Stirred for a bird,—the achieve of, the mastery of the thing!

Brute beauty and valour and act, oh, air, pride, plume, here
  Buckle! AND the fire that breaks from thee then, a billion
Times told lovelier, more dangerous, O my chevalier!

  No wonder of it: shéer plód makes plough down sillion
Shine, and blue-bleak embers, ah my dear,
  Fall, gall themselves, and gash gold-vermilion.

Kim Hyesoon, translated by Don Mee Choi

All The Garbage Of The World, Unite!

On the seat you left, two beer bottles, a cigarette butt, two pieces of scratch paper.
Why are you screening my calls, my messages? Don't you have anything else to do?
You are the bourgeoisie of communication. Why am I always afraid of the phone?
When you look at me, I always feel as if I should change into something else.
How about changing myself into a bundle of clothes dumped on the sofa
or a pale pink wad of bubble gum dangling from someone's lips
like the poor tummies of all the animals that flail about when they are turned over?
Do you know?
Eyesnavel god. Forearmsearflap god.
Sweetpotatokneesappleseed god. Pigstoenailschick god.
Dreamingdivingbeetlesashtree god. Lovelygirlsheelstoenail god.
Antsghostscatseyeball god. Ratholescatsrottingwater god.
Mrsdustingarmselephant god. Salivadropexplodeslikefreongas.
Salivafountainevenmoremortifyingnauseatingthanthesmelloflionsrotten breath god.
Do you know all the dearest gods that are hanging onto our limbs?
On the seat you left, a wet towel, a wad of gum, a crushed tomato.
Dear blackgarbagebags who thankfully lent each one of their bodies.
Dear foldedarms of the window and concrete and steel under my feet.
How high the armsofthemachinehammers that beat down steadily upon
those foldedarms.
All the pigs of the world unite god. All the cats of the world let's become a butter god.
Dear wrists escape from the arms god. Heap of curses, mackerel corpses spit out from a soccer player's mouth god. There are 3 million gods in India. How many people live there?
Dearest multiple gods that have swarmed in from the sky, land, sea.
On the seat you left, I sit like a garbage god, and do you or don't you know
that I wait for the green truck heading to the landfill like the dearest dirtiest loftiest god
who has long endured till now because of its hunger for humans?
Do you or don't you know that every day our hair falls and mixes with the melting water of an iceberg in the faraway sea?
Yournostrilssingledropofapricklynosehairearth god!

Inger Christensen, translated by Susanna Nied

From *Alphabet*

1

apricot trees exist, apricot trees exist

2

bracken exists; and blackberries, blackberries;
bromine exists; and hydrogen, hydrogen

3

cicadas exist; chicory, chromium,
citrus trees; cicadas exist;
cicadas, cedars, cypresses, the cerebellum

4

doves exist, dreamers, and dolls;
killers exist, and doves, and doves;
haze, dioxin, and days; days
exist, days and death; and poems
exist; poems, days, death

5

early fall exists; aftertaste, afterthought;
seclusion and angels exist;
widows and elk exist; every
detail exists; memory, memory's light;
afterglow exists; oaks, elms,
junipers, sameness, loneliness exist;
eider ducks, spiders, and vinegar
exist, and the future, the future

DISCUSSION

Field of work. Field of the page. To field a question. Questioning the field. To go afield. Field studies. "The absence / of field."

This last fragment here is from Mark Strand, from his poem, "Keeping Things Whole," in which he also writes, "I move / to keep things whole." We understand this well—moving through the field, the field moving through us, wholly.

When people ask Maya how she became a poet, she tells them that as a child, she learned about the music of language when she was fiercely hungry, listening to rain on a barn roof where she hid from her family, or watching the river's dents and ripples float around a snag, a salmon fry dart in the shallows; when she was curious how the broad bells of foxglove flowers or the aromatic, tight constellations of clover blossoms translated to taste, she placed them on her tongue. These experiences, she admits with a mix of wistfulness and self-deprecation for that wistfulness, were her first poetry—a combination of dreamspell and duende, a kind of embodied ecopoetics—and she heard them, felt them, her body humming with the need to act or imbibe. Rhythms and images of the natural world gave way organically to reading, mostly books from public libraries or classrooms. Maya found herself practicing close reading, and then writing, as she tried to recreate that magic she felt when immersed, by necessity—via all her senses—in the cow field, on her back, sometimes in wonder and others in terror, under the vast stitches of stars on the fabric underbelly of the firmament.

So when she read Gerard Manley Hopkins, and Walt Whitman's "Noiseless Patient Spider" ("Till the gossamer thread you fling catch somewhere, O my soul"), and Elizabeth Bishop's "The Fish" (where oil had spread a rainbow / around the rusted engine), and other oft-anthologized works in her high school English classes, it became clear that there were entire generations of poets celebrating and singing the rot and riot of season and place—situating their work with and in "the natural world" across the globe—and she was thrilled to find her people existed, too, among humans, and among those who love words.

You may be familiar with poems such as these, or the stark image-rhythms of Sappho and Lu Chi. These might all be considered "of the field," and in these cases, somewhat celebratory. As Maya learned when she left her rural upbringing, there are also poets writing antipastorals and necropastorals, and poets situating themselves specifically as bodies endangered by the same forces of power that endanger our planet. Bishop's begin to get closer to that impulse—we see the motor oil make a rainbow in the water—though we don't see the poisonous effects. Or we don't see how a poem that takes place in a café, questioning a compostable cup, or in a farmer's market, delighting in and yet being disturbed by the handling of "vegetable parts," is equally a poem of that wide meadow of nature that is also the human experience. We plan to show you some discussion of this braided and diverting lineage, and a short menu of such works here, which we hope offers a rhizomatic scope of what ecopoetics traditions exist and which might still be out there in the open field.

Attention, Wonder, and Some Global Origins

To write "in the field," one must set forth with equal amounts curiosity and listening, wonder and observing, attention to mystery and doubt (and, of course, with the considerations of our previous chapters in mind!). Writing in the field involves close attention, via one's sensory observations and perceptions, but it also involves the act of making something from place, of place, with place, *by* that specific place, nearly on its behalf—but also, in a sense, to become the "absence of field," through creation of a new entity—imagining that entity into being. One approach / critical lens to this process is called *ecopoetics*, from the Greek "oikos" and "poïesis," *house / family* plus *making / creating*, or making a home, and deals with humans' impact on or interaction with their environment. The term itself came into use in the late twentieth-century, coinciding with Jonathan Skinner's journal of the same name, and like many traditions, gave name to something with an existing and rich history, not just of theme and content, but as a way of mapping a system, even perhaps a form.

Sometimes called nature writing or environmental writing (and sometimes related to "writing about place"), ecopoetics isn't new. One may argue the tradition originates from ancient China's mountains and rivers poetry (Shanshui), or from the Greek, or from Indigenous oral traditions. We suspect it has not one, but many origins, and that each culture has its own historic "field" writing, its own manner of existing within imagination's swirl across time. In their introduction to *Native Voices: Indigenous American Poetry, Craft and Conversations,* CMarie Fuhrman and Dean Rader write "Indigenous poetry is not just a *field of subject matter,* but a way of being in the world" (xxv). And in Lu Chi's *Wen Fu*, or ars poetica, he recognizes that "In a single meter of silk, the infinite universe exists; language is a Great Flood from a small corner of the heart." This is ecopoetic if we've ever heard it; Lu Chi recognizing that silk isn't simply a metaphor, but rather, *is* language itself—the poem of the silkworm, the worm's writing being what it must do to live (and if you're interested in silk as sacred and received expression, check out Jen Bervin's *Silk: Poems,* an introduction to which is linked in our online companion). In silk is Ezra Pound's "natural object [as] adequate symbol," except, not merely a symbol: a *life*. And not an object, either: the Great Flood as it was, plainly, with its power as a force of communicating a feeling. From the Greek poet Sappho's "And her light / stretches over salt sea / equally and flowerdeep fields" to the Psalms of the King James Bible, ecopoetics stretches across the earth and through various cultures and time periods. But this history—from devotionals and pastoralism to observational, documentary, and inhabited nature writing, to writing nature and finally, ecopoetics—isn't, as you may imagine, easily championed by its privileged present. And, when a poet goes afield to make a home or simply commune among the plants and animals who also live in that space, the poet cannot ignore whose lands—plant, animal, cultural—they occupy, which ancestries belong to that place. Each poet walking into the field to observe, record, imagine, and create must map that place back through the blooms and thorns of time and human interaction.

There are many contemporary poets whose work one might consider ecopoetic. We suggest you check out those mentioned in this chapter, as well as anthologies such as *Black Nature* by Camille Dungy, or *Indigenous Literatures from Micronesia* by Craig Santos Perez, and the many poets listed and linked via our online anthologies.

Devotionals, Moments of Time, and other Celebratory Poetics

As partially noted above, there exist a wealth of poets from a hundred and even thousands of years ago whose work engages with the natural world in ways that have been variously classified as devotional and celebratory, what we might call odes, myths, and / or creation stories. Sometimes, these celebrations have couched within them complex critiques and reflections on humanity's trespasses. Think, for example, of the rhetorical capabilities of haiku, or hokku, you've read, which sometimes celebrate an image-moment, isolating and lifting, through a few brief words, a mountain peak or a pond or the movements of an animal. Some haiku also take on direct political moves, or speak back to ancestries. In his essay, "Haiku Poetics: Objective, Subjective, Transactional & Literary Theories," Randy Brooks notes that "Haiku are a rhetorical act—an attempt by the writer to share with a reader an observation or heartfelt insight referring to a perception or imagination of reality through the use of artistically-constructed language." He also notes that there are a multitude of ways to write haiku and a range of traditions that influence haiku poetics which have influenced many contemporary uses of form and brevity: Mita Mahato's abbreviated extinction limericks, in Sound, Shape, & Space, merge such nuances, while also celebrating what is possible with recycled form, language, and tangible materials.

In Western traditions, devotionals and reflections often take the shape of an intense focus on symbolic or natural image: consider British poet William Wordsworth's daffodils, which he saw "ten thousand . . . at a glance," "Beside the lake, beneath the trees, / Fluttering and dancing in the breeze," or American Modernist Emily Dickinson's deceptively simple descriptions of a bird, who "drank a Dew / From a convenient Grass - / And then hopped sidewise to the Wall / To let a Beetle pass." (Dickinson's poems, by the way, can all be sung to the hymn of the church tune, "Amazing Grace"—try it! . . . and Wordsworth believed that poems record those sacred "spots in time" when we are influenced by the gravity and levity of a moment.) No doubt you know H.D., as well, American Imagist poet and writer from the turn of the century who we can look to for essentializing and complicating the nature-canon tradition, whose poems, like Dickinson's, often celebrated the tangled wildness of both her own mind and body and the indeterminate spaces of the natural world, such as in "Sea Rose," or "Oread" (if you don't know them, you can find links to these via our online companion), both odes and also charms that draw us away from what's conjured to consider our minuteness and obfuscation in a planet whose magic mere humans could never begin to understand.

And then, of course, there's Gerard Manley Hopkins, British poet-priest whose verses were devotional, to be sure, but also—by his own goals—following the natural rhythms of speech, to document such body-felt moments as "the heart stirred / for a bird" or his pleasure and wonder at light "like shook foil." Hopkins is widely known for inventing "sprung rhythm," a style of prosody shaped not by counting every syllable but instead by marking and counting only stressed syllables—so a line might end up being 10 or 16 syllables but containing only five stressed ones. Hopkins also coined the term "inscape," which Denise Levertov, who you may remember reading about in Sound, Shape, & Space, later used to describe, at length, the ways organic form—through poems—offers a shape for what gathers in us, emotionally, and must be brought forth in language.

A bit of a tortured soul himself, upon entering the priesthood Hopkins first lit fire to his poems, believing his obsession with verses to be a sacrilegious distraction. However, walking the meadows of Oxfordshire, he found he couldn't stop writing; Hopkins oscillated between agony over his love for language and his love for God. His poem, "The Windhover," is dedicated by its epigraph "To Christ Our Lord," but without that, it could easily be a love poem to the bird itself, to how it hovers and trembles in the air, riding a warm breeze as it hunts. Or, it (the bird! / the poem!) could be an ars poetica, and therefore a love poem to language. A Petrarchan sonnet in sprung rhythm, the poem dips and rolls through the air of the page, winging itself to us in the first five lines thus:

> I caught this morning morning's minion, king-
> dom of daylight's dauphin, dapple-dawn-drawn Falcon, in his riding
> Of the rolling level underneath him steady air, and striding
> High there, how he rung upon the rein of a wimpling wing
> In his ecstasy! then off, off forth on swing,

Hopkins' language is over-full of sound and therefore celebration: "I caught this morning morning's minion, king-," he begins; couldn't he have simply said, "I saw a bird this morning"? However, he "caught" it, as in a brief capture, by eye and with words. Repeating "morning" underscores the time of day and reiterates that the bird is the follower—or minion—of morning, personifying morning as one who has power and agency. Too, breaking on "king," fracturing "kingdom" in two allows the half-word to become an appositive for the bird, which is now a follower of morning but also "king" of it, both servant and leader, until the word enjambs to become "kingdom of daylight's dauphin," dauphin being, of course, the son of a king, here as in, son of daylight, and the bird also a kingdom of daylight's son. Without time to pause and digest these appositives (or renamings), Hopkins plows forward with "dapple-dawn-drawn Falcon," offering not only the alliteration for momentum and playfulness, but also an internal slant rhyme (the echo surely a sign of parallelism!) between "dauphin" and "Falcon," giving them each a kind of leaping resonance, and calling back to "minion" by ending in the "n" sound, so all three namings become image rhymes, too. One could learn a lot about odes from Hopkins—picking up on the use of appositives, sound rhyme to indicate image rhyme, line break as hinge-image, allowing for imagistic and narrative pause, and conceptual accretion—as each image builds on the last, we "see" the windhover hovering on the wind, and in the poet's heart, also hovering, whirling its wings about, making him wonder and spill his wonder into words.

The Three E's: Ecopoetics, Ethnopoetics, and Ethical Positionality

You know, of course, that rhythm is an essential part of poetics, and that poetry has a long history of oral and other performative traditions. One such culturally specific intersection with ecopoetics is *ethnopoetics,* the study of language in oral literature. It exists both behind and adjacent to "nature writing," itself an ecotone (area of convergence between ecosystems) if you will, as a genre. Poet and scholar Christopher Arigo notes that an ecopoet is "an interdisciplinary creature, whose purview includes science and the arts," and that a good ecopoem is "a house made founded on the tension between the cutting edge of innovation and ecological thinking." These concerns recall our first chapter, on space, shape, and form, and our second one, which picks up a form of voice with the lyric "I," as well as our later chapter (next to this one), on documentary poetics. We would also point you here to poets such as Jen Bervin, with her seven-year international research project on silkworms, ending in a poem composed—in the voice of a mother silkworm!—on a silk genome, which, compatible with human tissue, is implanted in a person, the "listener" or recipient of the book-length silkworm - monologue. We also recommend you check out the ethnobotanist Irish poet Siobhan Campbell, whose poems embed oral traditions of Ireland as well as her botanical understandings. You'll also find, linked in our online companion, the work of Sherwin Bitsui, who begins his 2009 book, *Flood Song,* with the Navajo word for water: *tó,* repeated five times, so both in isolation and accumulation it sounds like raindrops. Lovely, right? But Bitsui is also wary of having his work overly romanticized. In an interview with *Guernica,* he notes: "as a native writer, there's the politics of having to represent nature as somehow idealized and somehow still existing in its pure state. And I think that the world that I am aware of, that I am bringing into the poems, has elements of technology mixing with natural elements." Bitsui voices part of what we want to underscore, too—contemporary poets, writing in any tradition that exists at the intersection of cultures and influences, must consider the ethics of their own positionalities. What we mean by this is *who they are* in relation to *the subjects they approach* and *the ways they approach those subjects.*

Anyone wishing to write in ethnopoetic documentary traditions should consider the romance of myth, alongside the author's role as an "eye" gazing outward and an "I" sometimes looking inward, and also the ways that power and privilege play into such textual creations and disseminations. While this certainly begins with acknowledging and respecting the inherent value and—dare we say?—voice of the flora, fauna, and people afield, it also involves asking ourselves why we are the ones to tell this story, to celebrate this life circumstance. In her 2021 book *Appropriate: A Provocation*, composed as letters to students, addressing concerns regarding approximation and appropriation in literary writing (and which we also discuss in The Racial Imaginary), Paisley Rekdal provides a list of questions that might "help writers reevaluate the spirit and intent of their project, to clarify both their depiction of the identities on the page and perhaps their creative resolve." We find these questions helpful in our own classrooms and, frankly, in our discussions with peers, and recommend this book as a useful text for anyone who wishes to reflect upon their own writing ethics.

To understand how the ethics of positionality and identity might intersect with a participatory critique of a canon of white nature writers, we turn for a moment back to the pastoral. Remember Wordsworth's "I Wandered Lonely as a Cloud," or—though not brought up here yet—Marlowe's "The Passionate Shepherd to His Love?" Those poems are examples of pastoralism, that long tradition that romanticizes rural landscapes and living, tracing its roots back to Greek poet Hesiod's *Works and Days*, which followed farm labor and agrarian lifestyle, and Italian poet Virgil's *Georgics*, with those shining plow blades and straining oxen. These were largely poems of masculine labor and desire, which rarely represented the myriad experiences of genders beyond the cishet male. We hope to suggest here a few contemporary poems and lineages which, while certainly in the ecopoetic traditions, operate quite differently from these narratives, and, in fact, challenge them. We'll begin with Vievee Francis and "Another Antipastoral," which both embodies that critique and also offers a new way to consider the lineage altogether. We also invite you to go back to Josefina de la Torre in Duende, Deep Image, & the Poetics of Spells and Indigenous poet M.L. Smoker in Telling Secrets, each of whom reckons with ways of representing place and image.

The Antipastoral, Necropastoral, and Field of the Page

Writing into and against traditional pastoralism are contemporary poets like Vievee Francis. Her book, *Forest Primeval*, which inverts the phrase *primeval forest,* offers reversals that reckon her literary and cultural ancestry through ecology and myth. A primeval forest is an old growth forest, also called *virgin forest,* that has, for the most part, grown undisturbed for thousands of years, and therefore contains a symbiosis of native species in feedback loops, multiple canopies, and an overall balance in what's called a *climax community.* Grammatically inverting the term primeval forest, putting the noun first and modifier second, yet keeping the language intact, suggests both ode and elegy to that ecological balance, and a linguistic reversal of colonial language, asking us to reconsider other structures: human and animal. Participating in and equally challenging received traditions, Francis opens the book with an almost-sonnet, 14 irregular lines, "Another Antipastoral," which rewrites history and acknowledges, with "another," that she is part of a broad movement addressing and remaking a canon.

Francis's speaker begins in the shadow of a mountain—perhaps evoking the tradition of mountain poetry—and puts down what that "mountain has awakened." The physical caesura of that space between strophes acts as a colon might, signifying what comes after is a list of what that speaker lays down, what she owns and lets go: "My mouthful of grass. / My curious tale." Moving immediately into animal consciousness, Francis's speaker has a "mouthful of grass," "a bleat in [her] throat," inhabiting that non-human mind, even before telling us she's morphing into it: "a paper hive, / a wolf spider, / the creeping ivy, the ache of a birch, a heifer, a doe." The language of humans "fails [her] here." That speaker "now know[s] the ragweed from the goldenrod," the former being wind pollinated and the latter insect pollinated; ragweed is the allergen, goldenrod good for ecosystems. Part of shedding the Christian allegory of Bunyan's "Pilgrim's Progress" as well as Milton's "Paradise Lost," that speaker "fall[s] from [her] dream of progress," which is the modernist urban: "the clear-cut glass, the potted and balconied tree, the lemon-waxed wood" (which we can imagine, is polished with store-bought Pledge, that domestic toxin sold as a beautifier of homes). Instead, the speaker goes into her "own nocturne," asking / invoking the listener with pleas, all along: "Can you understand?" "Don't you see?" and finally, as if to herself: "How could I know what slept inside?" The poem moves away from the external world, into something more primal, those forgotten lullabies awakening and surging forth. The gut biome *becomes* the field, as that speaker "rend[s] [her] fantasies to cud and up," from it, suggesting the cud is fantasies digested in a bovine or Cervidae stomach (deer, like cows, have four stomachs). This return to "animal" existence involves science and a deep knowledge of how the body works, recalling by soundings.

As Francis so aptly demonstrates, writing in the field—and in the absence of field—is like being alive: it isn't always easy or beautiful; it isn't always about flourish and bloom. It involves, too, extinction, pollution, and human avarice. Enter in poetry the *necropastoral.* Writes Joyelle McSweeney in her Harriet (Poetry Foundation) blog on the subject, "The Necropastoral is a political-aesthetic zone in which the fact of mankind's depredations cannot be separated from an experience of 'nature' which is poisoned, mutated, aberrant, spectacular, full of ill effects and affects." This means presentation of the beautiful includes, in the same frame, the complicated.

One of our favorite works in this field is Danish poet Inger Christensen's *Alphabet,* a book whose structure is based on the mathematical Fibonnaci sequence (in which each number is the sum of the previous two numbers), following the pattern of an unfurling fern, or a snail, or a hurricane. Likewise, the book-length poem is an *abecedarian*, moving from a catalog of what exists in the natural world to including hydrogen bombs and other human-made atrocities, but with a kind of building momentum, grounding nostalgia, an ode to such complicated existence. Says Susanna Nied, Christensen's translator, "Part of Inger's gift is this uncanny ability to be simultaneously specific and universal." In her translation of *Alphabet,* an excerpt of which you can read in this chapter anthology, Nied is able to factor in attention to music as well as form, moving us into the poet's incantatory ecosystem of verse.

Merging the concrete and abstract, *Alphabet* participates in several traditions at once: ecopoetics, docupoetics (see the chapter "Docupoetics & Other Forms of Lyric Research" for more), science / nature poetry, organic form (which we discuss in, "Space, Sound, and Shape"), poetry in translation, political / activist verse, ode and elegy, and orality (this poem is definitely one to read aloud!). It asks us to consider humans' role in the planet's evolution and how our interference is both nature and anti-nature.

Yet another poet dealing in the necropastoral is Kim Hyesoon, as translated from the Korean by Don Mee Choice. In her title poem from *All the Garbage of the World Unite*, Hyesoon opens with beer bottles and a cigarette butt, but moves rather quickly through a series of questions to compound-noun-gods that evoke nature as detritus. The opening "breakup" imagery and narrative of "On the seat you left, two beer bottles, a cigarette butt, two pieces of scratch paper. / Why are you screening my calls, my messages? Don't you have anything else to do? / You are the bourgeoisie of communication. Why am I always afraid of the phone?" quickly becomes "Do you know? / Eyesnavel god. Forearmsearflap god. / Sweetpotatokneesappleseed god." This movement is certainly through a different kind of "field" than we see in

Bervin, Christensen, or Francis, but with those clinging Frankengods made of rat holes and pigs' toenails, of salivadrops and sweepotatoknees, it is nevertheless merging beauty with poison, claiming they are all artifact and all diety. Deifying nosehairs feels nearly transcendentalist, Romantic, calling back to those who might stand on a precipice over the sea, thinking themselves the center of the world, asking, "Do you or don't you know that every day our hair falls and mixes with the melting / water of an iceberg in the faraway sea?"

This reality of monstrous decomposition, of recomposing a self which remains nevertheless permeable, is one operative mode of much contemporary writing that merges human and nature. In a lot of her work, Hyesoon could be classified as confessional (see "Telling Secrets"), conversational (see "The Poem in the Telephone Lines"), Surrealist (see "Writing Out of Surrealism"), and, of course, ecopoetic. Hyesoon is emblematic of much contemporary verse that blends the external with the personal and infuses modes.

Related to Hyesoon in that pursuit is the last "in the field" poet we want to discuss in this chapter, Jos Charles, one example of poets who use the field of the page—that is, employing negative space as a grammar, invoking physical caesura as a form of punctuation. Jos Charles' *FEELD* engages a blend of Chaucerian influence and textspeak, as well as a variety of ways to create caesura: negative space, enjambment, and back slashes (employed in a poem how they would be in an academic paper). This variety of elision, omission, and ways to indicate breath or thought-gaps helps the reader listen / think about how a trans body and mind blend—the speaker beginning by walking into a street fair / farmers' market, where they ground us in orange and purple, colors opposite on the wheel, in fabrics and birds and the body, "hors," "sadeld:"

thees wite skirtes / & orang
sweters / i wont / inn the feedynge marte /
wile mye vegetable partes bloome /
inn the commen waye / a grackel

. . .

inn 1 virsion off thynges /
alarum is mye nayme
/ unkempt & handeld
i am hors /
i am sadeld / i am a brokn hors

Charles' embrace of animal as a way to be, "inn 1 version of thyngs," in the field, has her speaker confessing "i am hors / I am sadeld / I am a broken hors," implying by sonic echo—for this poem operates a much by sound as it does concept, in fact, inseparably—that the self is horse, hoarse, also whores—we aren't sure which of these is saddled, broken. But we know the field, including as it does a canon that disallows a trans body, necessitates a re-writing.

Writing "In the field" means studying the stitches from the back of the fabric, ripping out those we feel need restitching. This place is where each poet begins: questioning the field, moving into it with senses alert, going forth with curiosity and wonder, and with the desire to learn and interpret and imagine anew.

INVITATIONS TO REFLECT

Discuss Together

In this chapter we described how ecopoetics is a field that contains poems of praise and celebration alongside poems of lamentation and critique. In recent contemporary poems especially, these notes often exist side by side in the same poem. But what about your poetics? To what degree do you want your poems to uplift, call out, call in, or protest? To what degree do you see the poems at the beginning of this chapter responding to one or more of these impulses?

For Further Study

Choose a book or journal in the ecopoetic tradition and study it for how it engages with ecology, environment, etc. in form and subject. What moves does the author make in their pursuit of "field" writing? What do they add to the "field" of poetics? Do the poems' structures or that of the book's seem to match an ecological construct (in other words, how do they use the field of the page, and the field of the book object)? In addition to those poets and collections referenced in this chapter, check out our online companion.

Writing Exercises

If you find yourself wanting to write in these traditions, here are a few approaches you might try. Feel free to blend / overlap / mix these. For example, you might mix 1 & 5, or 2 & 3. You might also consider mixing these with some from the Docupoetics chapter or from the Telling Secrets chapter.

1 **The Lyric [M]Ode**

Odes are one of the oldest forms of lyric poetry and are often employed by those writing into nature as ways of zooming in on, celebrating, and singing, a plant, animal, or scientific occurrence. From Hopkins' "The Windhover" to Muriel Rukeyser's "Conjugation of the Paramecium" to Melissa Kwasny's catalog of Montana plants in her collection *Thistle,* to Ross Gay's joyful ruminations from his garden, to Dorianne Laux's "A Short History of the Apple," the ode allows for exuberance or meditative turns. Choose one species and observe it, research it, study it as a naturalist would. Take notes. In addition to whatever else you note, write down at least 10 appositives (renamings, usually concrete noun phrases) for that thing. (For example, in Kwasny's poem "Common Blue," she refers to the butterfly as "the comma whose wings look battered.") Then, any cultural or associative connotations—which we like to think of as subject clusters—that would go with the topic (in Laux's "A Short History," she mentions Eve, Milton, Snow White, Halloween, etc.). With a focus on sound, weave together the most delicious images into an ode to your species. Try it in tercets or couplets to offer a lyric shape.

2 **Ecosystem or Pattern as Form**

In creative nonfiction, the hermit crab essay—a term pioneered by writer and educator Brenda Miller—is any essay that, like the hermit crab, borrows an existing natural form in which to live. Inger Christensen's *Alphabet,* which applies the natural / mathematical Fibonacci Sequence, spiraling with a litany of images that match the form, is a poetic example. Choose a naturally occurring pattern and shape that into a poetic form; fill with details that match your field study.

3 **Necropastoral and Frankengarbage**

Go for a walk around your city or town or ruralscape, writing down every image you see, hear, smell, feel: the ditch full of knapweed and Arby's cups, the billboard of fryers for sale above the large pots of geraniums and wave petunias wafting their pollens, the coo of a pigeon or whir of a metal crane, the ripple of siding on an apartment.

List it all. Then, ask yourself what your emotional landscape is like right now—are you in mourning? Celebration? Working your way through the aftermath of a large global event? List on another page all the feelings / ruminations / observations / meditations you have. Then, weave these together, merging your field of emotional space with your field of place, like Kim Hyesoon.

4 **The Absence of Field**

In Vievee Francis's "Another Antipastoral," she both acknowledges—via implied allusions—and rejects, via her inversion of grammar and use of the anti- prefix, the tradition into which she writes. Join Francis or some other poet you admire in writing the "anti-tradition," as in Tommy Pico's *Nature Poem* or Kim Hyesoon's *All the Garbage of the World Unite*, both necropastoral. Be sure to include, though, a "return" in some way to the animal / natural as part of the rejection of human traditions.

5 **Fact and Imagined Narrative Fracture: the Random Integer Generator**

We didn't have space in this chapter for every approach, but if you're looking for more, go to our online companion and read the entirety of Australian poet Joan Fleming's "A History of the Tanamite People" and Anne Carson's "By Chance the Cycladic People," which served as Fleming's inspiration. Note some of their techniques that you might like to try, saving them for later. Then, choose a familiar field subject to research further, and complete a working ethnography of "facts" about that subject—it could be an ecosystem or place, plant or animal, or an experience you've had (please, as we note in other chapters, be thoughtful about your positionality in relation to the subject). Try to list at least thirty facts, employing some of Fleming and Carson's approaches to the type of information gathered from the field (and in their case, imaginations), syntax, and sound. Then, like Fleming, whose study of "facts" brought her to a space of greater uncertainty, and therefore, imagination, play with order by employing a "random integer generator"—either printing out and cutting up, selecting strips one at a time to determine new order, or some other way of randomizing. Note how your fracture tends to create its own energy, how the field subject you're studying takes on a new lensing through fracture and reimagining. Note, too, how imagining is its own kind of fact-making, how facts are dependent upon who is doing the imagining, how fact isn't really fact at all.

6 **Repetition as Embodiment of Image or Sonic Echo Creating Image Rhyme**

We discuss in this chapter how Sherwin Bitsui's *Flood Song* begins with the Navajo word for water, "tó," which drips five times to invoke the accumulation that will eventually become the deluge. What word might you repeat, to begin accretion of image that represents growth / accumulation? Or, try it as Hopkins does: sonic echoes that gather words, across lines, into image rhyme and therefore parallel concepts: "dauphin," "Falcon,"and "minion," for example, merging into the imagined small-bird-king. Think of three words that almost rhyme, that all describe a concept you wish to embody, and use all three in proximity to one another in a poem. What wild imagining you might contribute to the field!

10

Docupoetics & Other Forms of Lyric Research

A FEW POEMS TO START US OFF . . .

In this chapter we'll be looking at poets whose work is rooted in research processes and whose craft involves experimenting with the formal and thematic possibilities made possible by placing that research alongside and within poetic concerns like lyricism. Often with inspiration from techniques common in documentary filmmaking or investigative journalism, poets working in this mode push the limits of what a poem is and what we ask it to do. We'll say more about all of this in the chapter, but first we want you to experience some poems that are often thought of as Docupoetic works and give you a chance to make observations and formulate your own questions about this style of poetry.

Layli Long Soldier

38

Here, the sentence will be respected.

I will compose each sentence with care, by minding what the rules of writing dictate.

For example, all sentences will begin with capital letters.

Likewise, the history of the sentence will be honored by ending each one with appropriate punctuation such as a period or question mark, thus bringing the idea to (momentary) completion.

You may like to know, I do not consider this a "creative piece."

I do not regard this as a poem of great imagination or a work of fiction.

Also, historical events will not be dramatized for an "interesting" read.

Therefore, I feel most responsible to the orderly sentence; conveyor of thought.

That said, I will begin.

You may or may not have heard about the Dakota 38.

If this is the first time you've heard of it, you might wonder, "What is the Dakota 38?"

The Dakota 38 refers to thirty-eight Dakota men who were executed by hanging, under orders from President Abraham Lincoln.

To date, this is the largest "legal" mass execution in US history.

The hanging took place on December 26, 1862—the day after Christmas.

This was the *same week* that President Lincoln signed the Emancipation Proclamation.

In the preceding sentence, I italicize "same week" for emphasis.

There was a movie titled *Lincoln* about the presidency of Abraham Lincoln.

The signing of the Emancipation Proclamation was included in the film *Lincoln;* the hanging of the Dakota 38 was not.

In any case, you might be asking, "Why were thirty-eight Dakota men hung?"

As a side note, the past tense of hang is *hung,* but when referring to the capital punishment of hanging, the correct past tense is *hanged.*

So it's possible that you're asking, "Why were thirty-eight Dakota men hanged?"

They were hanged for the Sioux Uprising.

I want to tell you about the Sioux Uprising, but I don't know where to begin.

I may jump around and details will not unfold in chronological order.

Keep in mind, I am not a historian.

So I will recount facts as best as I can, given limited resources and understanding.

Before Minnesota was a state, the Minnesota region, generally speaking, was the traditional homeland for Dakota, Anishinaabeg, and Ho-Chunk people.

During the 1800s, when the US expanded territory, they "purchased" land from the Dakota people as well as the other tribes.

But another way to understand that sort of "purchase" is: Dakota leaders ceded land to the US government in exchange for money or goods, but most importantly, the safety of their people.

Some say that Dakota leaders did not understand the terms they were entering, or they never would have agreed.

Even others call the entire negotiation "trickery."

But to make whatever-it-was official and binding, the US government drew up an initial treaty.

This treaty was later replaced by another (more convenient) treaty, and then another.

I've had difficulty unraveling the terms of these treaties, given the legal speak and congressional language.

As treaties were abrogated (broken) and new treaties were drafted, one after another, the new treaties often referenced old defunct treaties, and it is a muddy, switchback trail to follow.

Although I often feel lost on this trail, I know I am not alone.

However, as best as I can put the facts together, in 1851, Dakota territory was contained to a twelve-mile by one-hundred-fifty-mile-long strip along the Minnesota River.

But just seven years later, in 1858, the northern portion was ceded (taken) and the southern portion was (conveniently) allotted, which reduced Dakota land to a stark ten-mile tract.

These amended and broken treaties are often referred to as the Minnesota Treaties.

The word *Minnesota* comes from *mni,* which means water; and *sota,* which means turbid.

Synonyms for turbid include muddy, unclear, cloudy, confused, and smoky.

Everything is in the language we use.

For example, a treaty is, essentially, a contract between two sovereign nations.

The US treaties with the Dakota Nation were legal contracts that promised money.

It could be said, this money was payment for the land the Dakota ceded; for living within assigned boundaries (a reservation); and for relinquishing rights to their vast hunting territory which, in turn, made Dakota people dependent on other means to survive: money.

The previous sentence is circular, akin to so many aspects of history.

As you may have guessed by now, the money promised in the turbid treaties did not make it into the hands of Dakota people.

In addition, local government traders would not offer credit to "Indians" to purchase food or goods.

Without money, store credit, or rights to hunt beyond their ten-mile tract of land, Dakota people began to starve.

The Dakota people were starving.

The Dakota people starved.

In the preceding sentence, the word "starved" does not need italics for emphasis.

One should read "The Dakota people starved" as a straightforward and plainly stated fact.

As a result—and without other options but to continue to starve—Dakota people retaliated.

Dakota warriors organized, struck out, and killed settlers and traders.

This revolt is called the Sioux Uprising.

Eventually, the US Cavalry came to Mnisota to confront the Uprising.

More than one thousand Dakota people were sent to prison.

As already mentioned, thirty-eight Dakota men were subsequently hanged.

After the hanging, those one thousand Dakota prisoners were released.

However, as further consequence, what remained of Dakota territory in Mnisota was dissolved (stolen).

The Dakota people had no land to return to.

This means they were exiled.

Homeless, the Dakota people of Mnisota were relocated (forced) onto reservations in South Dakota and Nebraska.

Now, every year, a group called the Dakota 38 + 2 Riders conduct a memorial horse ride from Lower Brule, South Dakota, to Mankato, Mnisota.

The Memorial Riders travel 325 miles on horseback for eighteen days, sometimes through sub-zero blizzards.

They conclude their journey on December 26, the day of the hanging.

Memorials help focus our memory on particular people or events.

Often, memorials come in the forms of plaques, statues, or gravestones.

The memorial for the Dakota 38 is not an object inscribed with words, but an *act.*

Yet, I started this piece because I was interested in writing about grasses.

So, there is one other event to include, although it's not in chronological order and we must backtrack a little.

When the Dakota people were starving, as you may remember, government traders would not extend store credit to "Indians."

One trader named Andrew Myrick is famous for his refusal to provide credit to Dakota people by saying, "If they are hungry, let them eat grass."

There are variations of Myrick's words, but they are all something to that effect.

When settlers and traders were killed during the Sioux Uprising, one of the first to be executed by the Dakota was Andrew Myrick.

When Myrick's body was found,

his mouth was stuffed with grass.

I am inclined to call this act by the Dakota warriors a poem.

There's irony in their poem.

There was no text.

"Real" poems do not "really" require words.

I have italicized the previous sentence to indicate inner dialogue, a revealing moment.

But, on second thought, the words "Let them eat grass" click the gears of the poem into place.

So, we could also say, language and word choice are crucial to the poem's work.

Things are circling back again.

Sometimes, when in a circle, if I wish to exit, I must leap.

And let the body   swing.

From the platform.

                    Out

                                        to the grasses.

Paisley Rekdal

Assemblage of Ruined Plane Parts, Vietnam Military Museum, Hanoi

My eye climbs a row of spoilers soldered
into ailerons, cracked bay doors haphazarded
into windows where every rivet bleeds
contrails of rust. An hour ago, the doctor's wand
waved across my chest and I watched blood
on a small screen get back-sucked
into my weakened heart. It's grown a hole
I have to monitor: one torn flap
shuddering an infinite ellipsis of gray stars
back and forth. *You're the writer,* the doctor said
in French. *Tell me what you see.* Easier to stand
in a courtyard full of tourists scrying shapes
from this titanic Rorschach. Here's a pump stub
shaped like a hand; something celled,
cavernously fluted as a lobster's
abdomen. How much work
it must have taken to drag these bits
out of pits of flame, from lake beds
and rice paddies, and stack them in layers:
the French planes heaped beneath
the American ones, while the Englishwoman
beside me peers into this mess
of metals, trying to isolate one image
from the rest. Ski boot buckle
or tire pump, she muses at me, fossilized
shark's jaw, clothespin, wasp's nest?
According to the camera, it's just a picture
changing with each angle, relic
turned to rib cage, chrome flesh
to animal: all the mortal details
enumerated, neutered. I watch her trace
an aluminum sheet torched across a thruster
as if wind had tossed a silk scarf
over a face. If she pulled it back, would I find
a body foreign as my own entombed
in here, a thousand dog tags
jangling in the dark? I tilt my head: the vision slides
once more past me, each plane reassembling

then breaking apart. Spikes of grief—
or is it fury?—throb across the surface.
Everything has a rip in it, a hole, a tear, the dim sounds
of something struggling to pry open
death's cracked fuselage. White sparks,
iron trails. My heart rustles
in its manila folder. How the doctor smiled
at the images I fed him: *A row of trees,* I said,
pointing at my chart. *Stone towers,*
a flock of backlit swallows—
                                        Now I kneel beside a cross
of blades on which the Englishwoman
tries to focus. *Do you think I'll get it*
all in the shot? she calls as she steps back.
Steps back and back. Something like a knife sheath.
Something like a saint's skull. The sky
floats past, horizon sucked into it. She won't.

Craig Santos Perez

From "*Understory*"

For my wife, Nālani, and our daughter, Kaikainali'i, on her first birthday

nālani clips
kaikainali'i's tiny

fingernails while
she sleeps—

"the rape
of oceania

began with
guam"—soldiers

invade okinawa,
hawai'i, the

philippines, and
south korea—

#yesallwomen
how do

[we] stop
kaikainali'i's body

from becoming
target practice—

bullets fragment
and ricochet—

nālani brushes
kaikainali'i's hair

when she
wakes, sings

the names
of body

parts in
hawaiian language—

who will
remember the

names of
girls disappeared

from reservations
and maquiladoras

from villages
and schools

#mmiw #mmaw
#bringbackourgirls

nālani gathers
the clippings

because even
[our] nails

are ten
percent water—

outside, mānoa
rain falls

as large
as eggs—

inside, nālani
lies on

her side
to breast-

feed kaikainaliʻi
in bed—

they fall
asleep facing

each other,
still latched—

i nestle
with them

and, for
a moment,

kaikainaliʻi smiles—
what does

she dream
about? her

deep breath
rises and

falls like
king tides—

her fragile
rib cage

appears and
disappears like

a coral
island crowning—

my daughter,
i know

our stories
are heavier

than stones,
but you

must carry
them with

you no
matter how

far from
home the

storms take
your canoe

because you
will always

find shelter
in our

stories, you
will always

belong in
our stories,

you will
always be

sacred in
our ocean

of stories—
hanom hanom

Philip Metres

Black Site (Exhibit I)

Whenever I saw

a fly in my cell

I was filled

with joy

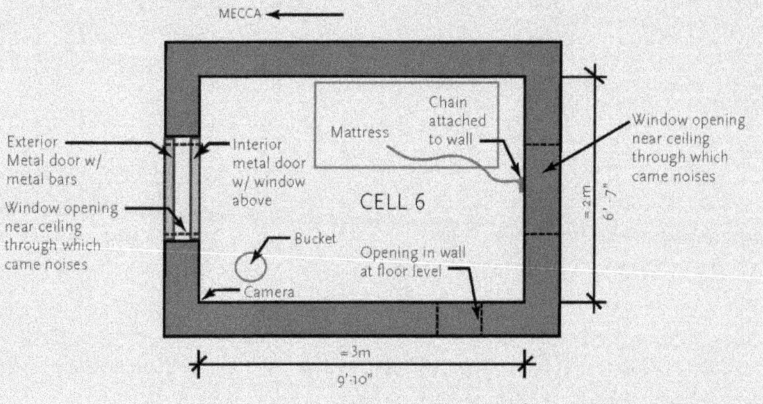

though I wished for it

to slip under the door

so it would not be

imprisoned itself

Marwa Helal

Census

Census. In the summer of 2000, there was a knock on our front door. Then the doorbell rang. My father answered it, "Hel-lo."

"Hi, I'm from the Census Bureau—do you have a few moments to answer a few follow-up questions about your Census form?"

"Shoor."

She looked down at her clipboard. "Well, Sir, it looks like you checked a few boxes for race, although it says there are only five people in your household."

"Yess?"

"How is that possible?"

Previously, my father had checked the form: White Non-Hispanic, African, African-American, Multiracial, and Other.

"Hang on, please. Just one second." He loudly called out, "yaa Aaazza, Maarrrwaa, Haaatem, Yaassserrr . . ." We gathered at the entrance in the order he had called us. "Look at my family and tell me what you see." A Biology professor, my father enjoyed challenging his students in the same way. She looked over our faces, each of us a different shade ranging from my mother's ivory skin to my father's dark summer brown—my brothers and me the gradients between.

My father went on with his lesson (she may as well have come over to ask about the binomial nomenclature of some plants in the yard)." We are from Egypt." A fan of the Socratic method, he went on. "Do you know where Egypt is?"

"Africa?" She replied hesitantly.

"Would this qualify us as African-American?" He didn't wait for her answer this time. "We get mistaken for just about everything around here and not one of us is the same color as the other. So," he paused. "I checked everything that applied . . ."

By 1924, there were about 200,000 Arabs living in the United States[1] and by 2000, at least 3.5 million Americans were of Arab descent[2].

It is 2010. A census form arrives in the mail.

I check OTHER and write-in: A-R-A-B.

In 2016, Obama wants to add a new racial category and has chosen an acronym to describe a group of people: MENA (Middle Eastern and North African)[3].

.

I note the absence of the word "Arab."

Still, they do not sense us[4].

1. "Arab-American History." 2010. Arab-American National Museum. N.p., Web. 29 Apr 2010.
2. "Arab-American Demographics." 2010. Arab American Institute. N.p., Web. 16 May 2010.
3. ". . . as it's called by population scholars—is broader in concept than Arab (an ethnicity) or Muslim (a religion). It would include anyone from a region of the world stretching from Morocco to Iran, and including Syrian and Coptic Christians, I[—]li Jews and other religious minorities." excerpt: "White House wants to add new racial category for Middle Eastern people," Korte, Gregory, USA Today. N.p., Web. 30 Sept 2016.
4. "US Census fails to add MENA category: Arabs to remain 'white' in count." 2018. N.p., Web. 27 Jan 2018.

Kiki Petrosino

Instructions for Time Travel

You must go through Mr. Jefferson
along his row of chinaberry trees

behind the ruined smokehouse
in unmarked tracts, under fieldstones

with no carvings, no monuments
with a few leaves shadowing the mulch

near scattered weeds, in sunken lines
while the sun walks in the day

at the end of the day
in an oval of brushed earth

just as the soft path finishes
under branches

where the dead are always saying
what they always say:

Write about me.

DISCUSSION

During the years we were writing this book we would often meet in Port Townsend, a little town on the Olympic Peninsula known for its writing residencies, writers' conference, and arts community. In one direction we could see Mt. Baker and the Cascade range stretched out on the other side of the Puget Sound. In the other direction the Salish Sea reaching into what seemed like the night sky at the edge of the world. Sometimes we took breaks to walk in the woods at Fort Worden State Park, a place filled with the ruins of army barracks, bunkers, defense batteries, hidden gun emplacements, and other signs of American militarization.

One of the reasons we love to wander in this place is because we watch with each passing year how the trees, the fungi, the rain, and the slugs soften these terribly sharp edges. One of the concrete walls is so thick with mosses and lichens now that passersby pick up sticks and etch their names or the names of their beloveds into the green. Whoever comes after them reads these wishes and longings, at first clearly, later as ghostly shadows, and finally just as the barely perceptible shade on which some new dream has been written or new plant has grown.

Everywhere you or I or any of us goes, we leave our mark. And the land remembers. Certainly, the S'Klallam land, stolen, militarized, extracted, and even now clutched and claimed by various layers of settler governments, remembers what has happened here. We try, always, to hear these memories on our walks, complicit beneficiaries as we are of settler colonialism; we read the interpretive plaques, the brochures, the Point No Point Treaty of 1855. We also read the field guides—the one Kate keeps in an app on her phone and the one a lifetime living in the Pacific Northwest has burnished within Maya's body (this, she says to Kate with some degree of self-deprecation for her complicity in ruin, is her own embodied poetics). We read the moss, the birds, the too-muchness of invasive poison hemlock, the absence of the sunflower sea stars and the scarcity of seals.

As we walk in this place, we talk about what poems to include in this chapter, what advice to give. One of us recounts for the other how fragments of Sappho's lost poems were found by archeologists combing through the ancient trash heap at Oxyrhynchus looking for documents, perhaps on papyrus or pottery or soup bones or talismans, that would show how these ancestors once lived. Inside a mummified crocodile, researchers found scraps of paper, used as stuffing. On one side, a shopkeeper's ledger counted the money that had come in and goods that had gone out. On the other side were lines of poetry that had been lost for 3,000 years.

One of us says docupoetics isn't even just about documents, though. It's about how everything we do is research. All experience is a kind of text you can read for meaning if you try. One of us worries that's too broad to be helpful to students. One of us thinks we don't give students enough credit for appreciating the murky, the inexplicable, the tidal zones of betweenness in poetry.

Both of us think you'll find it helpful to know a document is a recording of a transaction, interaction, or event. It might be a kind of evidence. If enough time has passed, a piece of trash might become a document. A document like a treaty might look like it documents rights, permissions, and entitlements. Read more closely, it might be understood as evidence of a land grab, war crimes, genocide.

An archive is a place where documents are collected. It might be the basement of a library or a box of photographs in a grandmother's attic, your family advice on beekeeping, or the file folder where someone who loves you stores all the little rhymes you ever wrote for them.

A documentary is a piece of art, like a film or an essay or a poem, crafted from documents like these.

We walked and we talked about poems and history and reclamation and restoration. We also talked about our children and people we missed and what we were afraid of. We talked about how grateful we are. And we chuckled to notice that all of this, too, is a kind of research; all of this knowledge is documented on a screen or on paper or in the rings of years at the heart of the madrona trees stretching their branches up the bluff and across the paths, and in the way we remember what each other said. This chapter too is a document and a documentary.

Written in the Grass

We have included Layli Long Soldier's "38" in this chapter as an example of a docupoetic work that draws on many kinds of sources. One of these sources is the grass, which holds a terrible memory many humans would rather forget. Long Soldier explains the significance of this source, writing:

> I started this piece because I was interested in writing about grasses. . . .
>
> One trader named Andrew Myrick is famous for his refusal to provide credit to Dakota people by saying, "If they are hungry, let them eat grass."

In this poem Long Soldier shows us how the grass itself holds one important part of the story of what happened to the Dakota people on the plains of Mnisota. The treaties the US government forced on the Dakota people also tell what happened, but you must learn to read them against their grain, to hear the violence and cruelty in the grammar of a language forced on a people by colonization. You must notice this grammar has separate words for murders and murders committed by the state, that this language obfuscates its commitment with legalistic loopholes.

> The US treaties with the Dakota Nation were legal contracts that promised money.
>
> It could be said, this money was payment for the land the Dakota ceded; for living within assigned boundaries (a reservation); and for relinquishing rights to their vast hunting territory which, in turn, made Dakota people dependent on other means to survive: money.
>
> The previous sentence is circular, akin to so many aspects of history.

Long Soldier's "38" does many things, and one of them is, through the use of poetic collaging and juxtaposition, to make these tricky and duplicitous documents reveal the truth of what happened. Another thing Long Soldier does with this poem is remind readers that this colonial language, with its uses of *hanged* and *hung* and *Indians* and *Let them eat grass*, is the same language many of us use when we try to make a poem. She writes:

> You may like to know, I do not consider this a "creative piece."
>
> I do not regard this as a poem of great imagination or a work of fiction.
>
> Also, historical events will not be dramatized for an 'interesting' read.

Throughout the poem the speaker resists any impulse to decorate or romanticize. She doesn't want to make the story dramatic (especially not in ways that center conflict, plot arcs, and resolution, as colonial narratives tend to) nor interesting (a trait of colonial journalism that follows principles like "if it bleeds, it leads"). Rather, the speaker wants to convey the circumstances of this atrocity in a way that untangles the colonizer myths of rights, entitlements, innocence, and heroism that government documents and the stories settler colonialists have told about those documents attempt to weave.

A Brief History of Docupoetics from Virgil's *Georgics* to the Present

There is a long tradition of poetry that combines nonfiction modes like investigative journalism, history, biography, etc. with the rhetorical tools and mood of lyric poetry. In his book about poetic forms, the poet Robert Hass suggested that the deeply researched, outward-facing, nonfiction poetry we currently call docupoetics is a modern-day incarnation of the Georgic. Georgics, which emerged in Ancient Greece, is a didactic or instructive poem intended to give information about a skill or important area of practical knowledge.

Though often associated with pastoral or nature poetry, Georgics only seem to be a form devoted to aspects of nature because they emerged during a pre-industrial age when all the skills a person could imagine required intimate engagement with the natural world. But really, both Georgics and Docupoetics are a type of poem that seeks to understand some facet of the world and a person's relationship to it.

To better understand how and why a poet might write a poem rooted in research, let's look at examples by the ancient Greek poet Virgil, and the contemporary US poet Paisley Rekdal. In his *Georgics*, Virgil devotes an entire book in verse to describing the work of beekeeping, offering practical advice like:

> First look for a site and position for your apiary,
> where no wind can enter (since the winds prevent them
> carrying home their food) and where no sheep or butting kids
> leap about among the flowers, or wandering cattle brush
> the dew from the field, and wear away the growing grass.

While, in her poem "Assemblage of Ruined Plane Parts, Vietnam Military Museum, Hanoi," Rekdal describes how a doctor monitors the speaker's heart condition in terms that are precise and attentive to the way a body works, as well as how someone might feel about living in it.

> [T]he doctor's wand
> waved across my chest and I watched blood
> on a small screen get back-sucked
> into my weakened heart. It's grown a hole
> I have to monitor.

Virgil uses descriptive detail, metaphors, and sound to make the bees seem as alive and their honey as delicious on the page as they are in life. He writes, "they keep the idle crowd of drones away from the hive. / The work glows, and the fragrant honey is sweet with thyme." Similarly, Rekdal seizes on opportunities to use lyric language that highlights beauty in the working of the world. She has the doctor say to the speaker, "*You're the writer . . . tell me what you see.*"

> *A row of trees*, I said,
> pointing at my chart. *Stone towers,*
> *a flock of backlit swallows—*

Classical Georgics are characterized by a certain degree of practicality—How wide should the entrance to a bee hive be? How much shade do they require? What should you do when they swarm? Docupoetics often has a similar note of pragmatism, as poets working in this vein don't want to merely describe beauty, but also to encourage action. Rekdal's poem is not just about a human heart that may be faltering. That imagery is juxtaposed against the wrenching and disturbing experience of visiting the Vietnam Military Museum in Hanoi, where she attempts to describe a sculpture made from pieces of machinery once used for death and destruction.

> Here's a pump stub
> shaped like a hand; something celled,
> cavernously fluted as a lobster's
> abdomen. How much work
> it must have taken to drag these bits
> out of pits of flame.

These observations serve the rhetorical purpose of building in readers a horror and resistance to the atrocities of war, which will hopefully have a galvanizing effect.

In this poem the reader can also see the poet questioning whether witnessing and recognizing these artifacts for what they are is really enough. She turns her attention to another woman in the museum who does not seem very deeply affected by the implications of a sculptural collage on display in the courtyard of a museum dedicated to commemorating a war without grief or apology. "*Do you think I'll get it / all in the shot?* she calls as she steps back. / Steps back and back. Something like a knife sheath." The reader is invited to wonder at the end whether the sculpture in the courtyard or this poem Rekdal has written does anything differently from what this woman does with her documentary eye. They are invited to consider whether they themselves in reading this poem have done anything more meaningful. Such questions, which are at the heart of docupoetics, provoke the reader to turn their gaze inward and undertake a meditation on accountability and complicity, to the important, practical work of identifying and confronting their own complicity in the ongoing machine of empire and war. For those of us living in a world with so many weapons of mass destruction, these questions of ethics and philosophy are not lofty, but are as pressing as how to care for the bees, goats, and grapes that would keep a family fed.

Like Virgil's Georgics, Craig Santos Perez's poem "Understory" seeks to convey crucial information about how to live as part of the human communities and beyond human ecosystems that shape and sustain the Pacific Islands. He writes,

> *you will*
> *always be*
>
> *sacred in*
> *our ocean*

of stories—
hanom hanom

Like Rekdal's poem, "Understory" also refuses to ignore the circumstances of this present moment in history, where colonialist violence and militarization threaten the speaker's communities. When thinking of how to prepare a child for adulthood, a parent must convey information about how to face violence and weapons, as much as they must remind a child how to know the tides and the corals.

#yesallwomen
how do

[we] stop
kaikainali'i's body

from becoming
target practice—

bullets fragment
and ricochet—

Though Perez's work is often described as "Ecopoetic," and would also fit comfortably in the chapter "Writing in the Field," we include his work here as an example of how poetry is often the vehicle through which Indigenous science and other forms of ancient knowledge, both nonfiction genres, are passed to the next generation. Because docupoetics is often understood as poetry shaped at the intersection of lyricism and nonfiction, we want to reflect on how this work is also distinct from the themes of celebration and protection that characterize Ecopoetic writing.

Putting the Documents in Docupoetics

A great many of the writers working in Docupoetics today place more emphasis than Hass does, with his comparison of docupoetry to Georgics, on the role actual documents play in their docupoetic work. A narrower definition would emphasize that docupoems exist in conversation with an archive of some kind and that the poetics involves a complex consideration of what documents exist, what documents have been erased or destroyed, what kinds of human experiences and feelings can be seen in these documents, as well as what parts of being human are not given space in the archive for full expression. Writers in this mode are often deeply influenced by Modernist poet Muriel Rukeyser's *Book of the Dead*, which chronicles attempts by West Virginia miners, most of whom were African Americans, to sue for damages after the Hawk's Nest Tunnel Disaster in 1930. Through a collage of documentary evidence and excerpts from testimony given by survivors, Rukesyer captures the massive scale of human suffering and environmental damage, as well as the callous disregard of the officials in the company. She writes, drawing from court testimony:

> This is the X-ray picture taken last April.
> I would point out to you : these are the ribs;
> this is the region of the breastbone;
> this is the heart (a wide white shadow filled with blood).

Philip Metres's *Sand Opera* also has many examples of how a poet might treat documentary evidence in lyric ways. In his series of poems, "The Abu Ghraib Arias," Metres creates a kind of dialogue between the Standard Operating Procedures manual for Camp Echo at the Guantanamo Bay prison camp, testimony from Abu Ghraib torture victims, accounts from whistleblowers inside the prison, and the damning words of US soldiers and contractors as they describe their own actions in their own words. Later in the book, Metres offers a series of poems called Black Sites which juxtapose architectural schematics of cells used to hold tortured prisoners, with accounts of what it was like to live inside those spaces, given by the people who had been held there. We have included an example of one of these Black Site poems with this chapter, but you will be able to appreciate the poem more fully if you realize it is not merely a standalone poem, but one in conversation with these other documents. In essays about the art of docupoetics, Metres has described why so many docupoetic works are often long or even book-length projects that prove difficult to excerpt. "The investigative poem opposes the idea of a poem as a closed system," he writes. Instead, these kinds of poems invite "'the real life outside the poem' into the poem, offering readers a double-journey—one that takes them further into the poem and beyond its limits." He adds that such poems are "a place of meeting between materiality and the imagination."

The text of the Black Site poem we've included in this chapter is a persona poem written in the voice of a prisoner noticing a fly in his cell and expressing both his gratitude for this small company in his isolation, and his desire to free the creature. "Whenever I saw / a fly in my cell / I was filled / with joy." Despite this joy, he wishes for the fly to escape through the crack under the door and be free in a way he cannot. "I wished for it / to slip under the door / so it would not be / imprisoned itself." These are lines of deep emotion and extraordinary lyrical beauty. On their own though, they risk turning torture into a muse in the way Rekdal worries about the treatment of war machines as art objects in "Assemablage of Ruined Plane Parts, Vietnam Military Museum, Hanoi." However, Metres's poem is more than just its words. At its core, it is a schematic of the cell's design overlaid by the prisoner's grace-filled and deeply humane words. The poem is driven by an awareness of the other humans who are part of this story, the ones who used their intelligence and talents to conceive of such a place, draft the architectural designs, pour the concrete, weld the bars, do the carpentry, and imagine the various torments. The poem documents the terrible human imagination required to design a space that ensures prisoners would hear certain noises, wouldn't hear others, would be deprived of or plunged into darkness, then deprived of or assaulted by light, all to ensure they would find in such a cell no moment of rest or peace.

With this poem, as is the case with many other docupoetic pieces, it is worth considering the impact of the visual design on meaning. In the book where this poem first appeared, the diagram that appears at the center of the poem is printed on vellum, an opaque paper which obscures the words of the prisoner, though those lines can still be read, even though it is the image of the cell that first leaps out as the darker and crisper text. But then readers turn that vellum page, and the cell disappears, while the prisoner's words of generosity and gentleness remain. By turning the page, readers have the power to remove that black site, as Metres surely wishes he could do. And as he likely understands, so many of his readers encountering these poems printed by a US publisher, distributed in US bookstores, taught in US university classrooms, have the power to demand and agitate for such removals, if only they could be inspired to use that power.

Questions of Voice & Witness

Another common attribute of docupoetic works is a deep sense of political import around the act of bearing witness. A principle underlying docupoetic work is that, even when an atrocity cannot be stopped, an artist or writer can do some good by documenting that it happened, given that it is the nature of oppressors to erase, obscure, and distort the truth. For this reason, you might sometimes hear docupoetic works referred to as Poetry of Witness.

The term Poetry of Witness was brought to prominence by Carolyn Forche, who edited the anthology *Against Forgetting: Twentieth Century Poetry of Witness,* which collected the voices of poets documenting their experiences in the 20th century with exile, state censorship, political persecution, house arrest, torture, imprisonment, military occupation, warfare, and assassination. Forche's own poem, "The Colonel," is considered an iconic example of this poetics. It is a poem rooted in her experience working with the human rights organization Amnesty International in El Salvador in 1978, during the Civil War between the US backed military and Farabundo Martí National Liberation Front. After describing the bourgeois comforts of the home—the food they were served, the American police drama on TV, the teenage daughter filing her nails, Forche writes, "The colonel returned with a sack used to bring groceries home. He spilled many human ears on the table. They were like dried peach halves." With lines like "What you have heard is true" and "Some of the ears on the floor caught this scrap of his voice. Some of the ears on the floor were pressed to the ground," Forche makes unbelievable atrocities register with audiences who may be numb to or numbed by such horror. (You can go to the online companion to find a link to this well-known poem in its entirety.)

However, there have been several compelling critiques of the uninterrogated power dynamics and privileges endemic to poetics of witness, as well as docupoetics more generally. It is important for poets to consider whether and why they might have the capacity to write with safety at a remove. As Metres has written, "The writers of investigative poetry must constantly confront both their epistemological limitedness and their position of privilege as text-workers, as makers in the language of contemporary empire." Poets working in this tradition must be careful to resist any self-aggrandizing narratives about writers giving voice to the voiceless, as if there were not plenty of survivors with voices of their own who might have space to speak if privileged people were not taking up all the oxygen in the room.

Kiki Petrosino's "Instructions for Time Travel" is an example of a poem that emerges from a writer's desire to tell or retell stories that oppressors erased, ignored, or papered over. This poem appears in *White Blood: A Lyric of Virginia*, a collection about lives of enslaved people on historic plantations, many of which have been transformed in the present-day into tourist destinations that celebrate slaveholders and whitewash the racist acts of violence those people perpetrated. Petrosino's speaker describes the experience of walking through Monticello, the plantation where Thomas Jefferson held hundreds of people, some his own multi-racial children, in bondage. We see the speaker pass by the monuments and landscaping with invasive species that are so characteristic of white settler aesthetics. Then we see her pass the more humble work spaces like smokehouses to the site of unmarked graves where Black people were buried. The speaker hears them calling "*Write about me*."

Many writers who are drawn to historical subjects may relate to this sense of hearing the past calling out, demanding to be remembered and written. However, we note that this poem is not merely a celebration of historical writing as an act of reclamation and memory. It is also a poem that sets and explains the poet's intentions. These are not Kiki Petrosino's stories and not her ancestors. A writer can cause harm imaging a way into lives that were not their own. Imagine how it might feel for a stranger to invent their own vision of your grandmother or grandfather's life? For their dreams to replace your own as the version of their story that people accept and believe?

In this poem Petrosino describes a feeling of being called by the dead to tell their stories. But it is also useful to know that in the collection where this poem appears, as well as in her broader body of work, she writes about the experience of being a multi-racial woman with Black, Italian, and other European ancestries. Elsewhere in *White Blood* she creates erasure poems out of the results from genetic testing that promises to reveal one's racial and ethnic ancestry. These erasures reveal the ways reducing one's racial identity to percentiles based on blood tests miss so much nuance about the true nature of identity. "Instructions for Time Travel" is a poem born not only of a deep interest in the lives of the enslaved people of Monticello and other plantations, but also a poem that establishes that when Petrosino writes about them she is also writing about her own history and the forces that shape her own experiences with privilege and oppression in this moment in history. We think Petrosino's work provides an excellent model for how poets working in docupoetic traditions can convey both their intentions and their preparedness to tell about the lives of others with sensitivity and integrity.

Marwa Helal's collection, *Invasive Species*, is another example of work that illustrates the extraordinary poetics that are possible when people who have experienced oppressions are given space to bear witness to their own story. In Helal's sequence of poems, "Immigration as Second Language," she interrogates both the language and the memories associated with documents submitted to and received from the US government during a speaker's attempts to obtain the permissions necessary to reside as an adult in the country where she was raised and where her parents still live. What might seem at first like a path through tedious bureaucratic paperwork becomes, thanks to Helal's analyses, augmentations, and translations, a clear and forthright account of cruelties and dehumanizations designed to protect white supremacy and assert imperial power.

The poems are presented as an abecedarian where A is for "aged out" and "asylum"; B is for "birthplace"; C is for "census"—the list goes on. R is for "Returning," a section of the poem that outlines the cruel choices an immigration system riddled with intentional inefficiencies and blatant racism forces on a family. Helal writes, "Returning to Egypt is hard and doesn't happen often enough." In addition to the expense, it is a risk for her and her parents to visit their homeland since it is increasingly the case that return visits can call their immigration status into question—just as such a trip became quite permanent for the speaker at one point in her past. She is forced to make a life for herself in Egypt, with extended family in a country she has had limited opportunities to know. She remarks, "Every time I see my parents while I am in Cairo they seem ages older. I am not used to this much time passing between visits. Six months. Eight months. Nine months in between."

The collection also illustrates how a poet who is rooted in their own story can bear witness to and establish solidarity with those who are subjected to the same systems. Helal frequently annotates the speaker's personal experience with other research to emphasize the ways that individual experiences are connected to a larger political context. In "Returning," she cites audio obtained by ProPublica from inside a US Customs and Border Protection facility where children are heard wailing. "Border patrol agent jokes, 'We have an orchestra here.'" O is for "One-800-IMMIGRATION. Payment Plans. Free Consultation." The poem moves between lines from this advertisement, personal experience, and reporting from *The New York Times*. The effect of Helal's docupoetic balance between lived experience, archival research, investigative journalism, and a poet's attention to the effects of language is a poem that explains the human rights crisis around immigration in ways that place the voices, experiences, emotions of people trying to build lives out a cruel system of inhumane bureaucracies.

There are many approaches to research, as well as many styles and forms available to writers working in docupoetic traditions. What lies at the core of this work is a commitment to finding, understanding, and then making your poetry tell those truths that the language of power and domination was designed to erase.

INVITATIONS TO REFLECT

Discuss Together

Look through your own trash and make a list of what you find there. How is your trash can an archive? What do the documents within reveal about power and justice in your place and moment in history? What do the documents within reveal about who you are, what you cherish, how you love, and how you live? How is your trashcan a poem?

For Further Study

In this chapter we mention how the docupoetic impulse can range from works that engage with an archive, to works that engage with a naturalist's library of field knowledge / immersive experiences, from Petrosino and Rukeyser to Virgil or Hass. Think of a poetry collection you've read and studied within other lineages, such as those described in Writing the Field or Racial Imaginary, which also relies on research. How is Jen Bervin's *Silk Poems,* for example, a merging of Lyric "I," Field, and Docupoetics traditions? How is Kiki Petrosino reckoning privilege and oppression within formal poetics in *White Blood: A Lyric of Virginia?* How does your own stack of poems—perhaps the ones you've written while studying this textbook, or perhaps the manuscript-in-progress you're revisiting as you write an artist statement for a grant or cover letter for submission—constitute a kind of merged poetics? What influences sing from your pages? What ancestors do you thank?

Writing Exercises

Like all the poets we have discussed in this chapter, you are a writer making your life in some degree of collaboration with and resistance to various political, monetary, and social institutions. Your daily navigations and negotiations have created a paper trail that hints at a story about relationships, power, memory, and forgetting. You have learned how to survive, to love, to rage, to be struck by beauty and fear and pain. You have figured out how to keep bees or change tires or prepare the food that comforted you when you were a child or reconstruct something lost across the generations. You have lived, you have learned, and you have a docupoetic project in you.

For each of the writing exercises below you will need a subject. We recommend that for a docupoetic project you find your subject by thinking of a force, institution, habit, pressure, or desire that has shaped your life. We also recommend that you stick with your subject over the course of many poems and try each of these exercises with that subject in mind, as a way to research your subject using a variety of different ways of knowing and understanding.

1 **Develop a (Soma)Tic Ritual**

A (soma)tic is a kind of ritual designed to engender poetry, though the rituals themselves can feel like poems or performance art pieces in their own right. CA Conrad developed the idea of (soma)tic poetry practice. We included an example of Conrad's work in the chapter on "Writing the Body," But we also think their work can be read as an example of docupoetry that instructs, informs, and demands action from the reader.

For this exercise, describe the steps for a ritual that would require you to engage with a force that shapes your life in a way you never have before. First describe the ritual step-by-step as if you were writing a how-to manual. Then do the ritual. Write a poem immediately after. Sometimes the instructions for the ritual will be a great poem, sometimes the poem the ritual brought out in you will be a great poem, sometimes they will both be great in very different ways.

2 **Visual Documentation**

Locate visual materials related to your subject—photographs, artworks, archival documents, advertisements, etc. Alter these primary sources in a lyrical way—that is, fragment them, distill images, erase and collage, add other sources, etc., to make the images and music in them sing. Consider, for example, how Philip Metres makes government documents tell a different truth through his use of layering, collaging, and vellum paper.

3 **Collaging Voices**

Collect quotes related to your subject—scholarly, difficult, jargon-rich—on index cards. Write what the quotes mean to you, or what memories they call to mind, on the back of those cards. Keep and grow this collection as you work on your docupoetic project. Then collage these cards into a poem composed entirely of quoted material or interweave them with other lyrical lines you've developed on this subject.

4 **Oral Histories**

Conduct or locate oral histories and / or affidavits related to your obsession. Make cuts, add interviewer questions, and use line breaks to highlight the poetic nature of these voices.

5 **The Research Is the Poem**

As you compile all these documents and learn more about your research through various primary and secondary sources, keep a process journal where you describe and observe yourself as a researcher. Keep track of the sensory details, the conversations, the feelings, and the memories that come to you as you research. Then combine and collage some of these details with the other archival materials you've collected into a poem.

Afterword: The Beginning & The End

An Invitation to Revisit Your *Ars Poetica*

When you finish the first ten chapters of this craft guide, you may have a new concept of yourself as a poet writing within a broader lineage. You may be rethinking your work and your relationship to it, and you might have new ideas about what you believe poetry is and can be. We invite you to revisit your initial ars poetica that you might have written after reading the forward to this book and write a new one. Consider how such ars poeticas create ongoing conversations with your evolving artist self. Consider, too, how those selves have been informed by an ever-expanding canon of your own making.

Mentor Poets and the Making of Personal Canons

When the authors of this textbook were young poets in an MFA program together, we used to meet at Kate's place to talk about poetry. We'd migrate with tea or wine to the mudroom at the back of the house, where Kate had cut open several paper grocery bags and spread them out across her wall, side to side in a large, sprawling poster. Sitting beneath this wall of entangled influences, we began to map a "family tree" of poetic lineages. Whenever one of us encountered a new poet, we'd try to figure out how that poet fit into the branches, roots, and leaves shooting off the tree—who their literary parents and cousins and stepchildren might be, how they connected, whether via direct relationship influence and / or via aesthetic. One such branch of Maya's poetry "poet-tree" (yep, we were that nerdy) was Richard Hugo → James Welch → M. L. Smoker, a lineage you might recognize from the chapter "Writing in the Field" and which helped Maya orient herself in a poetics of place (especially when that place is her beloved home in the Pacific Northwest) and epistolary poetics, a tradition we discuss in "Telling Secrets:

Confessions, Epistolaries, & the Lyric 'I'." One of Kate's was Frank O'Hara →. Barbara Guest → Daniel Borzutzky, a lineage that helped her articulate her interest in the poetics of conversational speech and ekphrastic writing, traditions we discuss in depth in "The Poem in the Telephone Lines" and "Duende, Deep Image, and the Poetics of Spells." We soon saw that this mapping system demanded necessary overlaps and drew dotted lines between those poets who were tangentially related, often labeling the lines with little narratives and funny bits of verse. Anyone who imitated anyone else was henceforth connected; anyone who studied with someone else was related by that circumstance; anyone who had a relationship—familial or otherwise—was part of the larger canonical drama. Sometimes we included titles of specific works, and sometimes we even drew little symbols that indicated romantic relationships or poetic schools and collectives. The tree eventually began to look more like a wild and tangled web.

Later, we would both give this assignment to our students, asking them to choose a mentor poet and study their work closely, as well as the work of one or more of that poet's literary ancestors, mapping these influences visually. Over the years, students came up with new concepts to describe their maps: rhizome, cafeteria, meadow, nightclub, delta, garden. All of these are useful ways to think about how rich canons of poetry influence each of us, and how we each ultimately create our own canons of influence, with myriad webbed lineages.

Below is an assignment you are welcome to use as-is, or otherwise adapt for your purposes. We personally recommend keeping the exercise casual and ongoing, with lots of freedom for how to approach making the visual elements—we've found many who love the tactile practice of drawing or collaging these on paper / textile, who see that embodiment as a crucial element of process. Others have thrived by engaging digitally, creating websites or Powerpoints. Whatever modalities you suggest, we recommend it be a "low risk" assignment that develops as the term progresses, and / or one with ample time to add and layer. This is a great way for poets to brainstorm or otherwise jump start a longer essay discussing and explicating poets most influential to one's own work.

Mentor Poet and Poetic Lineage Map: An Assignment

Your writer's lineage is, essentially, like a family tree / ancestry of writing influences. Begin by considering: Who are your literary parents / guardians? Grandparents? Aunts & uncles? Cousins? The relationships aren't always perfect, and don't always reflect this metaphor (maybe yours is, say, more like a rhizomatic root system), but the genealogy is there. Consider your major aesthetic influences, including who taught you what, and make a literary family tree (or other visual—you can name it using a different metaphor, such as "rhizome."). Begin, perhaps, with a central influence, or mentor poet, reading most or all of their work, interviews with them, reviews, and other ephemera, branching into reading the poets they note as influences and mentors and ancestors, and adding those to your map. You'll note that the map grows as you grow. The more you know, the less you know you know. You can begin anywhere and move in any global and temporal direction. Contemporary poet Jos Charles makes a good model for mapping ancestry—as she is in the canon of Chaucer or Hopkins (received rhythms and music), but also a contemporary of Kim Hyesoon or Cameron Awkward-Rich (innovative forms and disrupted narrative)—and rooted in lineages as varied as Writing in the Field to Poetics of the Body, diverging and converging, each branch of influence creates new texture, a new possibility for mapping a canon of influence.

Here is an example of a poetic lineage map created by a student:

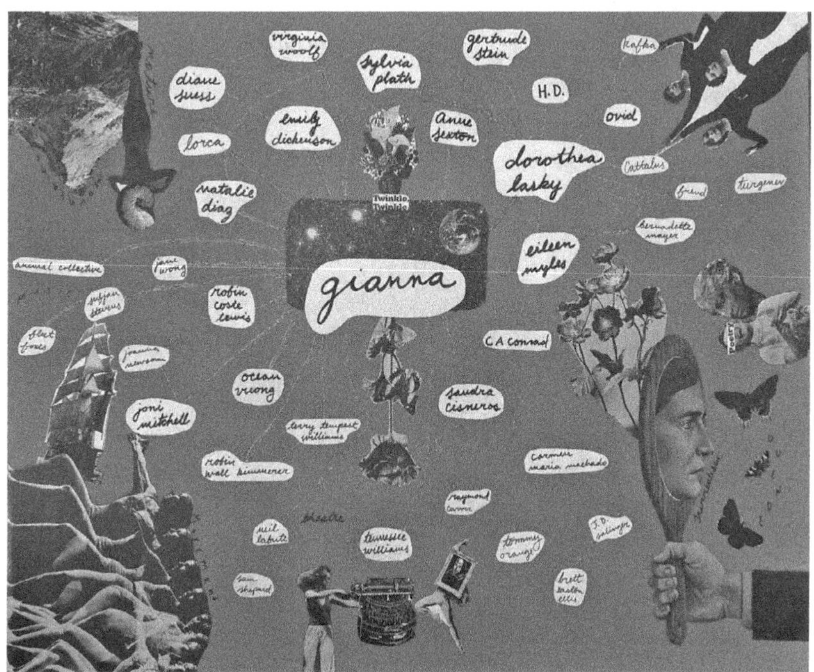

[Lineage map by Gianna Starble, a student in Maya's Advanced Poetry Workshop at Central Washington University, 2022. Used with permission.]

In discussing her map, Gianna spoke about the rewards of using a tactile process to create a collage, the influence of her mentor poet, Dorothea Lasky, and the connection between the literary and the performative. Here are some excerpts from Gianna's notes on this project:

> When I began the physical manifestation of [my poetic lineage map], I realized it felt more like a dizzying spider web. I wanted to connect the

> poets and artists loosely in a material that appeared faint and celestial, so I chose glitter glue. I love creating with my hands, so decided to incorporate collage work. The act of cutting and recontextualizing images represents how I think of inspiration and influence of writers who have come before me. I wanted to use images that reflected the eclectic energy of my aesthetic, and found a leisure catalog at my local antique mall with black and white images. Through the physical act of constructing my poetic lineage web on this red poster board, I felt a deeper understanding of my artistic style—how I glean from nostalgia, love to engage with the absurd, and enjoy leaning into the dark mystique. For my learning style, the tactile engagement also deepened my ability to see the process as part of the learning.
>
> The start of my lineage map was anchored in my mentor poet, Dorothea Lasky. In our advanced poetry class, we were asked to choose a mentor poet whose aesthetic most excited us and reflected a direction we aimed to go with our work. I chose Dorothea Lasky because of her distinct voice, unabashed themes, and how she manipulates the rhetorical situations of her poem, often blurring the lines between author, speaker, and the relation to the reader.
>
> In an interview with *Believer* magazine, Lasky describes her relationship to the lyric *I*, "I've always had the belief that the *I* in a poem is a sort of performance of the *I* of the poet writing the poem. That is to say, I still think a lot about the *I* in a poem as a sort of mask of a speaker and not something one might easily overlay on a real self in the world" (Dunn). Reading Lasky's poetry—and her commentary about it—has given me permission to be a performer in my own poems, to put my poetry, as she says, on the stage.
>
> . . .
>
> Through Lasky, I've found many predecessors that I realized, by relation, are vital parts of my poetic lineage. A big one being Federico García Lorca. Lasky is one of many poets inspired by Lorca's musing on *duende*, which can be defined as "the dark spirit and mystery of the earth." Lorca's ideas on duende have guided me in understanding one of my greatest influences, nature. Through the dark mysteries that I gravitate to in the outdoors, I have found that much of my poetic imagery is rooted in nature's magic.

Gianna went on to discuss writers in blurred and other genres, such as Borges and Cisneros, as well as musicians and others who perform their work on stage. Eventually, Gianna presented this map and her explanation of influence at a scholarly conference. But what perhaps brings our poet-teacher hearts the most joy is that she noted she plans to keep working on this kind of mapping as she embarks on graduate school, where she will study—wait for it!—literary fiction. Hooray for mentor lineage and genre blur, right?

We hope you'll give it a try, too, and include your true range of influences quite liberally. Start with a mentor poet whose work feels evocative and true to you, someone you are studying closely in or outside of a class, who pulls you further into writing and your creative self. Go from there.

If you aren't sure where to begin in tracing your mentor poets' lineage:

Look at a poet's acknowledgment page, and notes, in their book. From here you can find various communities and connections. For example, in Filipino-Jordanian poet Dujie Tahat's chapbook, *Salat,* you'll notice they list in their notes some other writers' pieces that Tahat's poems are "after" or "in response to." Among them are Mary Ruefle, Lena Khalaf Tuffaha, Marwa Helal, and Percy Bysshe Shelley. Tahat also notes in their acknowledgments some debts of gratitude, including Khalaf Tuffaha again, as well as Kaveh Akbar, Eve Ewing, and many more.

Another way to find lineage is to do a quick internet search on a poet and **listen to them read from their work at public events, noting who they mention in their Q & A; another trick is to read interviews or listen to podcasts with them**—poets often list who they are reading / admire when they answer questions. We would also venture that anyone who blurbs a book—unless a contest judge or assigned by a press—is someone the poet asked to offer words, and usually these are folks whose work they admire / learn from.

A third way would be to **look to their home press** . . . presses' authors often get to know one another. So, if you like BOA or Copper Canyon or Milkweed as a press, you may begin to see connections between authors, across genres.

A fourth approach: **find out where that writer / poet's "home community" is**, geographically, or in terms of their course of study or residency connections. Of which towns / arts systems are they a part? Which MFA or PhD or other programs do or did they grow from, or teach in? What is their social network like?

Finally—or maybe first!—**follow them on social media platforms** (Twitter, Instagram, Substack, etc.). Not all writers are on social media (and that's okay), but many are, and seeing who they seem to regularly re-share, respond to, quote, etc. can tell you at the very least something about how they operate in the social world. Sometimes this connects to influence and creative process, and sometimes it's just public PR . . . either way, you will undoubtedly learn something about the writer.

Making More Space in the Field

Throughout this book we've encouraged you to develop your own distinct voice as a poet by placing yourself in conversation with other writers who came before you, and those with whom you currently orbit the sun. This is just the beginning of a lifetime of reading and learning, writing to and for and after those poets that deepen your understanding of what a poem can do and how it can be. Ultimately, as you continue to engage in ever-expanding poetic communities, you will develop your own ideas about how to learn and grow as a writer, and you will, we hope, continue to make more space at the table / in the field / on the page for all the possible poetries and those who write them.

Appendices: Mapping Your Writing Life

CREATING AN INSPIRING AND SUPPORTIVE WORKSHOP COMMUNITY

In recent decades, many writers have come to find their most inspiring friendships and helpful first readers in writing workshops facilitated in universities, community writing centers, public libraries, or elsewhere. Sylvia Plath and Anne Sexton, two iconic confessional poets, met in a poetry seminar taught by another significant innovator of the Confessional mode, Robert Lowell. All three had spent time at the McLean Mental Hospital and their conversations about their experiences contributed to an atmosphere where each could find ways to write around taboos surrounding the themes of depression, suicide, and other mental health issues. Sandra Cisneros and Joy Harjo have both spoken publicly about how grateful they are to have found each other during their time at the Iowa Writers Workshop. Kate met her husband Brian, who is also conveniently her first and best editor, at an undergraduate poetry workshop. Kate and Maya found each other at a graduate MFA workshop.

We believe creative writing cohorts have the potential to evolve into fantastically supportive and nurturing communities. But we also wish to talk about how important it is to be mindful of the ways workshop groups can turn toxic, cruel, and creatively deadening. Sometimes participants place their own egos and fears at the center of conversations, and control discussions by attempting to dominate the group with a single aesthetic. More often still, writers can fail to appreciate how their race, gender, sexual orientation, or socioeconomic status might impact how they read and respond to work. Too often, white, male, cis, or hetero perspectives have been centered in workshops, even when the work under discussion is by someone who does not identify in those terms, leaving some members of the workshop group feeling alienated from their own voices or despairing there are not good readers out there for their work. We hope those of you working with this textbook will actively work to resist those problematic dynamics in your workshop. Some of the most innovative approaches to creating supportive and welcoming workshop communities have been generated by faculty and alums of places like Cave Canem, Canto Mundo, and Kundiman, which are organizations outside of Academia that emerged in response to the harm predominantly white creative writing programs and publishing houses have done to emerging writers. These organizations function far beyond repairing; they fund, lift, celebrate, and highlight a vast range of voices and styles that are changing the literary community for the better.

We also believe a workshop in any academic or community space, if planned carefully with a commitment to supporting each workshop member in the development of their own unique voice and vision, has the potential to be a successful space for incubating excellent poetry and poets. In this chapter we'll share some of the approaches to workshopping that have worked well in our classrooms or the classrooms of poet-teachers we admire. We recommend that workshop groups let each writer select the style of feedback and modality used on their own work. Teachers and workshop leaders can offer participants a "Workshop Menu" and invite them to choose from a list of possible approaches. Below is a non-comprehensive list of a few styles we've found useful. We recommend checking out Matthew Salesses' *Craft in the Real World* and Felicia Rose Chavez's *The Anti-Racist Writing Workshop* for more ideas about how to create supportive workshop communities.

Generative Writing Workshops

A generative writing workshop is one in which the workshop leader develops a series of writing prompts or experiments. Instead of focusing on one writer's piece as a focal point, everyone is generating new work in creative company with each other. You may recall our discussions of Surrealist writers and creative games they developed like Exquisite Corpse and Metaphor Machine, as well as their use of hypnosis and automatic writing to generate new work. These are all practices you might encounter in a generative writing workshop. Another way to approach this in a class is to use the work of the writer being workshopped as the prompt and then allow peers to write in response and share as a way of offering feedback to the writer.

Observations Only

With this approach classmates take turns stating objective observations about the poem in question, using "I notice" statements to offer specifics about the poem being workshopped. Some examples of the kinds of statements participants might offer in this workshop include: "I notice the poem uses a litany of metaphors," "I notice the poem is in couplets," "I notice a regular rhyme scheme," "I notice the speaker's tone and perspective shifts dramatically after the fourth stanza." This model works well to allow a class to gain comfort speaking aloud / making contributions and to practice talking about prosody or other technical craft elements. The method also reminds everyone that the poem they are discussing may be rooted in aesthetics or poetics different from the ones that guide their own writing. Such an approach helps workshop participants separate their understandable affection for those aesthetic aims guiding their own work from the way they respond to poems emerging from entirely different traditions or with entirely different aims from their own.

Fly-on-the-Wall Workshop

It is useful to be familiar with this workshop model, which was the one that dominated creative writing programs for generations. In these workshops, the writer whose work is "on the table" will usually open by reading a short excerpt; then they listen and take notes while their classmates talk amongst themselves about the work, often nearly pretending the writer isn't there (hence the "fly-on-the-wall").

Many people, Kate included, find having their work discussed while they listen silently to be very helpful. At its best, such a workshop gives a writer insight into how readers might perceive the work when they encounter it in a book or magazine without the author there to answer questions. The permission to be silent can allow a writer the space they need to process the feedback they are receiving. At its worst, though, the writer can feel erased, or the experience of being forced into silence can parallel other forms of cultural oppression or hegemony. For this reason, it is particularly important that this workshop approach be one among others from which a writer has the option to freely choose; it should never be forced on anyone.

To prepare for this workshop, each participant should write a letter to the writer whose work will be discussed, describing what is effective about the work in question, as well as offering some suggestions for improvement. When students elect to use this model in our classes, we ask those offering feedback to provide "revision challenges" to the writer, so the feedback does not become overly prescriptive in unhealthy or domineering ways.

The Unsilenced Workshop

In her essay, "Unsilencing the Writing Workshop," Beth Bich Nguyen describes the frustration of listening in silence as a workshop, largely composed of white people, discussed what dim sum was and whether it needed to be defined in a story written by an Asian American writer. She offers this anecdote as just one example of a major problem with the "Fly-on-the-Wall" workshop model, which is that it can advance a homogenous, and even white supremacist, notion of what makes for "good" literature. She writes, "the idea of what constituted basic knowledge did not include dim sum. They, the rest of the people in the workshop, decided what constituted basic knowledge . . . I was the outsider, the strange Asian who needed to adapt my work to what they understood. This wasn't intentional malice; it was baseline assumption."

In her essay, Nguyen proposes a different way of engaging with work that seeks to transform the power dynamic in workshop spaces. In the Unsilenced Workshop, workshoppers replace their critiques and advice with questions for the writer. They ask the writer questions like: Why did you use first-person? Or, what kinds of associations are we meant to have with a particular set of images? The benefits of such an approach are that "when the writer gets to talk about what they're trying to do, they discover something more about what they actually are doing. Almost always, they reveal information that they'd been holding back." To prepare for this workshop you should make a list of questions you could ask the writers about their work.

The Hooray All Day Workshop

The praise-based workshop has also been called a Bop workshop, Hallelujah workshop, and Signs of Life workshop. The practice here is to celebrate what readers find deeply resonant in a piece of writing. Readers can quote back to the writers their favorite lines. They can describe the moves they admired in the writing and explain why they think those moves are working so well. They flag beautiful images or highlight moments when the poetic form makes an interesting turn. Through these workshops writers often find inspiration and encouragement to pursue some facet of their voice or craft more deeply and fully. These kinds of workshops are a great way to find a sense of purpose or direction for newer work. They are also useful in helping writers safeguard the most beautiful or exciting parts of their work as they undertake major revisions—there is a very real danger in revising the spark out of a piece of writing. These workshops can also be healing experiences for writers whose creative process has been harmed by toxic feedback in the past—this method is great for restoring confidence or finding one's voice. To prepare for this workshop you should make a list of moments in the piece that excited you as a reader.

We find this kind of model works very well in early-term workshops, or when offering feedback on early drafts. (It also works well in private blog settings or in the discussion boards of online creative writing classes where students are building camaraderie and community, and not yet ready for critique.)

Critical Response Process

This workshop method was developed by Liz Lehrman as a way of giving feedback in a performing arts context, but it often translates easily into creative writing workshop groups. In this workshop the responders engage in dialogues with the writer, with a commitment to the writer's intent to make excellent work. The workshop begins with the responders offering Statements of Meaning. Responders state what was meaningful, evocative, interesting, exciting, and / or striking in the work they have just witnessed.

Then the writer asks questions about the work. In answering, responders stay on topic with the question and may express opinions in direct response to the artist's questions.

After that, responders ask neutral questions about the work, and the writer responds. Questions are neutral when they do not have an opinion couched in them. (We recommend teachers and workshop facilitators spend some time discussing the difference between a truly neutral question and one that veils criticism in the guise of a question. Practice asking questions of previously published work together before starting to workshop, because asking a truly neutral question is a skill that takes some time to develop.) After this period of questions and responses, the writer can ask the group to share opinions, if that is a kind of feedback the writer would like.

To prepare for this workshop, you should write a statement of meaning about what you thought the piece was doing, and a list of neutral questions about the work. The author will also write a set of questions about their own work, to ask their peers.

The Talk Show Host Method

Much like preparing for the unsilenced workshop, or the critical response process, in the Talk Show Host Method, classmates make a list of questions they want to ask the writer, who becomes a kind of "guest" on a talk show run by the class who serve as a collective "host." The entire workshop consists of the group asking the writer questions about their work. We recommend that participants consider how much care and preparation a good talk show host exercises—they carefully and closely read the work of the guest. They craft questions with the aim of drawing out ever more detailed answers and reflections, as well as encouraging them to talk through complex processes or decisions that may have been more intuitive than intentional in the early draft. Most great talk show hosts are not adversarial in their questioning; they create a supportive atmosphere where the guests feel invited to talk through their problems, processes, and struggles, all while clarifying and refining their great ideas.

The Q & A Method

Like a reverse of the Talk Show method described above, the author of the poem is in charge of asking questions about their own work. The author / writer prepares a list of concerns, questions, curiosities, and issues to address, and runs their workshop by asking peers to respond. This is a little different from the Critical Response Method in that the writer drives the conversation from the get-go.

Choosing the Best Workshop Style for You

This is not a comprehensive list of all potential workshop styles—we often cycle various interpretations and adaptations, as well as other methods, on and off our list of possibilities each term, depending on course demographics and needs. We also encourage students to invent new approaches specific to their class communities, to add to the ever-growing list of options.

STRATEGIES FOR REVISION

One of Kate's favorite in-class activities is to give her students photocopies of a marked-up, scratched-out first draft of a poem called "How to Lose Things The Gift of Losing Things." She reads aloud passages like, "I am such a / fantastic[a]lly good at losing things / I think everyone shd profit from my experiences" and "He who loseth his lif, etc.—but he who / loses his love never, no never never again—." Then Kate reads them Elizabeth Bishop's "One Art," one of the great villanelles in the English language, with lines like "The art of losing isn't hard to master; / so many things seem filled with the intent / to be lost that their loss is no disaster." At least sixteen drafts exist between the first version of this poem and its final form. And how encouraging is that? You can write something so mediocre and, through dedicated revision, transform it into a masterpiece.

When students ask us whether we think they are talented enough to become writers, first we tell them yes, of course. But then we tell them we don't believe in talent, only in revision. Figuring out an approach to revision that works for you is one of the central challenges of becoming a writer. Sometimes we see writers come out of a workshop who then try to answer every single question they heard or implement every single piece of advice they were given. This tends to bog down a poem, to make it wordy. Sometimes, if there were lots of cuts suggested, the writer can accidentally cut the heart right out. Other times, students become completely stymied by all the feedback and feel unable to revise at all because they can't remember anymore what they wanted the poem to do or be. We've ruined many of our own poems over the years by trying to stitch someone else's vision over our own.

While workshops can be a great place to gain a better understanding of how your readers interpret and respond to your piece, there are many ways to revise that go way beyond the kinds of suggestions that come up in such spaces. Sometimes a workshop will suggest that you cut or abandon a particularly distinct stylistic or voicy moment, but in revision the best solution for the poem is to amp up that style or voice twice or ten times as much. Sometimes the best way to implement a suggestion is to do its exact opposite. Sometimes you realize you need to cut lines or sections that the workshop group said they loved. As writers you'll need to practice revising creatively, which includes implementing suggested changes unexpectedly and idiosyncratically. It can sometimes mean discounting advice altogether.

One method we encourage you to try in order to develop a playful and creative revision practice is a project we call "The Big Revise." For this project, you should choose a poem in progress and write five drafts of it. Each draft should build on the previous one in some way, but also be as radically different as possible. And if you are thinking five drafts is a lot, excellent, that's the point! If you think five drafts is no big deal, bump it up to ten or fifteen, whatever number seems a little impossible. The reason for generating so many drafts is that, during the first one or two revisions, students tend to respond closely to feedback they received from a workshop cohort. But once they've exhausted that well, they start to think more deeply and weirdly about what the poem could be doing. They start to take risks and then experiment wildly. Sharing the results of these revisions with your workshop is also a great way to build towards an atmosphere of collaboration, risk taking, and radical revision, right from the get-go.

Here's a list of revision exercises you might consult for ideas as you approach each new draft:

- Add new images and reframe existing ones. Make the eye of the speaker a kind of camera that zooms in and out, pans around, and endlessly seeks unlikely angles.
- Choose the poem's strongest image and write it on a separate page; then, make a list of appositives (noun phrases that rename the original). Try to work several of these into the poem, in various contexts. These will create imagistic parallels, or implied metaphors, and may even generate new sister-poems!
- Economy of language: Make a Mad-Lib of your poem, replacing each noun with a blank / part of speech name (try including directives, such as "a noun which has to do with food"). Then ask a friend to supply words without seeing the poem.
- Alternatively, take the images you wrote down during "invitation to reflect" in the Surrealism chapter, and insert those into your poem, where language is flat.
- Complicate the chronology. Add three or more jumps in time.
- Change the point of view from first person to third, third to second, etc. Try a persona. Try a different persona.
- Enrich with research. Add a tangent that involves interesting factoids from science or history. Meditate on a story in the news that hangs heavy on your mind. All the better if the research seems unrelated to the poem at first glance.
- Make the poem twice as long. Then make it half as long. Your new half should not look like the old one.
- Make your whole poem into a serial list of questions. Or, if you tend to use a lot of questions, turn those questions into statements.
- Write the poem backwards, beginning with the ending. At some point you'll feel the impulse to swerve into new terrain, and you should follow that swerve and see where it leads you. This is an interesting strategy because endings in early drafts usually emerge from a moment during which we figured out something important and new. What happens to your thought process and imagination if

you start with that new idea? How much farther can the poem wander into realms you've never considered?

- Cut and salvage. After every draft, pause to notice what you might have lost from earlier drafts. Bring those beautiful lines, stanzas, and ideas forward, combining them with what you love best about newer versions. (Printing out the drafts and then cutting them into chunks that you tape together into the new poem can be a fun and productive way to approach this.)
- Cut up the entire poem into individual words and place them all in a pile, then assemble into a new poem. Leave out words that aren't interesting.
- As a class / cohort / friend group, make a quick list of energizing revision exercises you love; share them, and then try each other's as you revise.

These are strategies for major revisions that help you explore all of the potential a poem has to surprise readers, deepen themes, and draw upon form and craft in new ways. But what about polishing, fine-tuning, and tweaking poems? Line editing is another important skill that has its place in the writing process.

Once you've reached a point where you know the poem is doing all you want in terms of themes, imagery, and narrative arcs and it has a certain flair in terms of style or voice, then you are ready to tackle some drafts that focus more on fine-tuning the lines and form. Consider the drafts for Langston Hughes' poem "Harlem," which is linked in this book's online companion. The final version of this poem famously asks the question "What happens to a dream deferred?" But in earlier drafts, you can see how Hughes experiments with different ways of using line breaks to create the necessary pacing for sentences like "Does it dry up like a raisin in the sun." When he asks, does it "fester like a sore— / And then run?" he asks in the margins of his drafts about whether "and" is needed and if the word should be capitalized. These drafts are fascinating to review, both in terms of all the many, many lines he wrote, fiddled with, and ultimately cut over the course of all those drafts, but also to see the way he used each preposition, conjunction, line break, and comma with intention and care.

Here are some questions and prompts you can use when you've switched from revising with the roughest sandpaper to using the fine grain. We recommend focusing on just one of these exercises per draft and printing out a new version of the poem to mark up each time you switch to a different editorial strategy.

- Mark each of your sentences and notice how long they are and what structures they use. Generally, writers have a particular kind and length of sentence to which they default. In this draft, try to vary that sentence length and structure. Put a short periodic statement after a long and complex sentence with many subordinate clauses. Have a dependent-independent-clause sentence follow one with an independent-dependent-clause. Reframe one or two lines as questions. Can you get away with an exclamation point? Try some asides and learn to love the em dash.

- Circle all the adjectives and adverbs in your poem and consider whether you can cut them. Although adjectives and adverbs are describing words, so it would be reasonable to think they bring more detail into a piece, they often turn into filler and deplete an image or insight of its immediacy.
- Highlight all the verbs in your poem. Experiment with turning all the passive verbs into active ones.
- Are you using regular line breaks or irregular line breaks? Should the irregular line breaks be regular in their irregularity? Where does the silence go?
- Play with lines. Revisit the chapter "Sound, Shape, and Space" and try to imitate the lines of poets like Mai Der Vang, Rebecca Tamás, or Rosebud Ben-Oni. Try putting your poem into a range of types of lines.
- Let the poem lead you to its form. Has your voice fallen into a somewhat regular rhythm or line length? Try to make that pacing intentional throughout the whole poem. Maybe you notice your lines are quite ragged and unpredictable—be intentionally irregular and disrupt those spots where the line lengths are regularized. Have repetitions emerged that might lend themselves to becoming a refrain, or even a pantoum or villanelle? If you are in the 12–18–line range, ask yourself whether the poem wants to be a sonnet. Consider whether you are writing subtly in the tradition of odes or ballads or other familiar forms, and whether you might like to make that subtle influence more explicit.
- Take a closer look at your titles. Do they add anything to your poems? Do you like context-, or narrative-revealing, titles, that allow you to dive into the poem with some information already established, or do you like those that seem to ask a question that seeks to be answered? Does your title work nicely to provide some tension between itself and the first lines? Should you consider a read-in title (one that is part of the first sentence of the poem)? Does your title invite a re-read after finishing the poem?
- Look at your first line and last line—do they read together? Would it be more helpful to the poem if they spoke to one another?
- Look just at your last few lines and see if they make you draw in your breath and make you want to read your own poem again. If not, find a line somewhere else in the poem that has that effect, and figure out how to make the poem end there.

SOME NOTES ON ASSEMBLING A COLLECTION

Given the demographic range for this book—undergraduate students, graduate students, and folks writing and learning outside of academic institutions—we realize you may be at the point in your writing career where you are ready to compile a chapbook or book manuscript for publication / submission. Here are a few tips we have found useful for approaching that process.

First, we cannot stress enough that if you have the resources, try printing out your poems and pinning them to a wall or arranging them on a flat surface (some people use large tables; Maya likes to use her floor, or, on a nice day, a field or large patch of moss). The physical enactment of moving poems around as you consider their relationship to one another is one way to both make a book and to create new energies within and between existing poems, as well as to inspire new poems. As you play with order, you will notice new throughlines and ideas coalescing in front of you.

The order of your poems, like a poem's form, should serve / contribute to the content & movement of the poems themselves. That might mean juxtaposing the form (order) & content, or it might mean making it fit in expected ways. Though if you go with what you consider to be an "expected" order, such as chronological by time or season, consider finding ways to introduce some juxtaposition in the form of the poems themselves, so the book doesn't feel too samey-samey or plodding to readers. Or don't! Sometimes seamless projects are incredibly immersive and pleasurable.

Another way to think about the structure of a book is to look to the structure of a crown of sonnets. In that form, the first line of each sonnet picks up the last line of the previous. When looking at manuscript order, consider how each new poem could pick up on something from the last poem—a theme, a question, a narrative moment, an image, a speaker, or listener, etc.

Other common strategies for ordering we've seen poets use include:

- by date written
- by date occurred (chronological in time)
- alphabetical order of titles
- by season
- by finding a set of related poems to open different sections. The subsequent poems in each section are chosen to correspond with themes in the sectioning opening poem or to advance a narrative the section opening poem introduces.

Further Questions to Consider as You Develop Your Own Manuscript

On first & last poems: Readers screening piles of manuscripts for publication often begin by reading the first, say, three poems in a manuscript to see if that manuscript goes in the Yes, Maybe, or No pile. After that, they read the first six, and sort again. Then they might read the first six and last three. (These numbers are a little arbitrary, but many screeners have a set number or page count like this that they try to apply universally to all manuscripts, for equity.) What they're looking for is strength, sure, but they are also taking notes on whether the first poems set up the manuscript's questions, tensions, themes, characters, etc., and then whether the concluding poems answer those. When reading a manuscript for the first time, you might consider the first poem / poems as one(s) that make promises and then the rest of the manuscript as living up to those promises while also continuing to surprise us.

We suggest you put your most compelling, exhilarating, and gripping poems at the front to ensure you are catching the full attention of a busy screener. Remember the first person at a press who looks at your submission has probably been asked to review a pile of dozens, even hundreds, of manuscripts they must sort in a short period of time. Considering their undertaking, it helps to be greeted by some poems that intentionally set out to woo them and remind them they agreed to read thousands of pages of poetry a week because it's a real pleasure.

On speaker / listener: Think back to our discussion of the rhetorical situation in Chapter 2. Who is the speaker? What is the speaker saying? Are there multiple points of view? Why? Are they necessary? Is it clear when you are working in persona, and does it need to be? Who is the listener / who are the listeners? Reflect on how your speakers / framing of speakers engages the arc of your book.

On tone: How does each poem contribute to tone? Should any tones shift to create a balance that works for the central forces?

On setting: If the manuscript is somehow place-based, why? How does place / setting inform the manuscript?

On a poem's fit: Do the poems all fit the manuscript? Including a poem "because it is good" or "because it is published" may not be the best reasons. Including a poem "because it fits the arc or cohesiveness of the collection" is a great reason.

Finding Your Way into Your Manuscript: A Suggested Exercise

Choose a collection of poems you admire, perhaps by a poet you consider a mentor, and study this book's structure closely. (Because they are not always designed by the author with an intentional cohesiveness beyond authorship, we do not suggest using a "collected works" or "selected works" for this purpose). Ask yourself of this collection:

- How does the author set up the arc of their book?
- Would this be useful as a pattern for your own manuscript? Why or why not?

If you already have a manuscript completed, compare your answers to these questions to your own work. What is your organizational pattern? What other patterns of structure can you imagine working for your poems?

SUBMITTING POEMS FOR PUBLICATION

After spending so much time writing and revising your poems, you may start to wonder how you can get them published. Before thinking about publishing a book, we recommend you start by submitting poems to literary magazines, journals, and other venues you admire. Once you've published 20 or 30 pages of poetry in such places, then it's a good time to start thinking about whether you are ready to assemble and submit a full-length poetry collection.

How do you know if you are ready to submit your work for publication? The answer to that question has a lot to do with what fuels you as an artist and how you respond to rejection. Most poets submitting to magazines get rejected most of the time. A common acceptance rate for magazines is just 2 per cent of all submissions. We tell students you are ready to submit if you know that, even if you get a rejection, you'll keep writing. If you think a rejection might discourage you to the point that you will give up, we suggest waiting until you feel stronger in your relationship with poetry and more confident in your voice, regardless of how others respond. We also remind students that traditional publication isn't the only route to accessing and joining a poetry community—it is just one way to pursue this goal. Once you have thoughtfully considered your reasons for seeking publication, as well as your readiness for the whole process—in terms of your relationship to your work, your work's audience, your growth as an artist, etc.—then you can decide whether to embark.

There are some very real benefits to submitting to magazines. Finding an audience and having your work validated through the selection process are some obvious benefits, among others that involve community-building through publication. But another benefit of submitting is that it can change your relationship to your poems. Even if the poems are rejected, once you start submitting them to magazines, you are signaling to yourself that your writing is intended for an audience beyond yourself and your immediate writing cohort. This sense of writing in a way that can connect and resonate with strangers can invigorate and transform your writing process. It can also change the perspective you bring to your work when you sit down to revise. Submitting poems for publication is a way of transforming your writing process from a private practice into a public art.

Where to Submit

There are thousands of literary magazines. Some are online, some are print only. Some are zines distributed locally or regionally, others are distributed nationally or internationally. This abundance is exciting, because it means there are many communities of writers with diverse aesthetics finding space to flourish, read each other's work, and inspire each other. It can be an overwhelming abundance, though, because how will you ever know which venues are the right ones?

We recommend submitting to journals and other venues who are publishing / lifting writers you admire. That increases your odds of acceptance, because if you like the writers they endorse, there's a good chance they will like the work you are creating. It also makes your experience of submitting more meaningful, because it means you are starting a conversation with editors and readers whose taste and judgment you already trust and appreciate.

We recommend you find these journals by choosing a few favorite poets and looking up what magazines their work has appeared in. We then suggest you go to those magazines' websites and read the poems you find there. Look at the biography notes for writers in the magazine whose work you also enjoyed reading. Those bio notes will probably list other journals in which those poets have published. Go read these journals, looking for new voices that resonate with you, check those bio notes, and follow them to other journals. With this method it won't be long before you have a great list of new writers you love and journals that are supporting them. This is one way to begin—conduct your own literary market analysis by dropping down rabbit-holes of curiosity.

Both Kate and Maya ask their students in advanced classes to practice such market analysis. Kate often gives her students an assignment to research literary magazines in the way we describe here, and she asks them to create a tree chart of the works and magazines they discover. They look something like this:

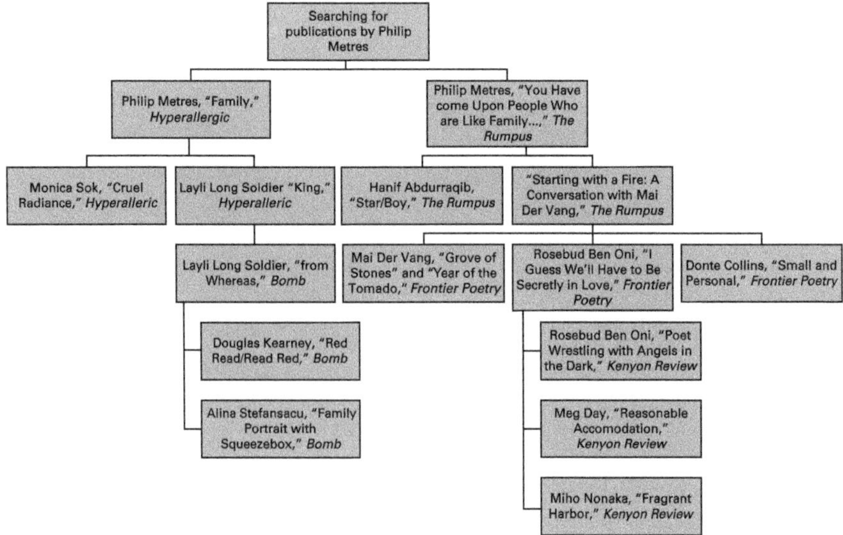

Maya assigns students in graduate publication classes to complete a market survey, to match their own works' aesthetics, with quick details on several categories. That assignment looks like this:

Literary Market Survey
For this assignment, research and provide an annotated bibliography of 10–15 potential literary or other publication venues appropriate to your goals and genre(s), with notes on the rhetorical fit. These can be online or in print, journals or presses. For each, research and complete the following analysis:

- Name who they are and how we find them; their publishing format / frequency / recent issue(s), as applicable
- Social media presence
- Venue's overall mission, aesthetic, and ethos (look at About Us / Mission pages and "masthead" [to study editors])
- Genre / niche / how you'd describe them in relation to other journals or presses—where do they situate in publishing?
- What draws you to this venue / what you admire about their editorial ethos and the work / authors they publish
- Why they are a good fit for your work
- Anything else you would like to note (when they are open for publication, what you might do to prepare to submit, etc).

How to Submit

This brings us to the next step in the process: Once you have found the journals to which you would like to submit, you should take a look at their submission guidelines, which will probably be easy to find on their website. Submissions typically consist of 4–6 poems, though if you have a very long poem, it may be appropriate to send just the one. Be mindful to stay at or under the maximum number of poems or pages, as this is respectful of the editors' time. And speaking of being respectful—as of this writing, the vast majority of editors working for most literary magazines are volunteers. Be kind and patient towards those people who are working to create a vibrant literary community.

In addition to the poems, you should also include a cover letter. A cover letter for a submission like this will be short and include just a few basic elements:

- A short note thanking the editors for taking the time to read your work

- A line about your admiration for their journal that mentions specific pieces in past issues that you enjoyed
- A brief bio note: You can see an example of such bios by reading the contributor notes in a recent issue of the journal to which you're submitting. You'll probably want to include pronouns and other identity markers, a short list of your most impressive previous publications, and your current occupation. Sometimes, folks list where they live and notes on their families or community groups. Occasionally, they list current projects—such as "is currently seeking a home for her memoir, [. . .]," or "is working on a book about bats."

Sometimes people think it might help their chances to make their cover letter stand out by making jokes, lyrical language or other flourishes. In our experiences as editors, it is better to let the creativity of your work speak for itself. Sometimes emerging writers feel self-conscious about not having much to say in their bio notes. Our experience as former editors and from what we've heard from others is that it's very exciting to be the first person to offer publication to an emerging writer. Don't be ashamed to say in your bio note, "If accepted this would be my first publication." There's a good chance the editors will give your submission a little extra care and attention—after all, it's wonderful to see a new generation of writers emerging with their fresh perspectives.

Finally, make sure you keep track of all the places where you are submitting poems. If your work is accepted by one magazine, it is important to send a note to all the other journals where you submitted and let them know you must withdraw that poem, as it is being published elsewhere. You may also have the option to withdraw your poem through their submissions manager. Unless otherwise stated (as in the case of reprints), it is not acceptable to publish a poem in more than one magazine. It is also generally considered in poor taste to withdraw a poem after it's been accepted if a magazine you consider better accepts it instead. Be careful if you submit a poem to more than one magazine that you will be equally happy to have the poem appear in any of their pages.

WRITING AN ARTIST STATEMENT

An artist statement is a common creative writing class assignment, a regular feature of grant and fellowship applications, and often a part of applications for MFA programs or other opportunities.

We often ask students to write artist statements to go along with individual poems or manuscripts they bring to workshop, or as part of their final portfolios at the end of our classes, because the process of articulating their choices within, and aspirations for, their own work helps writers develop intention about their own writing and revision processes.

In addition to this potential to invite reflection, a well-written artist statement also has the potential to help you gain access to financial resources that can support your artistic pursuits. For this reason, we want to name some of the expectations and rhetorical conventions associated with artist statements. However, we also must acknowledge that every grant, fellowship, and application will be unique, so there is no one-size-fits-all formula we can offer. With these caveats in mind, we offer some general principles to help you approach writing such a document.

First let's tackle some of the terms you might encounter when you apply for a grant from a state or regional arts board or a fellowship from a major foundation like Creative Capital, Sustainable Arts Foundation, or the National Endowment for the Arts. You may be asked to submit a "Project Proposal," a "Personal Statement," an "Artist Statement," and "Work Sample." You may also be asked to submit a resume or curriculum vitae, as well as a budget.

Project proposals, personal statements, and artist statements all serve very similar purposes for selection committees—they help people understand what your strengths and goals are as an artist. Sometimes they'll want you to focus on the work you propose to complete in the future; other times they'll want you to focus more on what you've already accomplished. But whether you are asked to submit three different statements, which might be as short as 300 words each, or one single artist statement that is quite long, your goal will be the same: use these documents to tell a story about who you've been as a writer and where you are going.

Structuring an Artist Statement

Try opening your artist statement with a brief summary of your current work-in-progress (often referred to as a WIP). Maybe you are writing a series of linked poems, or you are in the process of revising a chapbook centered around a particular theme. Or maybe you've been experimenting with different received forms or visual poetry. Devote two to three sentences to describing this work. If you've had success publishing poems in magazines or received awards for your work, this is a great time to flex a little and mention that your WIP is not only exciting to you, but also that you've had success finding publishers for it. A little bragging can feel uncomfortable, but it is an important part of these kinds of documents.

But don't brag too much! We recommend pivoting from an exclusive focus on your own work to a paragraph or two where you discuss your relationship to literary influences with which the selection committee is likely to be familiar. Talking about who inspires you and how you have learned from their work helps people considering your application to not only appreciate the work you've submitted but also to imagine your potential for growth. One or two historical influences is appropriate, but you'll want to be sure to include contemporary writers as well. You might take a look at previous recipients of the grant or fellowship and mention how your work is specifically in conversation with theirs, since you can feel pretty confident the selection committee will be familiar with and appreciate those writers' aesthetics.

After talking a bit about other writers and literary communities that have influenced you, you'll want to bring the conversation back to your work: how it is going to be as good as these influences, but also how it's going to be new, different, and groundbreaking. After all, a selection committee will want to support writers who are pushing the art form into the future, not just repeating what's already been done. We suggest talking a bit more about the works you mentioned in your introduction. Try reflecting on how you are adding to or extending the existing conversations you've mentioned. This is a great time to tell the selection committee about why you feel your work is urgent or what gives you a sense of purpose as a writer.

After hitting on these key points—what you are writing, who you are in conversation with, and why your work matters—you'll want to conclude. Be sure your conclusion includes a note of gratitude for the time the selection committee will spend reviewing these applications. You may also want to mention what a difference this award will make in your life as a writer.

Other Frequently Asked Questions about Applications

Most applications that ask for an artist statement will also ask you to include a work sample. It can be hard to decide which work sample to pick. If you are proposing a project you are only just beginning, the work that relates to that project may still be in rough form. We suggest always choosing the work you feel is strongest, even if it's not totally related to the project proposal. If your work has been previously published in magazines, you might consider including a cover sheet in front of your work that says something like "Pieces from this work sample have previously appeared in. . . ." If members of the selection committee have not looked closely at your resume, this can help remind them of your previous success as a writer. In your statement you might include a paragraph where you discuss what ideas and techniques were guiding you when you wrote the materials in the work sample and then talk about how the new work will build on what you've already accomplished.

But don't let all our talk of prior publications discourage you if you haven't started publishing yet. Lots of opportunities exist for emerging writers and you should not feel ashamed to be at the beginning of your career. That's an exciting place to be! And lots of selection committees will be eager to give support and encouragement to someone starting out.

If you decide the current work-in-progress is the best choice for your work sample, another strategy you can use in your artist statement is to name the areas of weakness you hope to improve with the support of the grant or fellowship. For example, if you are hoping to infuse your poems with more formal innovations or more wildly surreal imagery, you can add a paragraph to your artist statement where you talk about how you will use the time and support to devote yourself to that kind of revision. You might think that naming the areas you want to improve undermines you, but in fact the opposite is true. The selection committee will probably think your work is great and then have even more admiration for your ambition as a writer to keep pushing yourself to achieve something else with your work. They will also appreciate the fact that you have such a concrete plan for project development.

If your grant application asks for a budget, you may have an opportunity to clarify aspects of your project. For example, if you are applying for funding to support travel, you might add a sentence about what you will be researching or experiencing while you are on the road. Or, if the budget includes funding so you can take time off work to focus on your writing, you can include a line or two about the specific poems you will be revising or writing during that period. Sometimes grant applications have frustratingly small word counts, so you should consider whether there's an opportunity in the budget documents to make the story of you and your work a little clearer to the committee.

Never Let a Rejection Get You Down

Most grants you apply for will be very competitive and the chances are high that even your fantastic project proposal will be rejected. We cope with this frustrating reality by assuming we won't get the grants we apply for and focusing on the benefits of engaging in the process instead. By applying for a grant, you must think about your work, your goals, your trajectory as a writer in new ways. That reflection process is great for finding new ways to think about your work and inspiration to explore new territories. On more than one occasion we've written entire books of poetry based on an idea we described in a grant application that was rejected. Rejections are part of writing, so please remember don't give up, don't get discouraged, and know that we're rooting for you.

ACKNOWLEDGMENTS

The authors and publisher gratefully acknowledge the permissions granted to reproduce the copyrighted material in this book. The third-party copyrighted material displayed in the pages of this book is done so on the basis of "fair dealing for the purposes of criticism and review" or "fair use for the purposes of teaching, criticism, scholarship or research" only, in accordance with international copyright laws, and is not intended to infringe upon the ownership rights of the original owners.

Every effort has been made to trace copyright holders and to obtain their permission for the use of copyrighted material. However, if any have been inadvertently overlooked, the publishers will be pleased, if notified of any omissions, to make the necessary arrangement at the first opportunity.

Chapter Acknowledgments

Chapter 1

Douglas Kearney, "Afrofuturism (Blanche Says 'Meh')" from *The Black Automaton* (Fence, 2009). Reproduced with the permission of the author.

Mai Der Vang, "Dear Exile" from *Afterland* © Mai Der Vang, 2017. Reproduced with the permission of the Permissions Company, LLC on behalf of Graywolf Press, Minneapolis, Minnesota. Available at: www.graywolfpress.org.

Mita Mahato, excerpts from "The Extinction Limericks" in *In Between: Poetry Comics* (Pleiades Press, 2017). Reproduced with the permission of the author.

Rebecca Tamas, "Interrogation (1)" from *WITCH*, Penned in the Margins March 2019.

Rosebud Ben-Oni, "Poet Wrestling with Atonement." This first appeared in *Hayden's Ferry Review*, Issue 63, Fall / Winter 2018.

Jawdat Fakhreddine, "Bird" from *Lighthouse for the Drowning*, translated by Jayson Iwen and Huda Fakhreddine © Jawdat Fakhreddine, 1996.

English translation © Jayson Iwen and Huda Fakhreddine, 2017. Reproduced with the permission of the Permissions Company, LLC on behalf of BOA Editions, Ltd. Available at: www.boaeditions.org.

Chapter 2

Christopher Soto, "Those Sundays" in *Sad Girl Poems* © Christopher Soto, 2016. (Sibling Rivalry Press). Reproduced by permission of the author.

Jorge Luis Borges "Borges and I", in *Labyrinths*, translated by James E. Irby (New Directions Publishing Corporation, 1962, 1964). Reproduced with the permission of the publisher and the Estate of Jorge Luis Borges.

Margaret Attwood, "Siren Song" from Selected Poems, 1965–1975. Reproduced with the permission of HarperCollins Publishers.

M. L. Smoker, "Letter to Richard Hugo (1)" in *Another Attempt at Rescue* © M. L. Smoker, 2005. Reproduced with the permission of Hanging Loose Press and the author.

Toi Derricotte, "Speculations about I" from *"I": New and Selected Poems* © Toi Derricotte, 2019. Reproduced with the permission of the University of Pittsburgh Press.

Chapter 3

Barbara Guest, "Eating Chocolate Ice Cream: Reading Mayakovsky" from *The Collected Poems of Barbara Guest* © Barbara Guest, 2016. Reproduced with the permission of the Wesleyan University Press.

Debora Kuan, "Minority Assignment #2" from *Xing*. Copyright © Debora Kuan, 2011. Reproduced with the permission of Saturnalia Books.

Craig Morgan Teicher, "Why Poetry: A Partial Autobiography ["How Tense it Makes Me, Reading"] from *The Trembling Answers* © Craig Morgan Teicher, 2017. Reproduced with the permission of the Permissions Company, LLC on behalf of BOA Editions Ltd. Available at: www.boaeditions.org.

Daniel Borzutzky, "Lake Michigan, Scene 18" from *Lake Michigan* © Daniel Borzutzky, 2018. Reproduced with the permission of the University of Pittsburgh Press.

Halfe, Louise B.—Sky Dancer, "ê-kwêskît–Turn-Around Woman" from The Crooked Good (Keegedonce Press, 2021). Reproduced with the permission of Keegedonce Press.

Chapter 4

Eduardo Corral, "Self Portrait with Tumbling and Lasso" from *Slow Lightning* (Yale University Press, 2012). Reproduced with the permission of the author.

Zbigniew Herbert, "Hermes, Dog, and Star," in *Collected Poems of Zbigniew Herbert 1956–1998,* translated by Alyssa Vales. Reproduced with the permission of the Wylie Agency.

Gérard de Nerval, "Lines in Gold," from *Modern Poets of France: A Bilingual Anthology* translated by Louis Simpson (Story Line Press, 1997). Translation © Louis Simpson, 1997. Reproduced with the permission of the Permissions Company, LLC on behalf of Matthew Simpson.

Marosa Di Giorgio, Excerpt from "Funeral carriages laden with watermelons" of *The Moth (La falena)* in *Los papeles salvajes*, the collected poems of Marosa Di Giorgio (2017). Translated by Peter Boyle. Reproduced with the permission of the translator.

Penelope Rosemont, Excerpt from the introduction to *Surrealist Women: An International Anthology* (University of Texas Press, 1998). Reproduced with the permission of the University of Texas Press.

Jose Hernandez Diaz, "The West," in *The Rumpus*. Reproduced with the permission of the author. Available at: https//.the rumpus.net.

Chapter 5

Brigit Pegeen Kelly, "Song" in *Song* © Brigit Pegeen Kelly, 1995. Reproduced with the permission of the Permissions Company, LLC on behalf of BOA Editions Ltd. Available at: www.boaeditions.org.

Diane Seuss, "[I dreamed I had to find my way]" from *frank: sonnets*, © Diane Seuss, 2015. Reproduced with the permission of the Permissions Company, LLC on behalf of Graywolf Press, Minneapolis, Minnesota. Available at: www.graywolfpress.org.

James Wright, "Milkweed" from *The Branch Will Not Break* (Wesleyan University Press, 1963). Reproduced with the permission of the publisher.

Jennifer Givhan, "Desert Duende," from *Landscape with Headless Mama* (Pleiades Press, 2016). Reproduced with the permission of the author.

Josefina de la Torre, Excerpts from *Poemas de la Isla,* (University of Washington Press, 2000). translated by Carlos Reyes. Reproduced with the permission of the translator.

Rachelle Cruz, "Self Portrait as Blood," in *Self Portrait as Rumor and Blood* (Dancing Girl Press, 2012). Reproduced with the permission of the author.

Chapter 6

Kenji C. Liu, "Warding Spell Against Trump v. Hawaii :: 585 US ___ (2018)." First published on Unmargin.org.

Laura Hershey, "In the Way" from *In the Way: ADAPT* Poems* (Dragonfly Press, 1992). Reproduced with the permission of Robin Stephens.

Monica A. Hand, "Black is Beautiful" from *me and Nina*, © Monica A. Hand, 2016. Reproduced with the permission of the Permissions Company, LLC on behalf of Alice James Books. Available at: www.alicejamesbooks.org.

Roy G. Guzman, "Queerodactyl" from *Catrachos* © Roy G. Guzman, 2021. Reproduced with the permission of the Permissions Company, LLC on behalf of Graywolf Press. Available at: www.graywolfpress.org.

Naomi Shahib Nye, "A Palestinian Might Say" in *The Tiny Journalist*, © Naomi Shihab Nye, 2019. Reproduced with the permission of the Permissions Company, LLC on behalf of BOA Editions, Ltd. Available at: www.boaeditions.org.

Chapter 7

Bruce Snide, "Frutti di Mare" in *Fruit* © Bruce Snider, 2020 (Board of Regents of the University of Wisconsin System, 2020). Reproduced with the permission of the University of Wisconsin Press.

CA Conrad, "Storm SOAKED Bread" and "One Day I Will Step from the Beauty Parlor and Enlist in the Frequency of Starlings" in *A Beautiful Marsupial Afternoon* ... (Wave Books, 2012). Reproduced with the permission of the author.

Cameron Awkward-Rich, "[Black Feeling]" in *Dispatch*. (Persea Books, (New York), 2019). Available at: www.perseabooks.com. Reproduced with the permission of the author. All rights reserved.

Debjani Chatterjee, "What I Did Today" in *Stairs and Whispers: D / deaf and Disabled Poets Write Back* (Nine Arches Press, 2017). Reproduced with the permission of the publishers.

Meg Day, "10AM Is When You Come to Me." Originally appeared in the Academy of American Poets "Poem-a-Day" digital poetry series, July 1, 2019.

Ama Codjoe, "On Seeing and Being Seen" in *Bluest Nude* © Ama Codjoe, 2022. Reproduced with the permission of the Permissions Company, LLC on behalf of Milkweed Editions. Available at: www.milkweed.org.

Chapter 8

Leanne Betasamosake Simpson "This Accident of Being Lost" in *This Accident of Being Lost* © Leanne Betasamosake Simpson, 2017. (House of Anansi Press, Toronto, 2017). Available at: www.houseofanansi.com. Reproduced with the permission of the publishers.

Aracelis Girmay, "& When We Woke," in *Kingdom Animalia* (BOA Editions, 2011). Reproduced with the permission of the Permissions Company, LLC on behalf of BOA Editions, Ltd. Available at: www.boaeditions.org.

Jaswinder Bolina, "Partisan Poem," from *The 44th of July* (Omnidawn, 2019). Reproduced with the permission of the author.

Roger Reeves, "In a Brief, Animated World: The Marriage of Anne of Denmark to James of Scotland, 1589" in *King Me* © Roger Reeves, 2013. Reproduced with the permission of the Permissions Company, LLC on behalf of Copper Canyon Press. Available at: www.coppercanyonpress.org.

Tess Taylor, "Downhill White Supremacists March on Sacramento" in *Rift Zone* (Red Hen Press, 2020). Reproduced with the permission of the publisher.

Chapter 9

Gerard Manley Hopkins, "The Windhover." Public domain.

Inger Christensen, in *ALPHABET*, translated by Susanna Nied, © Inger Christensen, 1981, 2000, translation © Susanne Nied, 2000. Reproduced with the permission of New Directions Publishing Corp. Reproduced in the British Commonwealth with the permission of Bloodaxe Books.

Jos Charles, excerpt from *Feeld* (Milkweed Editions, 2018). Reproduced with the permission of the author and the publisher.

Kim Hyesoon, translated by Don Mee Choi, "All the Garbage of the World, Unite!" in *All the Garbage of the World, Unite!* (Action Books, 2011). Reproduced with the permission of the translator and publisher.

Vievee Francis, "Another Antipastoral" in *Forest Primeval:* Poems. (TriQuarterly Books / Northwestern University Press, 2016), © Vievee Francis, 2016. All rights reserved.

Chapter 10

Craig Santos Perez "Understory" in *Habitat Threshold* (Omnidawn Publishing, 2020). The poem appears with the permission of the publisher. All rights reserved.

Layli Long Soldier, "38" in *Whereas* © Layli Long Soldier, 2017. Reproduced with the permission of the Permissions Company, LLC on behalf of Graywolf Press, Minneapolis, Minnesota. Available at: www.graywolfpress.org.

Marwa Helal, "Census" from *Invasive Species* (Nightboat Books, 2019). Reproduced with the permission of the author.

Paisley Rekdal, "Assemblage of Ruines Plane Parts, Vietnam Military Museum, Hanoi" in *Imaginary Vessels* © Paisley Rekdal, 2016. Reproduced with the permission of the Permissions Company, LLC on behalf of Copper Canyon Press. Available at: www.coppercanyonpress.org.

Philip Metres, "Black Site (Exhibit I)" in *Sand Opera*, © Philip Metres, 2015. Reproduced with the permission of the Permissions Company, LLC on behalf of Alice James Books. Available at: alicejamesbooks.org.

Kiki Petrosino, "Instructions for Time Travel" in *White Blood*, © Kiki Petrosino, 2020. Reproduced with the permission of Sarabande Books.

Afterword

Gianna Starble, "Lineage Map." Visual and discussion of influences, as student example of "Mentor Poet and Poetic Lineage Map: An Assignment." Reproduced with the permission of the author.

Authors' Acknowledgments

We are indebted first and foremost to poets, those writing now (most especially including those reading this book), and those whose ghosts haunt all poems.

Thank you, Lucy Brown and Aanchal Vij, our editors at Bloomsbury Academic (UK), as well as to Joe Wilkins and Sean Prentiss, editors for the *Bloomsbury Writer's Guides and Anthologies* series.

We wish to thank the writers whose works appear in these pages, including those to whom we allude and paraphrase, as well as friends who generously read, discussed, and / or offered notes on chapters or the conversations herein, including Brian Blair, Peter Campion, Natalie Dalea, CMarie Fuhrman, Merle Geode, Ray Gonzalez, Brandon Hackbarth, Greg Langen, Chi Kyu Lee, Matt Martinson, Nen Ramirez, Laura Read, Amalia Tenuta, Chaun Webster, Ellen Welcker, Kachina Yeager, and Jordan Young. We're also grateful to the "Workshopping the Workshop" group at University of Minnesota for ideas that appear explicitly in our appendix on approaches to workshopping and inform our thinking about pedagogy throughout this book. Special thanks to Douglas Kearney for facilitating those conversations, as well as Tarik Dobbs, torrin a. greathouse, and Mariela Lemus, along with guest facilitators Tisa Bryant, Felicia Rose Chavez, Erika Meitner, and Terrion Williamson, whose ideas were particularly influential on our work here. Further thanks to May Lee-Yang, whose grant-writing workshop collaborations with Kate inspired some of the advice and recommendations we give in the appendixes.

We also owe a debt of gratitude to editorial assistants Madison Flint, Lum Chi, and Haily Zauner. Thanks to the Dean's First-Year Research and Creative Scholars program at University of Minnesota for funding and supporting much of Lum and Haily's work. Thanks also to the students in our classes who so generously allowed us to beta test earlier versions of this textbook with them. Maya would like to thank especially the following students in her Winter 2022 Advanced Poetry Workshop at Central Washington University, who offered responses and / or conversations about these chapters: Gianna Starble, Austin Fricke, Tiffany Nelson, Susan Wenzel, and Aubrey Higdon; and her Spring 2022 Poetry II Workshop at Western Colorado's MFA program: Cheryl Slover-Linett, Erica Reid, Sarah Ward, Emily Eads, and Camelia Finley. Kate is grateful to the students in her Fall 2021 course Experiments in Voice & Poetry and Fall 2022 Graduate Poetry Workshop for sharing feedback about their experience with these chapters. Maya also offers gratitude to librarian extraordinaire Wendy Spaček for help sleuthing a translator's name.

Finally, we wish to thank the organizations who offered us space, time, and/or funding during the writing of this project: The H.J. Andrews Experimental Forest Artists' Residency and the Centrum Port Townsend Writers' Conference; as well as our families for their support when we said we were too busy garnering permissions to join in playing Birdspottingopoly or to hunt for fossils.

INDEX

abecedarian 190, 222
abstract expressionist (paintings), 61
accessible 127–8
Akbar, Kaveh
  as ancestor poet to Dujie Tahat 231
  "Apology" 45
alliteration 17, 37, 187
allusions 18, 64, 195
Americans with Disabilities Act 127
Ammons, A. R. , 61
Andalusian Romantic 104
antipastoral 77
antistrophe 12
Apollinaire, Guillaume 79
apostrophe (direct address) 24, 37, 168
archive 18, 214, 218, 224
Arigo, Christopher 187
ars poetica
  as Hopkin's "Windhover" 186
  invitation to compose xi
  invitation to revisit 227
  Lu Chi's *Wen Fu* 184
  and reflexivity 34, 36
  as surrealist theory 79
Ashbery, John
  "The One Thing that Can Save America" 59
Asian American Writers Workshop 127
assonance, 15
Atwood, Margaret 35, 36, 38
  "Siren Song" 30, 45, 46
audience
  in experimental voices 62
  liberatory poetics' response to 122
  as part of a poem's rhetorical situation 34, 36
  for poetry performance 16
authorial intrusion 32, 36
automatic writing 61, 64, 67, 77, 88, 235
avant garde 64, 78, 86, 100, 101
Awkward-Rich, Cameron
  "[Black Feeling]" 143, 152
Ayyad, Janna Jihad 129

Baraka, Amiri 125
Ben-Oni, Rosebud 17, 243
  "Poet Wrestling with Atonement" 8
Bitsui, Sherwin 188, 195
Black Arts Movement (BAM) 125, 126, 127
Black, Sheila 149
Blunk, Jonathan 104
Bly, Robert 82, 104, 105, 106
Bolina, Jaswinder
  "Partisan Poem" 159
Borzutzky, Daniel
  Lake Michigan
  "Lake Michigan, Scene 18" 53
Breton, Andre 79, 123
Brooks, Gwendolyn
  and the Black Arts Movement 126
  and The Reclaiming Power of Collective Confession 46
Browning, Robert
  "My Last Duchess" 58, 63
Buñuel, Luis 100
Button Poetry, 18

CA Conrad
  "(Soma)tic 5: Storm SOAKED Bread" 140, 150
cante jondo 100
Canto Mundo 234
Carrington, Leonora 44, 80, 81
Carson, Anne 43, 108, 112, 195
Cave Canem 126, 234

Cento 78, 87
Césaire, Aimé 80, 88, 123
Césaire, Suzanne 123
"Surrealism and Us: 1943" 123
Charles, Jos
  feeld 179, 191
Chatterjee, Debjani
  "What I Did Today" 136, 146, 153
Chaucerian influence 191, 229
Chi, Lu 183, 184
Christensen, Inger
  Alphabet 182, 190, 194
climax community 189
Clare, Eli
  "Stolen Bodies, Reclaimed Bodies: Disability and Queerness" 150
Codjoe, Ama
  "On Seeing and Being Seen" 138, 148
colonialism 41, 65, 155, 169, 171, 213
conditionals 77, 87
confessional mode xiii, 23, 33, 234
confessional poetry 33, 38, 58, 60
Confessionalism 20, 39, 40
contemporary (poetry) xiv, 16, 18, 19, 22, 39, 43, 59, 61, 64, 82, 83, 84, 103, 107, 135, 173, 185, 188, 189, 191, 193, 229
Corral, Eduardo
  "After Bei Dao/ After Jean Valentine" 83
  "Self Portrait with Tumbling and Lasso" 73
couplets 12, 13, 16, 17, 194
Cruz, Rachelle 98
cultural appropriation 171

Dali, Salvador 100
Day, Meg
  "10 a.m. Is When You Come to Me" 139, 147
decolonization 172
de la Torre, Josefina 91, 107, 189
de Nerval, Gérard
  "Lines in Gold" 71, 82
deep image 14, 82, 89–99, 100, 103, 105–6, 108, 110
Derricotte, Toi
  "Speculations About I," 25, 38
Desnos, Robert 124, 125
devotionals 13, 177, 185
Di Giorgio, Marosa 72, 80
Diaz, Jose Hernandez
  "The West" 76, 84
Diaz, Natalie 99, 110
  and Ada Limon 44
Didion, Joan 33
docupoetics 190
  "Docupoetics and Other Forms of Lyric Research" 197–226
dominant culture 64, 129
dream diary 88
duende/ dwende 89–104, 183, 230
  "Play and Theory of" 100
Dungy, Camille 185

ecopoetics 122, 131, 177, 183, 184, 185, 187, 190, 193
ecotone 111, 187
elegy 12, 16, 19, 40, 45, 82, 112, 189, 190
Eliot, T.S.
  "Love Song of J. Alfred Prufrock" 37
elision 191
embodied poetics 135, 145, 146, 147, 148, 152, 183, 213
Enheduanna 36–7
enjambment 191
  see also "line break"
Enzer, Julie R. 150
Epic of Sundiata 18
epistolary/epistole/epistle 16, 24, 37, 40, 42, 43, 44, 45, 101, 227
epode 12
erasure poems 221
erotic poetry 147, 148
  in ghazal 12
Espada, Martin 45
ethical positionality 187
ethnopoetics 187
eurocentrism 165
experimental poetry 64
exquisite corpse 78, 87, 235

Fanon, Frantz 123
Fibonacci sequence 194
"field of the page" 18, 19, 151, 177, 183, 189, 191, 193

field studies 183
Fleming, Joan 195
Forche, Carolyn 44, 220, 221
form(s), poetic 11–22
Four Guns 11, 15
fragmentation 19
Francis, Viviee
  "Another Antipastoral" 178, 188, 189, 195
Forest Primeval 189
Francisco, Ariel 105
French Symbolism 70
Freudian theory 38, 79
Fuhrman, CMarie 184, 260

Gay, Ross 194
genre blur 152, 231
ghazal 12
Girmay, Aracelis 133, 174
  "& When We Woke" 157, 165, 166
Givhan, Jennifer
  "Desert Duende" 97, 108, 109, 110
Guest, Barbara
  "Eating Chocolate Ice Cream: Reading Mayakovsky" 49, 60
Guzmán, Roy G. 118, 132
  "Queerodactyl" 124

haibun 12
haiku 12, 112, 185
Halfe, Louis B.—Sky Dancer
  "*ê-kwêskît*—Turn-Around Woman" 56, 65, 256
Hand, Monica A. 126, 132
  "Black Is Beautiful" 115
Happenings 62–3
Harlem Renaissance 18, 82, 126
Hass, Robert 106, 215
Hayden, Robert 38, 39
Hearing Trumpet, The 81
H.D. 37, 43, 108, 186
hegemonic 124, 170
Helal, Marwa
  "Census" 210
  "Immigration as Second Language" 222
  Invasive Species 222
Herbert, Zbigniew
  "Hermes, Dog, and Star" 75, 83
Hershey, Laura
  "Getting Comfortable" 145
High Modernism 38
hinge image 104, 187
Hopkins, Gerard Manley 186
  "The Windhover" 180, 183, 187, 194, 196, 229
Hong, Cathy Park
  "Delusions of Whiteness in the Avant-Garde" 64
Horna, Kati 80
Hugo, Richard 40, 44
  and M.L. Smoker 29, 41, 101, 227
Hyesoon, Kim
  "All the Garbage of the World, Unite!" 70, 181, 190, 195

iambic pentameter 12
implicit biases 171
implied audience 166
implied listener 36, 58
incantatory 15, 175, 190

jazz poetry 18
Jones, LeRoi 125
juxtaposition 64, 77, 86, 215, 244

Karenya, Rob 125
Kazuo, Shiraga
  Challenge to the Mud 62
Kearney, Douglas 18, 255
  "Afrofuturism (Blanche Says, 'Meh')" 10
Kinnell, Galway 105
Kuan, Debora
  "Minority Assignment #2" 55
Kundiman 126, 234
Kwasny, Melissa 43, 194
Kwv txhiaj 12

Lecoq, Jacques 145, 153
Levertov, Denise 17, 186
Lewis, Robin Coste 46
liberatory Poetics, see also "the Poetics of Liberation" 122–3, 127, 129, 150
Limerick
  "Extinction Limericks," Mita Mahato 9, 19, 70, 87, 108, 185, 255

Limon, Ada 44
line break 108, 187, 242
lineation 22
listener (poetic) 32, 34–6, 37, 39, 40, 42, 44, 45, 58, 187, 245
litany
  as poetic form 13
as literary device/effect 15, 17, 45, 168, 174, 194, 235
literary predecessor 41, 44
Litoral 100
Liu, Kenji C.
  "Warding Spell Against Trump v. Hawaii :: 585 US _____ (2018)" 131
"Living Metaphor" 102
Lofreda, Beth
  The Racial Imaginary: Writers on Race in the Life of the Mind 163
Long Soldier, Layli
  "38" 199
Lorca, Federico Garcia 100–4, 230
Lowell, Robert 38, 234
Loy, Mina 37, 77, 80
lyric mode 24, 36, 39
lyric poetry 37, 194, 215

Machado, Antonio 99, 103, 104
Madness, Rack, & Honey 32
magpie rhymes 11
Mahato, Mita
  "Extinction Limericks" 9, 19, 70, 87, 108, 185, 255
manifesto 60, 79, 88
Max King, Cap
  The Racial Imaginary: Writers on Race in the Life of the Mind 163
membranes (poetic, rhetorical) 33–40, 43, 58
Merwin, W.S. 45
metaphor, parts of: tenor & vehicle 37, 149, 151
#MeToo Movement 46
Metres, Philip
  "Black Site (Exhibit I)" 219–20
  Sand Opera 219
microaggression 148, 174
Miller, Janie Elizabeth 112
mimesis 22, 84
Modernist 37, 78, 185, 218
Modernist urban 189

narrative cohesion 101
Neal, Larry
  "The Black Arts Movement" 125
necropastoral 177, 183, 190, 194, 195
  "The Antipastoral, the Necropastoral, and the Field of the Page" 189–92
negative space 111, 191
Nelson, Maggie 40
Neruda, Pablo 82
New Criticism 38
New York School, The 59–64, 122, 125
Nied, Susanna 182, 190
Nuyorican Poets 18, 127
Nye, Naomi Shihab
  "A Palestinian Might Say" 119, 129

occasional poetry 130, 132
ode 12, 37, 40
O'Hara, Frank
  "Lana Turner Has Collapsed" 59
omission 191
Ono, Yoko 62
oral tradition 11, 14–16, 18, 20, 175
"Oread" 108, 186
organic form 17, 186, 190

Pan-African 123
pantoum 13, 243
Papa Dada 80, 87
Parallelism 13, 187
pastoral, pastoralism 177, 188, 216
Pegeen Kelly, Brigit
  "Song" 95, 100, 103, 110
pentatonic 13
Perez, Craig Santos
  "Understory" 206
permeability 33–4
persona 33, 38, 45, 58, 170, 219, 241, 245
persona poem 170, 219
Personist poetry 60
Petrosino, Kiki
  "Instructions for Time Travel" 212

Phillips, Carl 83
physical caesura 103, 111, 189, 191
Pico, Tommy 195
poetic exchange 32
poetry comics 19, 86, 110
poetry of witness 220
political poetry 122, 127
Pollard, Cherise A.
New Thoughts on the Black Arts Movement 125
Prados, Emilio 100, 102
Praxis 38, 101, 108
primeval forest 189
prose poem 12, 40, 83, 84, 88, 151
Pythagoras 71, 82

quatrains 13
queer theory 147, 151

Rader, Dean 184
racial identity 163, 170, 171, 222
racial imaginary 154–75
radif 12
radius of action 102, 104
see also "Living Metaphor"
Rankine, Claudia
The Racial Imaginary: Writers on Race in the Life of the Mind 163
Ray, Man 78
recontextualizing 13, 230
Reeves, Roger
"In a Brief, Animated World: The Marriage of Anne of Denmark to James of Scotland, 1589" 156
King Me 164
refrain 11, 17, 243
Rekdal, Paisley
Appropriate: A Provocation 171, 188
"Assemblage of Ruined Plane Parts, Vietnam Military Museum, Hanoi" 204
repetition 15, 17, 85, 122, 175
anaphoric 84
and Douglas Kearney 18
and image rhyme 195
as part of Laura Hershey's writing process 145–6
and Phillipe Soupault 83
in spells 108
resource extraction 177
rhetorical exchange 46
rhetorical situation 32–6, 245
rhyme 11, 96
in Hopkins 187
image rhyme 195
internal 84
rhyme scheme 12, 19, 235
vowel rhyme 108
rhythm 11, 36, 108
sprung rhythm 186
Rich, Adrienne 39
rim of the wound 111
Roethke, Theodore 41
Romantic 80, 82
Andalusian Romantic 104, 191
Rosemont, Penelope 79, 80
Rosenthol, M. L. 38
Rothenberg, Jerome 82, 105
Ruefle, Mary 32, 231
Rukeyser, Muriel 194, 224
Book of the Dead 218

Santoz Perez, Craig
from "Understory" 206, 217, 218
Sappho 37, 43, 183, 184, 213
self-reflexivity 36, 38, 173
Seuss, Diane
"[I dreamed I had to find my way from the city where I live now]" 94
Sexton, Anne
and Chris Soto, 39
as confessional poet, 38, 234
Shadow Self 105
Shakur, Assata 122
Simpson, Leanne Betasamosake 170
"this accident of being lost" 161, 169
Skinner, Jonathan 184
slam poetry 127
Smith, Tracy K. 105
Smoker, M.L. 41, 101, 189
"Letter to Richard Hugo (1)" 29
Snider, Bruce
"Frutti de Mari" 137
speaker (poetic) 48
in epistolary 40, 44, 45

and the Lyric "I" 32–4, 37
and Margaret Atwood 35–6
"More Experiments with first-person speaker" 65
in ordering a collection 245
"Race and Relationships between Author, Speaker, and Reader" 166–7
and reflexivity 38
speaker and poet 58
socialism 60
soliloquies 38
Song Poet, The 11
sonic 18, 82
sonic echo 84, 191, 195, 196
sonnet 12–13, 82, 186, 189
crown of, 244
Frank Sonnets by Diane Seuss 20, 67, 105
Petrarchan 13, 186
Soto, Christopher (Loma)
"Those Sundays" 31
Soupault, Phillipe 83
spells 14, 20, 89–110
spoken word 16, 18, 127
staccato 108
stanzas 12, 13, 17, 35, 242
Strand, Mark 183
strophe 12, 189
Surrealism
"Writing Out of Surrealism" 69–85
syntactical 13, 22, 46, 108
syntax 84, 104, 108, 112, 175, 195

talismanic nouns 106
Tamás, Rebecca 20, 243
"Interrogation (1)" 3, 14, 70
tanka 13
Taylor, Tess
"Downhill White Supremacists March on Sacramento" 162
Teicher, Craig Morgan 51, 61
"Why Poetry: A Partial Autobiography: ['How tense it makes me, reading. . .'] 51
temple hymns (of Enheduanna) 36
tercet 35, 194
textspeak 191
Titchkosky, Tony
"Life with Dead Metaphors" 150
tone 48, 59, 62, 67, 166, 245
"The Poem in Telephone Lines & Other Thoughts on Tone, Talk, and Voice in Poetry" 47
and spells 112
traditional forms 12, 16, 19, 21
traditional hmong song poem 11, 14, 16
Transcendentalist 191
typography 18, 28, 46
Tzara, Tristan 80, 87

Vang, Mai Der
"Dear Exile," 6, 16, 17
Varo, Remedios 43, 44, 78, 80, 81
Virgil
Georgics 188, 215–16, 217, 218
voice 11, 16, 19, 24, 32, 33, 45, 46–8, 58–9, 243
collective voice 175
experimental voice 62
Questions of Voice & Witness 220

Welch, James 41, 227
Werner's Nomenclature of Colors 99
white savior complex 172
white supremacy 64, 155, 165, 222
whitewashing 126, 165
Wordsworth, William 185, 186, 188
Wright, James 104, 105, 106
"Duende, James Wright, and Deep Image" 103 104
"Milkweed" 93

Yang, Kao Kalia 11, 13